The
Oxford Book
Of American Verse

The
Oxford Book
Of American Verse

Chosen & Edited by
Bliss Carman

NEW YORK
OXFORD UNIVERSITY PRESS
AMERICAN BRANCH: 35 WEST 32ND STREET
LONDON, TORONTO, MELBOURNE, & BOMBAY
1927

PREFACE

THE chief purpose of a prefatory note to an anthology is to make due acknowledgment to the poets and publishers who have permitted the use of their property. For their courteous co-operation in the present instance, I am glad to join The Oxford University Press in this expression of thanks.

A brief word may be added as to the work itself. The Oxford Book of American Verse does not attempt to be in the least encyclopaedic. It is a comparatively small anthology, and cannot pretend to compete with a work such as Mr. Stedman's invaluable book was in its day, and still is for the period it covers; nor does it compare for our own time with the thorough and extensive compendium of Miss Monroe and Mrs. Henderson.

The Oxford Book, after the manner of anthologies, takes a much more skimming view of the whole field of American verse, and it must be confessed a rather more irresponsible one. Not that I have felt licensed to indulge any waywardness or perversity of preference in making the selections. On the contrary, since I have been given so free a hand, I have felt all the more a need for judicious care, and for a fineness of poetic judgment much more accurate than will here appear.

Some years ago I was employed with others in compiling a ten-volume work entitled The World's Best Poetry. A number of eminent men were to be engaged to edit the various volumes, and we wanted James Whitcomb Riley to take charge of the volume of Humorous Verse.

PREFACE

" Oh, no! " he said. " No, I couldn't do that! Why, there are four hundred poets right here in Indiana, and every one of them is a personal friend of mine! "

I must confess to feeling a keen sympathy with Mr. Riley's embarrassing state of mind.

If the making of an anthology could be put in the hands of an ideal anthologist of infallible taste, how happy we should all be! At least theoretically. As a matter of fact we must usually put up with a taste that is anything but infallible, as I am uneasily aware. There will doubtless be many lovers of poetry and students of this Oxford Book who will wish in their disappointment and dissatisfaction that they could have had the task of making the selections themselves. I can only reply that in moments of misgiving I sincerely wish they had.

I would gladly have included here many beautiful poems of which I am fond, particularly among those of more recent years, and yet I have had to refrain for one reason or another. Sometimes our courteous copyright allowance for any one author was exhausted, and sometimes I had to check my enthusiasm for this favorite author or that from an unwillingness to run into an undue excess. I shall never open the Oxford Book without missing " The Blue Flag in Bog " and other poems which I perhaps too extravagantly admire, nor without grudging the space given to a number of productions of an earlier age " which no gentleman's library should be without." For after all an anthologist, no matter how much leeway he may be accorded, is not commissioned to please himself alone.

In reading the final proofs of the Book I have been struck again by what seemed to me the most significant difference between the old poetry and the new. The old poetry by

iv

PREFACE

comparison was to so great an extent imbued with a doleful spirit, or with a desperate resignation at best. In spite of the orthodoxy of the conventional age which produced it, the poetry of those days shows for the most part little of the valiant and joyous spirit which we find in the verse of our own times. And in view of our present spiritual needs I could not help recalling Matthew Arnold's declaration that "the future of poetry is immense," and the saying of Emerson, that serene seraph and our first prophet of a larger life of the spirit, that poetry has by no means all been written, but rather is still only in its beginning.

With the more confidence, then, I offer this modest compilation to that younger generation of poetry lovers, so many of whom I have had the pleasure of knowing in schools and universities through Canada and the United States, and to whom I for one entrust the future of American poetry without misgiving.

B. C.

New Canaan,
Connecticut,
    June, 1927.

ACKNOWLEDGMENTS

THE editor and publishers herewith offer thanks to the following, who have kindly given permission to include recent poems:

Elaine Goodale Eastman, George Edward Woodberry, J. P. McCaskey, Alice Corbin Henderson, Hermann Hagedorn, Thomas S. Jones, Jr., A. M. Robertson for three poems by George Sterling, Mary Perry King, Katharine Lee Bates, Langdon Mitchell, Thomas Fleming Day, Hamlin Garland, Carrie H. Moulton for three poems by Francis S. Saltus, Joseph Clarke, Mildred Howells for poems by W. D. Howells, copyright 1923 by Mildred Howells and J. M. Howells, William Winter, John J. Piatt, Harrison S. Morris, Arthur Colton, James Ryder Randall.

To Messrs. Charles Scribner's Sons and the authors for poems from *Children of the Night* and *The Town down the River* by Edwin Arlington Robinson; for poems from *The Builders and Other Poems* by Henry Van Dyke; for poems from *The Coast of Bohemia* by Thomas Nelson Page; for selections from *Poems* by H. C. Bunner; for selections from *Poems* by Sidney Lanier; for poems from *Poems of Childhood* and *The Second Book of Verse* by Eugene Field; for poems from *Chinese Lyrics* by Frederick Peterson; for selections from *Poems* by Richard Henry Stoddard; for a selection from *Poems* by Alan

ACKNOWLEDGMENTS

Seeger; for a selection from *Poems* by Edward S. Martin; for a selection from *Poems* by George P. Lathrop.

To the Macmillan Company and John Wiley for "The Faun," from *Poems Lyrical and Dramatic* by Sarah King Wiley; to the Macmillan Company and the authors for poems copyright by the Macmillan Company by Edgar Lee Masters, Ridgely Torrence, Edwin Arlington Robinson, Vachel Lindsay, John G. Neihardt, Sara Teasdale, Marguerite Wilkinson, Hervey Allen, and Harriet Monroe.

To the Century Company and the author for poems by Harrison S. Morris, John H. Boner, and S. Weir Mitchell. To the Yale University Press and the author for "Ecce in Deserto" from *Collected Poems* by Henry A. Beers. To Mr. John J. McVey for two poems by John Boyle O'Reilly. To the Whittaker and Ray Wiggin Company for permission to print from the complete poetical works of Joaquin Miller. To Messrs. P. J. Kenedy and Sons for "The Conquered Banner" by Abraham Joseph Ryan. To Funk & Wagnalls Company for "Indirection" by Richard Realf. To Messrs. James Pott and Company and the author for two poems by Clinton Scollard. To the Harvard University Press and Mr. Robert Hillyer for two poems. To Messrs. Dodd Mead & Company and the authors for "A Corn Song" from *Lyrics of Lowly Life* by Paul Laurence Dunbar, and "A Portrait" by Miss Caroline Duer from *Poems by Caroline Duer and Alice Duer*.

To The Bobbs-Merrill Company for "A Plantation Ditty" from *Comes One With a Song* by Frank L. Stanton, copyright 1898, used by special permission of the publishers, The Bobbs-Merrill Company. For the following poems by James Whitcomb Riley: For "The Old Man and

ACKNOWLEDGMENTS

Jim " from *Poems Here at Home,* copyright 1893–1920, used by special permission of the publishers, The Bobbs-Merrill Company. For " A Life Lesson " from *Rhymes of Childhood,* copyright 1890–1918, used by special permission of the publishers, The Bobbs-Merrill Company. For " On the Death of Little Mahala Ashcraft " from *Neighborly Poems,* copyright 1891–1925, used by special permission of the publishers, The Bobbs-Merrill Company. For " Bereaved " from *Poems Here at Home,* copyright 1893–1920, used by permission of the publishers, The Bobbs-Merrill Company. For " Little Orphant Annie " from *Afterwhiles,* copyright 1887, used by special permission of the publishers, The Bobbs-Merrill Company.

To Messrs. Harper & Brothers for five poems by Dana Burnet from *Poems by Dana Burnet,* published by Harper & Brothers. To Messrs. Duffield & Company and the author for " Under the Stars " by Wallace Rice. To Messrs. D. Appleton and Company for " A Little Way " from *Songs of the Soil* by Frank L. Stanton. To Messrs. G. P. Putnam's Sons and the authors for two poems from *Ships in Harbor* by David Morton; for selections from *Poems* by Grace D. Litchfield; for poems from *The Shadow Garden and Other Plays* by Madison Cawein. To Messrs. Lippincott and the author for " Always " by Harrison Smith Morris. To Messrs. Small, Maynard & Company for " An Immorality " by Ezra Pound, for poems by John Banister Tabb, John Vance Cheney, Charlotte Perkins Stetson, Lilla Cabot Perry, and George Santayana. To the McClure Publications, Inc. and the author for poems by Willa S. Cather. To the Lothrop Lee & Shepard Company and the author for two poems by Paul Hamilton Hayne. To Messrs. Henry Holt & Company and the

CONTENTS

CONTENTS

CONTENTS

CONTENTS

CONTENTS

CONTENTS

CONTENTS

CONTENTS

The mid-tide meets in the Channel waves that flow from
    shore to shore,
And the mist hung heavy upon the land from Feather-
    stone to Dunmore,
And that sterling light in Tusker Rock where the old
    bell tolls each hour,
And the beacon light that shone so bright was quench'd
    on Waterford Tower.

The nightly robes our good ship wore were her whole
    topsails three,
Her spanker and her standing jib — the courses being
    free,
" Now, lay aloft! my heroes bold, not a moment must
    be passed! "
And royals and top-gallant sails were quickly on each mast.

What looms upon our starboard bow? What hangs upon
    the breeze?
'Tis time our good ship hauled her wind abreast the old
    Saltees,
For by her ponderous press of sail and by her consorts four
We saw our morning visitor was a British man-of-war.

Up spake our noble Captain then, as a shot ahead of us
    past —
" Haul snug your flowing courses! lay your topsail to the
    mast! "
Those Englishmen gave three loud hurrahs from the deck
    of their covered ark,
And we answered back by a solid broadside from the decks
    of our patriot bark.

2

"Out booms! out booms!" our skipper cried, "out booms
    and give her sheet,"
And the swiftest keel that was ever launched shot ahead
    of the British fleet,
And amidst a thundering shower of shot, with stun'-sails
    hoisting away,
Down the North Channel Paul Jones did steer just at the
    break of day.

PHILIP FRENEAU

1752–1832

2. *The Indian Burying Ground*

IN spite of all the learned have said,
    I still my old opinion keep;
The posture, that we give the dead,
    Points out the soul's eternal sleep.

Not so the ancients of these lands —
    The Indian, when from life released,
Again is seated with his friends,
    And shares again the joyous feast.

His imaged birds, and painted bowl,
    And venison, for a journey dressed,
Bespeak the nature of the soul,
    Activity, that knows no rest.

His bow, for action ready bent,
    And arrows, with a head of stone,
Can only mean that life is spent,
    And not the old ideas gone.

Thou, stranger, that shalt come this way,
  No fraud upon the dead commit —
Observe the swelling turf, and say
  They do not lie, but here they sit.

Here still a lofty rock remains,
  On which the curious eye may trace
(Now wasted, half, by wearing rains)
  The fancies of a ruder race.

Here still an aged elm aspires,
  Beneath whose far-projecting shade
(And which the shepherd still admires)
  The children of the forest played!

There oft a restless Indian queen
  (Pale Shebah, with her braided hair)
And many a barbarous form is seen
  To chide the man that lingers there.

By midnight moons, o'er moistening dews;
  In habit for the chase arrayed,
The hunter still the deer pursues,
  The hunter and the deer, a shade!

And long shall timorous fancy see
  The painted chief, and pointed spear,
And Reason's self shall bow the knee
  To shadows and delusions here.

PHILIP FRENEAU

Retirement

A HERMIT'S house beside a stream,
With forests planted round,
Whatever it to you may seem
More real happiness I deem
Than if I were a monarch crown'd.

A cottage I could call my own,
Remote from domes of care;
A little garden walled with stone,
The wall with ivy overgrown,
A limpid fountain near,

Would more substantial joys afford,
More real bliss impart
Than all the wealth that misers hoard,
Than vanquish'd worlds, or worlds restored —
Mere cankers of the heart!

Vain, foolish man! how vast thy pride,
How little can your wants supply! —
'Tis surely wrong to grasp so wide —
You act as if you only had
To vanquish — not to die!

SAMUEL WOODWORTH

1785–1842

4. *The Bucket*

HOW dear to this heart are the scenes of my childhood,
 When fond recollection presents them to view!
The orchard, the meadow, the deep-tangled wild-wood,
 And every loved spot which my infancy knew!
The wide-spreading pond, and the mill that stood by it,
 The bridge, and the rock where the cataract fell,
The cot of my father, the dairy-house nigh it,
 And e'en the rude bucket that hung in the well —
The old oaken bucket, the iron-bound bucket,
The moss-covered bucket which hung in the well.

That moss-covered vessel I hailed as a treasure,
 For often at noon, when returned from the field,
I found it the source of an exquisite pleasure,
 The purest and sweetest that nature can yield.
How ardent I seized it, with hands that were glowing,
 And quick to the white-pebbled bottom it fell;
Then soon, with the emblem of truth over-flowing,
 And dripping with coolness, it rose from the well —
The old oaken bucket, the iron-bound bucket,
The moss-covered bucket arose from the well.

How sweet from the green mossy brim to receive it,
 As poised on the curb it inclined to my lips!
Not a full blushing goblet could tempt me to leave it,
 The brightest that beauty or revelry sips.
And now, far removed from the loved habitation,
 The tear of regret will intrusively swell,

6

SAMUEL WOODWORTH

As fancy reverts to my father's plantation,
　And sighs for the bucket that hangs in the well —
The old-oaken bucket, the iron-bound bucket,
The moss-covered bucket that hangs in the well!

EMMA HART WILLARD
1787–1870
5. *Rocked in the Cradle of the Deep*

ROCKED in the cradle of the deep
　I lay me down in peace to sleep;
Secure I rest upon the wave,
For thou, O Lord! hast power to save.
I know thou wilt not slight my call,
For Thou dost mark the sparrow's fall;
And calm and peaceful shall I sleep,
Rocked in the cradle of the deep.

When in the dead of night I lie
And gaze upon the trackless sky,
The star-bespangled heavenly scroll,
The boundless waters as they roll, —
I feel thy wondrous power to save
From perils of the stormy wave:
Rocked in the cradle of the deep,
I calmly rest and soundly sleep.

And such the trust that still were mine,
Though stormy winds swept o'er the brine,
Or though the tempest's fiery breath
Roused me from sleep to wreck and death.

In ocean cave, still safe with Thee
The germ of immortality!
And calm and peaceful shall I sleep,
Rocked in the cradle of the deep.

JOHN PIERPONT

1785–1866

6. *My Child*

I CANNOT make him dead!
   His fair sunshiny head
Is ever bounding round my study-chair;
   Yet, when my eyes, now dim
   With tears, I turn to him,
The vision vanishes — he is not there!

   I walk my parlor floor,
   And through the open door
I hear a footfall on the chamber stair;
   I'm stepping toward the hall
   To give the boy a call;
And then bethink me that — he is not there!

   I thread the crowded street;
   A satchelled lad I meet,
With the same beaming eyes and colored hair:
   And, as he's running by,
   Follow him with my eye,
Scarcely believing that — he is not there!

8

JOHN PIERPONT

I know his face is hid
  Under the coffin-lid;
Closed are his eyes; cold his forehead fair;
  My hand that marble felt;
  O'er it in prayer I knelt;
Yet my heart whispers that — he is not there!

I cannot make him dead!
  When passing by the bed,
So long watched over with parental care,
  My spirit and my eye
  Seek it inquiringly,
Before the thought comes that — he is not there!

When, at the cool, gray break
  Of day, from sleep I wake,
With my first breathing of the morning air
  My soul goes up with joy,
  To Him who gave my boy,
Then comes the sad thought that — he is not there!

When at the day's calm close,
  Before we seek repose,
I'm with his mother, offering up our prayer,
  Whate'er I may be saying,
  I am, in spirit, praying
For our boy's spirit, though — he is not there!

Not there! Where, then, is he?
  The form I used to see
Was but the raiment that he used to wear;

The grave that now doth press
Upon that cast-off dress,
Is but his wardrobe locked; — he is not there!

He lives! In all the past
He lives; nor, to the last,
Of seeing him again will I despair;
In dreams I see him now;
And, on his angel brow,
I see it written, " Thou shalt see me there! "

Yes, we all live to God!
Father, thy chastening rod
So help us, thine afflicted ones, to bear,
That in the spirit-land,
Meeting at thy right hand,
'Twill be our heaven to find — that he is there!

FITZ–GREENE HALLECK

1790–1867

7. *Marco Bozzaris*

AT midnight, in his guarded tent,
    The Turk was dreaming of the hour
When Greece, her knee in suppliance bent,
    Should tremble at his power:
In dreams, through camp and court, he bore
The trophies of a conqueror;
    In dreams his song of triumph heard;
Then wore his monarch's signet ring:
Then pressed that monarch's throne — a king;
As wild his thoughts, and gay of wing,
    As Eden's garden bird.

FITZ–GREENE HALLECK

At midnight, in the forest shades,
  Bozzaris ranged his Suliote band,
True as the steel of their tried blades,
  Heroes in heart and hand.
There had the Persian's thousands stood,
There had the glad earth drunk their blood
  On old Platæa's day;
And now there breathed that haunted air
The sons of sires who conquered there,
With arm to strike and soul to dare,
  As quick, as far as they.

An hour passed on — the Turk awoke;
  That bright dream was his last;
He woke — to hear his sentries shriek,
" To arms! they come! the Greek! the Greek! "
He woke — to die midst flame, and smoke,
And shout, and groan, and sabre-stroke,
  And death-shots falling thick and fast

As lightnings from the mountain-cloud;
And heard, with voice as trumpet loud,
  Bozzaris cheer his band:
" Strike — till the last armed foe expires;
Strike — for your altars and your fires;
Strike — for the green graves of your sires;
  God — and your native land! "

They fought — like brave men, long and well;
  They piled that ground with Moslem slain,
They conquered — but Bozzaris fell,
  Bleeding at every vein.

JOHN HOWARD PAYNE

Let others delight 'mid new pleasures to roam,
But give me, oh, give me, the pleasures of home!
   Home, Home, sweet, sweet Home!
There's no place like Home! there's no place like Home!

To thee I'll return, overburdened with care;
The heart's dearest solace will smile on me there;
No more from that cottage again will I roam;
Be it ever so humble, there's no place like home.
   Home! Home! sweet, sweet Home!
There's no place like Home! there's no place like Home!

JOSEPH RODMAN DRAKE

1795-1820

10.   *The American Flag*

WHEN Freedom from her mountain height
   Unfurled her standard to the air,
She tore the azure robe of night,
   And set the stars of glory there.
She mingled with its gorgeous dyes
The milky baldric of the skies,
And striped its pure celestial white
With streakings of the morning light;
Then from his mansion in the sun
She called her eagle bearer down,
And gave into his mighty hand
The symbol of her chosen land.

Majestic monarch of the cloud,
   Who rear'st aloft thy regal form,
To hear the tempest trumpings loud

16

And see the lightning lances driven,
  When strive the warriors of the storm,
And rolls the thunder-drum of heaven,
Child of the sun! to thee 'tis given
  To guard the banner of the free,
To hover in the sulphur smoke,
To ward away the battle stroke,
And bid its blending shine afar,
Like rainbows on the cloud of war,
  The harbingers of victory!
Flag of the brave! thy folds shall fly,
The sign of hope and triumph high,
When speaks the signal trumpet tone,
And the long line comes gleaming on.
Ere yet the life-blood, warm and wet,
Has dimmed the glistening bayonet,

Each soldier eye shall brightly turn
To where thy sky-born glories burn,
And, as his springing steps advance,
Catch war and vengeance from the glance.
And when the cannon-mouthings loud
Heave in wild wreaths the battle shroud,
And gory sabres rise and fall
Like shoots of flame on midnight's pall,
  Then shall thy meteor glances glow,
And cowering foes shall shrink beneath
  Each gallant arm that strikes below
That lovely messenger of death.

Flag of the seas! on ocean wave
Thy stars shall glitter o'er the brave;

When death, careering on the gale,
Sweeps darkly round the bellied sail,
And frighted waves rush wildly back
Before the broadside's reeling rack,
Each dying wanderer of the sea
Shall look at once to heaven and thee,
And smile to see thy splendors fly
In triumph o'er his closing eye.

Flag of the free heart's hope and home!
   By angel hands to valor given;
Thy stars have lit the welkin dome,
   And all thy hues were born in heaven.
Forever float that standard sheet!
   Where breathes the foe but falls before us,
With Freedom's soil beneath our feet,
   And Freedom's banner streaming o'er us?

11. *Elfin Song*

OUPHE and goblin! imp and sprite!
   Elf of eve! and starry Fay!
Ye that love the moon's soft light,
   Hither — hither wend your way;
Twine ye in a jocund ring,
   Sing and trip it merrily,
Hand to hand, and wing to wing,
   Round the wild witch-hazel tree.

Hail the wanderer again,
   With dance and song, and lute and lyre.

Pure his wing and strong his chain,
   And doubly bright his fairy fire.
Twine ye in an airy round,
   Brush the dew and print the lea;
Skip and gambol, hop and bound,
   Round the wild witch-hazel tree.

The beetle guards our holy ground,
   He flies about the haunted place,
And if mortal there be found,
   He hums in his ears and flaps his face;
The leaf-harp sounds our roundelay,
   The owlet's eyes our lanterns be;
Thus we sing, and dance, and play,
   Round the wild witch-hazel tree.

WILLIAM CULLEN BRYANT
1794-1878

12.   *Thanatopsis*

TO him who in the love of Nature holds
  Communion with her visible forms, she speaks
A various language; for his gayer hours
She has a voice of gladness, and a smile
And eloquence of beauty, and she glides
Into his darker musings, with a mild
And healing sympathy, that steals away
Their sharpness, ere he is aware. When thoughts
Of the last bitter hour come like a blight
Over thy spirit, and sad images

Of the stern agony, and shroud, and pall,
And breathless darkness, and the narrow house,
Make thee to shudder, and grow sick at heart; —
Go forth, under the open sky, and list
To Nature's teachings, while from all around —
Earth and her waters, and the depths of air —
Comes a still voice — Yet a few days, and thee
The all-beholding sun shall see no more
In all his course; nor yet in the cold ground,
Where thy pale form was laid, with many tears,
Nor in the embrace of ocean, shall exist
Thy image. Earth, that nourished thee, shall claim
Thy growth, to be resolved to earth again,
And, lost each human trace, surrendering up
Thine individual being, shalt thou go
To mix for ever with the elements,
To be a brother to the insensible rock
And to the sluggish clod, which the rude swain
Turns with his share, and treads upon. The oak
Shall send his roots abroad, and pierce thy mould.

  Yet not to thine eternal resting-place
Shalt thou retire alone, nor couldst thou wish
Couch more magnificent. Thou shalt lie down
With patriarchs of the infant world — with kings,
The powerful of the earth — the wise, the good,
Fair forms, and hoary seers of ages past,
All in one mighty sepulchre. The hills
Rock-ribbed and ancient as the sun, — the vales
Stretching in pensive quietness between;
The venerable woods — rivers that move

WILLIAM CULLEN BRYANT

In majesty, and the complaining brooks
That make the meadows green; and, poured round all,
Old Ocean's gray and melancholy waste, —
Are but the solemn decorations all
Of the great tomb of man. The golden sun,
The planets, all the infinite host of heaven,
Are shining on the sad abodes of death,
Through the still lapse of ages. All that tread
The globe are but a handful to the tribes
That slumber in its bosom. — Take the wings
Of morning, pierce the Barcan wilderness,
Or lose thyself in the continuous woods
Where rolls the Oregon, and hears no sound,
Save his own dashings — yet the dead are there:
And millions in those solitudes, since first
The flight of years began, have laid them down
In their last sleep — the dead reign there alone.
So shalt thou rest, and what if thou withdraw
In silence from the living, and no friend
Take note of thy departure? All that breathe
Will share thy destiny. The gay will laugh
When thou art gone, the solemn brood of care
Plod on, and each one as before will chase
His favorite phantom; yet all these shall leave
Their mirth and their employments, and shall come
And make their bed with thee. As the long train
Of ages glide away, the sons of men,
The youth in life's green spring, and he who goes
In the full strength of years, matron and maid,
The speechless babe, and the gray-headed man —
Shall one by one be gathered to thy side,
By those, who in their turn shall follow them.

Thy sports, thy wanderings, when a child,
Were ever in the sylvan wild;
And all the beauty of the place
Is in thy heart and on thy face.

The twilight of the trees and rocks
Is in the light shade of thy locks;
Thy step is as the wind, that weaves
Its playful way among the leaves.

Thine eyes are springs, in whose serene
And silent waters heaven is seen;
Their lashes are the herbs that look
On their young figures in the brook.

The forest depths, by foot unpressed,
Are not more sinless than thy breast;
The holy peace, that fills the air
Of those calm solitudes, is there.

18. *"I Broke the Spell that Held Me Long"*

I BROKE the spell that held me long,
The dear, dear witchery of song.
I said, the poet's idle lore
Shall waste my prime of years no more,
For Poetry, though heavenly born,
Consorts with poverty and scorn.

I broke the spell — nor deemed its power
Could fetter me another hour.
Ah, thoughtless! how could I forget
Its causes were around me yet?
For whereso'er I looked, the while,
Was Nature's everlasting smile.

Still came and lingered on my sight
Of flowers and streams the bloom and light,
And glory of the stars and sun; —
And these and poetry are one.
They, ere the world had held me long,
Recalled me to the love of song.

19.   The Death of the Flowers

THE melancholy days are come, the saddest of the year,
   Of wailing winds, and naked woods, and meadows
   brown and sere.
Heaped in the hollows of the grove, the autumn leaves
   lie dead;
They rustle to the eddying gust, and to the rabbit's tread;
The robin and the wren are flown, and from the shrubs
   the jay,
And from the wood-top calls the crow through all the
   gloomy day.

Where are the flowers, the fair young flowers, that lately
   sprang and stood
In brighter light and softer airs, a beauteous sisterhood?

Alas! they all are in their graves, the gentle race of
    flowers
Are lying in their lowly beds, with the fair and good of
    ours.
The rain is falling where they lie, but the cold November
    rain
Calls not from out the gloomy earth the lovely ones again.

The wind-flower and the violet, they perished long ago,
And the brier-rose and the orchis died amid the summer
    glow;
But on the hills the golden-rod, and the aster in the
    wood,
And the yellow sun-flower by the brook in autumn beauty
    stood,
Till fell the frost from the clear cold heaven, as falls the
    plague on men,
And the brightness of their smile was gone, from upland,
    glade, and glen.

And now, when comes the calm mild day, as still such days
    will come,
To call the squirrel and the bee from out their winter
    home;
When the sound of dropping nuts is heard, though all the
    trees are still,
And twinkle in the smoky light the waters of the rill,
The south wind searches for the flowers whose fragrance
    late he bore,
And sighs to find them in the wood and by the stream no
    more.

And then I think of one who in her youthful beauty died,
The fair meek blossom that grew up and faded by my
     side.
In the cold moist earth we laid her, when the forests cast
     the leaf,
And we wept that one so lovely should have a life so
     brief:
Yet not unmeet it was that one, like that young friend of
     ours,
So gentle and so beautiful, should perish with the flowers.

20.   *The Past*

THOU unrelenting Past!
     Strong are the barriers round thy dark domain,
   And fetters, sure and fast,
Hold all that enter thy unbreathing reign.

   Far in thy realm withdrawn,
Old empires sit in sullenness and gloom,
   And glorious ages gone
Lie deep within the shadow of thy womb.

     ildhood, with all its mirth,
     , Manhood, Age that draws us to the ground,
     d last, Man's Life on earth,
     o thy dim dominions, and are bound.

     ast my better years;
     st my earlier friends, the good, the kind,
     ielded to thee with tears —
The venerable form, the exalted mind.

                                              33

My spirit yearns to bring
The lost ones back — yearns with desire intense,
And struggles hard to wring
Thy bolts apart, and pluck thy captives thence.

In vain; thy gates deny
All passages save to those who hence depart;
Nor to the streaming eye
Thou giv'st them back — nor to the broken heart.

In thy abysses hide
Beauty and excellence unknown; to thee
Earth's wonder and her pride
Are gathered, as the waters to the sea;

Labors of good to man,
Unpublished charity, unbroken faith,
Love, that midst grief began,
And grew with years, and faltered not in death.

Full many a mighty name
Lurks in thy depths, unuttered, unrevered;
With thee are silent fame,
Forgotten arts, and wisdom disappeared.

Thine for a space are they —
Yet shalt thou yield thy treasures up at last,
Thy gates shall yet give way,
Thy bolts shall fall, inexorable Past!

All that of good and fair
Has gone into thy womb from earliest time,
Shall then come forth to wear
The glory and the beauty of its prime.

They have not perished — no!
Kind words, remembered voices once so sweet,
  Smiles, radiant long ago,
And features, the great soul's apparent seat,

  All shall come back; each tie
Of pure affection shall be knit again;
  Alone shall Evil die,
And Sorrow dwell a prisoner in thy reign.

  And then shall I behold
Him, by whose kind paternal side I sprung,
  And her, who, still and cold,
Fills the next grave — the beautiful and young.

21.   *An Evening Revery*

THE summer day is closed — the sun is set:
    Well they have done their office, those bright hours,
The latest of whose train goes softly out
In the red west. The green blade of the ground
Has risen, and herds have cropped it; the young twig
Has spread its plaited tissues to the sun;
Flowers of the garden and the waste have blown
And withered; seeds have fallen upon the soil,
From bursting cells, and in their graves await
Their resurrection. Insects from the pools
Have filled the air awhile with humming wings,
That now are stilled for ever; painted moths
Have wandered the blue sky, and died again;
The mother-bird hath broken for her brood

Good-bye

31.

GOOD-BYE, proud world! I'm going home:
  Thou are not my friend, and I'm not thine.
Long through thy weary crowds I roam;
A river-ark on the ocean brine,
Long I've been tossed like the driven foam;
But now, proud world! I'm going home.
Good-bye to Flattery's fawning face;
To Grandeur with his wise grimace;
To upstart Wealth's averted eye;
To supple Office, low and high;
To crowded halls, to court and street;
To frozen hearts and hasting feet;
To those who go, and those who come;
Good-bye, proud world! I'm going home.

I am going to my own hearth-stone,
Bosomed in yon green hills alone, —
A secret nook in a pleasant land,
Whose groves the frolic fairies planned;
Where arches green, the livelong day,
Echo the blackbird's roundelay,
And vulgar feet have never trod
A spot that is sacred to thought and God.

O, when I am safe in my sylvan home,
I tread on the pride of Greece and Rome;
And when I am stretched beneath the pines,
Where the evening star so holy shines,
I laugh at the lore and the pride of man,
At the sophist schools and the learned clan;
For what are they all, in their high conceit,
When man in the bush with God may meet?

RALPH WALDO EMERSON

32.   *The Rhodora*
              On being asked, whence is the Flower?

IN May, when sea-winds pierced our solitudes,
   I found the fresh Rhodora in the woods,
Spreading its leafless blooms in a damp nook,
To please the desert and the sluggish brook.
The purple petals, fallen in the pool,
Made the black water with their beauty gay;
Here might the red-bird come his plumes to cool,
And court the flower that cheapens his array.
Rhodora! if the sages ask thee why
This charm is wasted on the earth and sky,
Tell them, dear, that if eyes were made for seeing,
Then Beauty is its own excuse for being:
Why thou wert there, O rival of the rose!
I never thought to ask, I never knew:
But, in my simple ignorance, suppose
The self-same Power that brought me there brought you.

33.   *The Humble-Bee*

BURLEY, dozing humble-bee,
   Where thou art is clime for me.
Let them sail for Porto Rique,
Far-off heats through seas to seek;
I will follow thee alone,
Thou animated torrid-zone!
Zigzag steerer, desert cheerer,
Let me chase thy waving lines;
Keep me nearer, me thy hearer,
Singing over shrubs and vines.

RALPH WALDO EMERSON

Insect lover of the sun,
Joy of thy dominion!
Sailor of the atmosphere;
Swimmer through the waves of air;
Voyager of light and noon;
Epicurean of June;
Wait, I prithee, till I come
Within earshot of thy hum, —
All without is martyrdom.

When the south wind, in May days,
With a net of shining haze
Silvers the horizon wall,
And with softness touching all,
Tints the human countenance
With a color of romance,

And infusing subtle heats,
Turns the sod to violets,
Thou, in sunny solitudes,
Rover of the underwoods,
The green silence dost displace
With thy mellow, breezy bass.

Hot midsummer's petted crone,
Sweet to me thy drowsy tone
Tells of countless sunny hours,
Long days, and solid banks of flowers;
Of gulfs of sweetness without bound
In Indian wildernesses found;
Of Syrian peace, immortal leisure,
Firmest cheer, and bird-like pleasure.

Aught unsavory or unclean
Hath my insect never seen;
But violets and bilberry bells,
Maple-sap and daffodels,
Grass with green flag half-mast high,
Succory to match the sky,
Columbine with horn of honey,
Scented fern and agrimony,
Clover, catchfly, adder's-tongue
And brier-roses, dwelt among;
All beside was unknown waste,
All was picture as he passed.

Wiser far than human seer,
Yellow-breeched philosopher!
Seeing only what is fair,
Sipping only what is sweet,
Thou dost mock at fate and care,
Leave the chaff, and take the wheat.
When the fierce northwestern blast
Cools sea and land so far and fast,
Thou already slumberest deep;
Woe and want thou canst outsleep;
Want and woe, which torture us,
Thy sleep makes ridiculous.

34. *The Snow-Storm*

A NNOUNCED by all the trumpets of the sky,
   Arrives the snow, and, driving o'er the fields,
Seems nowhere to alight: the whited air
Hides hills and woods, the river, and the heaven,

43.   *Days*

DAUGHTERS of Time, the hypocritic Days,
    Muffled and dumb like barefoot dervishes,
And marching single in an endless file,
Bring diadems and fagots in their hands.
To each they offer gifts after his will,
Bread, kingdoms, stars, and sky that holds them all.
I, in my pleached garden, watched the pomp,
Forgot my morning wishes, hastily
Took a few herbs and apples, and the Day
Turned and departed silent. I, too late,
Under her solemn fillet saw the scorn.

44.   *Waldeinsamkeit*

I DO not count the hours I spend
    In wandering by the sea;
The forest is my loyal friend,
    Like God it useth me.

In plains that room for shadows make
Of skirting hills to lie,
Bound in by streams which give and take
Their colors from the sky;

Or on the mountain-crest sublime,
Or down the oaken glade,
O what have I to do with time?
For this the day was made.

RALPH WALDO EMERSON

Cities of mortals woe-begone
Fantastic care derides,
But in the serious landscape lone
Stern benefit abides.

Sheen will tarnish, honey cloy,
And merry is only a mask of sad,
But, sober on a fund of joy,
The woods at heart are glad.

There the great Planter plants
Of fruitful worlds the grain,
And with a million spells enchants
The souls that walk in pain.

Still on the seeds of all he made
The rose of beauty burns;
Through times that wear and forms that fade,
Immortal youth returns.

The black ducks mounting from the lake,
The pigeon in the pines,
The bittern's boom, a desert make
Which no false art refines.

Down in yon watery nook,
Where bearded mists divide,
The gray old gods whom Chaos knew,
The sires of Nature, hide.

Aloft, in secret veins of air,
Blows the sweet breath of song,

O, few to scale those uplands dare,
Though they to all belong!

See thou bring not to field or stone
The fancies found in books;
Leave authors' eyes, and fetch your own,
To brave the landscape's looks.

Oblivion here thy wisdom is,
Thy thrift, the sleep of cares;
For a proud idleness like this
Crowns all thy mean affairs.

WILLIAM GILMORE SIMMS

1806–1870

45.   *The Lost Pleiad*

NOT in the sky,
   Where it was seen
So long in eminence of light serene, —
Nor on the white tops of the glistering wave,
Nor down in mansions of the hidden deep,
Though beautiful in green
And crystal, its great caves of mystery, —
Shall the bright watcher have
Her place, and, as of old, high station keep!

Gone! gone!
Oh! nevermore, to cheer
The mariner, who holds his course alone
On the Atlantic, through the weary night,

WILLIAM GILMORE SIMMS

When the stars turn to watchers, and do sleep,
Shall it again appear,
With the sweet-loving certainty of light,
Down shining on the shut eyes of the deep!

The upward-looking shepherd on the hills
Of Chaldea, night-returning with his flocks,
He wonders why his beauty doth not blaze,
Gladding his gaze, —
And, from his dreary watch along the rocks,
Guiding him homeward o'er the perilous ways!
How stands he waiting still, in a sad maze,
Much wondering, while the drowsy silence fills
The sorrowful vault! — how lingers, in the hope that
    night
May yet renew the expected and sweet light,
So natural to his sight!

And lone,
Where, at the first, in smiling love she shone,
Brood the once happy circle of bright stars.
How should they dream, until her fate was known,
That they were ever confiscate to death?
That dark oblivion the pure beauty mars,
And, like the earth, its common bloom and breath,
That they should fall from high;
Their lights grow blasted by a touch, and die,
All their concerted springs of harmony
Snapt rudely, and the generous music gone!

Ah! still the strain
Of wailing sweetness fills the saddening sky;
The sister stars, lamenting in their pain
That one of the selectest ones must die, —

Must vanish, when most lovely, from the rest!
Alas! 'tis ever thus the destiny.
Even Rapture's song hath evermore a tone
Of wailing, as for bliss too quickly gone.
The hope most precious is the soonest lost,
The flower most sweet is first to feel the frost.
Are not all short-lived things the loveliest?
And, like the pale star, shooting down the sky,
Look they not ever brightest, as they fly
From the lone sphere they blest!

HENRY WADSWORTH LONGFELLOW

1807–1882

46. *Evangeline*

THIS is the forest primeval. The murmuring pines and
the hemlocks,
Bearded with moss, and in garments green, indistinct in
the twilight,
Stand like Druids of eld, with voices sad and prophetic,
Stand like harpers hoar, with beards that rest on their
bosoms.
Loud from its rocky caverns, the deep-voiced neighboring
ocean
Speaks, and in accents disconsolate answers the wail of the
forest.

This is the forest primeval; but where are the hearts
that beneath it
Leaped like the roe, when he hears in the woodland the
voice of the huntsman?

66

Where is the thatch-roofed village, the home of Acadian
    farmers, —
Men whose lives glided on like rivers that water the wood-
    lands,
Darkened by shadows of earth, but reflecting an image of
    heaven?
Waste are those pleasant farms, and the farmers forever
    departed!
Scattered like dust and leaves, when the mighty blasts of
    October
Seize them, and whirl them aloft, and sprinkle them far
    o'er the ocean.
Naught but tradition remains of the beautiful village of
    Grand Pré.

Ye who believe in affection that hopes, and endures, and
    is patient,
Ye who believe in the beauty and strength of woman's de-
    votion,
List to the mournful tradition, still sung by the pines of
    the forest;
List to a Tale of Love in Acadie, home of the happy.

In the Acadian land, on the shores of the Basin of
    Minas,
Distant, secluded, still, the little village of Grand
    Pré
Lay in the fruitful valley. Vast meadows stretched to the
    eastward,
Giving the village its name, and pasture to flocks without
    number.

But their dwellings were open as day and the hearts of the
    owners;
There the richest was poor, and the poorest lived in abun-
    dance.

    Somewhat apart from the village, and nearer the Basin
    of Minas,
Benedict Bellefontaine, the wealthiest farmer of Grand
    Pré,
Dwelt on his goodly acres; and with him, directing his
    household,
Gentle Evangeline lived, his child, and the pride of the
    village.
Stalwart and stately in form was the man of seventy
    winters;
Hearty and hale was he, an oak that is covered with snow-
    flakes;
White as the snow were his locks, and his cheeks as brown
    as the oak-leaves.
Fair was she to behold, that maiden of seventeen summers.
Black were her eyes as the berry that grows on the thorn
    by the wayside,
Black, yet how softly they gleamed beneath the brown
    shade of her tresses!
Sweet was her breath as the breath of kine that feed in the
    meadows.
When in the harvest heat she bore to the reapers at noon-
    tide
Flagons of home-brewed ale, ah! fair in sooth was the
    maiden.
Fairer was she when, on Sunday morn, while the bell from
    its turret

Sprinkled with holy sounds the air, as the priest with his
hyssop

Sprinkles the congregation, and scatters blessings upon
them,

Down the long street she passed, with her chaplet of beads
and her missal,

Wearing her Norman cap, and her kirtle of blue, and the
ear-rings,

Brought in the olden time from France, and since, as an
heirloom,

Handed down from mother to child, through long genera-
tions.

But a celestial brightness — a more ethereal beauty —

Shone on her face and encircled her form, when, after
confession,

Homeward serenely she walked with God's benediction
upon her.

When she had passed, it seemed like the ceasing of exquisite music.

Introduction

47.   *The Song of Hiawatha*

SHOULD you ask me, whence these stories?
    Whence these legends and traditions,
With the odors of the forest,
With the dew and damp of meadows,
With the curling smoke of wigwams,
With the rushing of great rivers,
With their frequent repetitions,
And their wild reverberations,

As of thunder in the mountains?
I should answer, I should tell you,
   " From the forests and the prairies,
From the great lakes of the Northland,
From the land of the Ojibways,
From the land of the Dacotahs,
From the mountains, moors, and fen-lands
Where the heron, the Shuh-shuh-gah,
Feeds among the reeds and rushes.
I repeat them as I heard them
From the lips of Nawadaha,
The musician, the sweet singer."

   Should you ask where Nawadaha
Found these songs so wild and wayward,
Found these legends and traditions,
I should answer, I should tell you,
" In the bird's-nests of the forest,
In the lodges of the beaver,
In the hoof-prints of the bison,
In the eyry of the eagle!

   " All the wild-fowl sang them to him,
In the moorlands and the fen-lands,
In the melancholy marshes;
Chetowaik, the plover, sang them,
Mahng, the loon, the wild-goose, Wawa,
The blue heron, the Shuh-shuh-gah,
And the grouse, the Mushkodasa! "

   If still further you should ask me,
Saying, " Who was Nawadaha?
Tell us of this Nawadaha,"
I should answer your inquiries
Straightway in such words as follow.

HENRY WADSWORTH LONGFELLOW

" In the vale of Tawasentha,
In the green and silent valley,
By the pleasant water-courses,
Dwelt the singer Nawadaha.
Round about the Indian village
Spread the meadows and the cornfields,
And beyond them stood the forest,
Stood the groves of singing pinetrees,
Green in Summer, white in Winter,
Ever sighing, ever singing.

" And the pleasant water-courses,
You could trace them through the valley,
By the rushing in the Spring-time,
By the alders in the Summer,
By the white fog in the Autumn,
By the black line in the Winter;
And beside them dwelt the singer,
In the vale of Tawasentha,
In the green and silent valley.

" There he sang of Hiawatha,
Sang the Song of Hiawatha,
Sang his wondrous birth and being,
How he prayed and how he fasted,
How he lived, and toiled, and suffered,
That the tribes of men might prosper,
That he might advance his people! "

Ye who love the haunts of Nature,
Love the sunshine of the meadow,
Love the shadow of the forest,
Love the wind among the branches,
And the rain-shower and the snowstorm,
And the rushing of great rivers

Through their palisades of pinetrees,
And the thunder in the mountains,
Whose innumerable echoes
Flap like eagles in their eyries; —
Listen to these wild traditions,
To this Song of Hiawatha!

Ye who love a nation's legends,
Love the ballads of a people,
That like voices from afar off
Call to us to pause and listen,
Speak in tones so plain and childlike,
Scarcely can the ear distinguish
Whether they are sung or spoken; —
Listen to this Indian Legend,
To this Song of Hiawatha!

Ye whose hearts are fresh and simple,
Who have faith in God and Nature,
Who believe that in all ages
Every human heart is human,
That in even savage bosoms
There are longings, yearnings, strivings
For the good they comprehend not,
That the feeble hands and helpless,
Groping blindly in the darkness,
Touch God's right hand in that darkness
And are lifted up and strengthened; —
Listen to this simple story,
To this Song of Hiawatha!

Ye, who sometimes, in your rambles
Through the green lanes of the country,
Where the tangled barberry-bushes
Hang their tufts of crimson berries

Over stone walls gray with mosses,
Pause by some neglected graveyard,
For a while to muse, and ponder
On a half effaced inscription,
Written with little skill of song-craft,
Homely phrases, but each letter
Full of hope and yet of heart-break,
Full of all the tender pathos
Of the Here and the Hereafter; —
Stay and read this rude inscription,
Read this Song of Hiawatha!

48. *Hermes Trismegistus*

As Seleucus narrates, Hermes describes the principles that
rank as wholes in two myriads of books; or, as we are in-
formed by Manetho, he perfectly unfolded these principles
in three myriads six thousand five hundred and twenty-five
volumes. . . .

. . . Our ancestors dedicated the inventions of their wisdom to this deity, inscribing all their own writings with the
name of Hermes. — IAMBLICUS.

STILL through Egypt's desert places
    Flows the lordly Nile,
From its banks the great stone faces
    Gaze with patient smile.
Still the pyramids imperious
    Pierce the cloudless skies,
And the Sphinx stares with mysterious,
    Solemn, stony eyes.

75

But where are the old Egyptian
    Demi-gods and kings?
Nothing left but an inscription
    Graven on stones and rings.
Where are Helios and Hephæstus,
    Gods of eldest eld?
Where is Hermes Trismegistus,
    Who their secrets held?

Where are now the many hundred
    Thousand books he wrote?
By the Thaumaturgists plundered,
    Lost in lands remote;
In oblivion sunk forever
    As when o'er the land
Blows a storm-wind, in the river
    Sinks the scattered sand.

Something unsubstantial, ghostly,
    Seems this Theurgist,
In deep meditation mostly
    Wrapped, as in a mist.
Vague, phantasmal, and unreal
    To our thought he seems,
Walking in a world ideal,
    In a land of dreams.

Was he one, or many, merging
    Name and fame in one,
Like a stream, to which, converging,
    Many streamlets run?

Till, with gathered power proceeding,
    Ampler sweep it takes,
Downward the sweet waters leading
    From unnumbered lakes.

By the Nile I see him wandering,
    Pausing now and then,
On the mystic union pondering
    Between gods and men;
Half believing, wholly feeling,
    With supreme delight,
How the gods, themselves concealing,
    Lift men to their height.

Or in Thebes, the hundred-gated,
    In the thoroughfare
Breathing, as if consecrated,
    A diviner air;
And amid discordant noises,
    In the jostling throng,
Hearing far, celestial voices
    Of Olympian song.

Who shall call his dreams fallacious?
    Who has searched or sought
All the unexplored and spacious
    Universe of thought?
Who, in his own skill confiding,
    Shall with rule and line
Mark the border-land dividing
    Human and divine?

Trismegistus! three times greatest!
   How thy name sublime
Has descended to this latest
   Progeny of time!
Happy they whose written pages
   Perish with their lives,
If amid the crumbling ages
   Still their name survives!

Thine, O priest of Egypt, lately
   Found I in the vast,
Weed-encumbered, sombre, stately,
   Grave-yard of the Past;
And a presence moved before me
   On that gloomy shore,
As a waft of wind, that o'er me
   Breathed, and was no more.

49. *The Chamber Over the Gate*

IS it so far from thee
   Thou canst no longer see,
In the Chamber over the Gate,
That old man desolate,
Weeping and wailing sore
For his son, who is no more?
   O Absalom, my son!

Is it so long ago
That cry of human woe
From the walled city came,
Calling on his dear name,

And sheltering boughs with all their leaves implore,
And say in language clear as human speech,
   "The peace of God, that passeth understanding,
   Be and abide with you forevermore!"

52.   *Nature*

AS a fond mother, when the day is o'er,
   Leads by the hand her little child to bed,
   Half willing, half reluctant to be led,
And leave his broken playthings on the floor,
Still gazing at them through the open door,
   Nor wholly reassured and comforted
   By promises of others in their stead,
Which, though more splendid, may not please him
   more;
So Nature deals with us, and takes away
   Our playthings one by one, and by the hand
   Leads us to rest so gently, that we go
Scarce knowing if we wish to go or stay,
   Being too full of sleep to understand
   How far the unknown transcends the what we know.

53.   *Chimes*

SWEET chimes! that in the loneliness of night
   Salute the passing hour, and in the dark
And silent chambers of the household mark
The movements of the myriad orbs of light!

Through my closed eyelids, by the inner sight,
    I see the constellations in the arc
    Of their great circles moving on, and hark!
I almost hear them singing in their flight.
Better than sleep it is to lie awake,
    O'er-canopied by the vast starry dome
    Of the immeasurable sky; to feel
The slumbering world sink under us, and make
    Hardly an eddy, — a mere rush of foam
    On the great sea beneath a sinking keel.

54. *The Sound of the Sea*

THE sea awoke at midnight from its sleep,
    And round the pebbly beaches far and wide
    I heard the first wave of the rising tide
Rush onward with uninterrupted sweep;
A voice out of the silence of the deep,
    A sound mysteriously multiplied
    As of a cataract from the mountain's side,
Or roar of winds upon a wooded steep.
So comes to us at times, from the unknown
    And inaccessible solitudes of being,
    The rushing of the sea-tides of the soul;
And inspirations, that we deem our own,
    Are some divine foreshadowing and foreseeing
    Of things beyond our reason or control.

55.   *Chaucer*

AN old man in a lodge within a park;
    The chamber walls depicted all around
    With portraitures of huntsman, hawk, and hound,
    And the hurt deer. He listeneth to the lark,
Whose song comes with the sunshine through the dark
    Of painted glass in leaden lattice bound;
    He listeneth and he laugheth at the sound,
    Then writeth in a book like any clerk.
He is the poet of the dawn, who wrote
    The Canterbury Tales, and his old age
    Made beautiful with song; and as I read
I hear the crowing cock, I hear the note
    Of lark and linnet, and from every page
    Rise odors of ploughed field or flowery mead.

56.   *Divina Commedia*

I

OFT have I seen at some cathedral door
    A laborer, pausing in the dust and heat,
    Lay down his burden, and with reverent feet
    Enter, and cross himself, and on the floor
Kneel to repeat his paternoster o'er;
    Far off the noises of the world retreat;
    The loud vociferations of the street
    Become an undistinguishable roar.
So, as I enter here from day to day,
    And leave my burden at this minster gate,

85

Kneeling in prayer, and not ashamed to pray,
The tumult of the time disconsolate
  To inarticulate murmurs dies away,
  While the eternal ages watch and wait.

II

How strange the sculptures that adorn these towers!
  This crowd of statues, in whose folded sleeves
  Birds build their nests; while canopied with leaves
Parvis and portal bloom like trellised bowers,
  And the vast minster seems a cross of flowers!
  But fiends and dragons on the gargoyled eaves
  Watch the dead Christ between the living thieves,
  And, underneath, the traitor Judas lowers!
Ah! from what agonies of heart and brain,
  What exultations trampling on despair,
  What tenderness, what tears, what hate of wrong,
What passionate outcry of a soul in pain,
  Uprose this poem of the earth and air,
  This mediæval miracle of song!

III

I enter, and I see thee in the gloom
Of the long aisles, O poet saturnine!
And strive to make my steps keep pace with thine.
The air is filled with some unknown perfume;
The congregation of the dead make room
For thee to pass; the votive tapers shine;
Like rooks that haunt Ravenna's groves of pine
The hovering echoes fly from tomb to tomb.

From the confessionals I hear arise
   Rehearsals of forgotten tragedies,
     And lamentations from the crypts below;
And then a voice celestial that begins
   With the pathetic words, "Although your sins
     As scarlet be," and ends with "as the snow."

IV

With snow-white veil and garments as of flame,
   She stands before thee, who so long ago
     Filled thy young heart with passion and the woe
   From which thy song and all its splendors came;
And while with stern rebuke she speaks thy name,
   The ice about thy heart melts as the snow
     On mountain heights, and in swift overflow
   Comes gushing from thy lips in sobs of shame.
Thou makest full confession; and a gleam,
   As of the dawn on some dark forest cast,
     Seems on thy lifted forehead to increase;
Lethe and Eunoë — the remembered dream
   And the forgotten sorrow — bring at last
     That perfect pardon which is perfect peace.

V

I lift mine eyes, and all the windows blaze
   With forms of Saints and holy men who died,
     Here martyred and hereafter glorified;
   And the great Rose upon its leaves displays
Christ's Triumph, and the angelic roundelays,
   With splendor upon splendor multiplied;
     And Beatrice again at Dante's side
   No more rebukes, but smiles her words of praise.

And then the organ sounds, and unseen choirs
　　Sing the old Latin hymns of peace and love
　　And benedictions of the Holy Ghost;
And the melodious bells among the spires
　　O'er all the house-tops and through heaven above
　　Proclaim the elevation of the Host!

VI

O star of morning and of liberty!
　　O bringer of the light, whose splendor shines
　　Above the darkness of the Apennines,
　　Forerunner of the day that is to be!
The voices of the city and the sea,
　　The voices of the mountains and the pines,
　　Repeat thy song, till the familiar lines
　　Are footpaths for the thought of Italy!
Thy flame is blown abroad from all the heights,
　　Through all the nations, and a sound is heard,
　　As of a mighty wind, and men devout,
Strangers of Rome, and the new proselytes,
　　In their own language hear thy wondrous word,
　　And many are amazed and many doubt.

57.　　　　　　*Sandalphon*

HAVE you read in the Talmud of old,
　　In the Legends the Rabbins have told
　　Of the limitless realms of the air,
Have you read it, — the marvellous story
Of Sandalphon, the Angel of Glory,
　　Sandalphon, the Angel of Prayer?

How, erect, at the outermost gates
Of the City Celestial he waits,
 With his feet on the ladder of light,
That, crowded with angels unnumbered,
By Jacob was seen, as he slumbered
 Alone in the desert at night?

The Angels of Wind and of Fire
Chant only one hymn, and expire
 With the song's irresistible stress;
Expire in their rapture and wonder,
As harp-strings are broken asunder
 By music they throb to express.

But serene in the rapturous throng,
Unmoved by the rush of the song,
 With eyes unimpassioned and slow,
Among the dead angels, the deathless
Sandalphon stands listening breathless
 To sounds that ascend from below; —

From the spirits on earth that adore,
From the souls that entreat and implore
 In the fervor and passion of prayer;
From the hearts that are broken with losses,
And weary with dragging the crosses
 Too heavy for mortals to bear.

And he gathers the prayers as he stands,
And they change into flowers in his hands,
 Into garlands of purple and red;
And beneath the great arch of the portal,
Through the streets of the City Immortal
 Is wafted the fragrance they shed.

It is but a legend, I know, —
A fable, a phantom, a show,
   Of the ancient Rabbinical lore;
Yet the old mediæval tradition,
The beautiful, strange superstition,
   But haunts me and holds me the more.

When I look from my window at night,
And the welkin above is all white,
   All throbbing and panting with stars,
Among them majestic is standing
Sandalphon the angel, expanding
   His pinions in nebulous bars.

And the legend, I feel, is a part
Of the hunger and thirst of the heart,
   The frenzy and fire of the brain,
That grasps at the fruitage forbidden,
The golden pomegranates of Eden,
   To quiet its fever and pain.

58.   *The Fiftieth Birthday of Agassiz*

May 28, 1857

IT was fifty years ago.
   In the pleasant month of May,
In the beautiful Pays de Vaud,
   A child in its cradle lay.

And Nature, the old nurse, took
   The child upon her knee,
Saying: " Here is a story-book
   Thy Father has written for thee."

"Come, wander with me," she said,
 " Into regions yet untrod;
And read what is still unread
 In the manuscripts of God."

And he wandered away and away
 With Nature, the dear old nurse,
Who sang to him night and day
 The rhymes of the universe.

And whenever the way seemed long,
 Or his heart began to fail,
She would sing a more wonderful song,
 Or tell a more marvellous tale.

So she keeps him still a child,
 And will not let him go,
Though at times his heart beats wild
 For the beautiful Pays de Vaud;

Though at times he hears in his dreams
 The Ranz des Vaches of old,
And the rush of mountain streams
 From glaciers clear and cold;

And the mother at home says, " Hark!
 For his voice I listen and yearn;
It is growing late and dark,
 And my boy does not return!"

59. *My Lost Youth*

OFTEN I think of the beautiful town
    That is seated by the sea;
Often in thought go up and down
The pleasant streets of that dear old town,
    And my youth comes back to me.
        And a verse of a Lapland song
        Is haunting my memory still:
        " A boy's will is the wind's will,
And the thoughts of youth are long, long thoughts."

I can see the shadowy lines of its trees,
    And catch, in sudden gleams,
The sheen of the far-surrounding seas,
And islands that were the Hesperides
    Of all my boyish dreams.
        And the burden of that old song,
        It murmurs and whispers still:
        " A boy's will is the wind's will,
And the thoughts of youth are long, long thoughts."

I remember the black wharves and the ships,
    And the sea-tides tossing free;
And Spanish sailors with bearded lips,
And the beauty and mystery of the ships,
    And the magic of the sea.
        And the voice of that wayward song
        Is singing and saying still:
        " A boy's will is the wind's will,
And the thoughts of youth are long, long thoughts."

HENRY WADSWORTH LONGFELLOW

I remember the bulwarks by the shore,
   And the fort upon the hill;
The sunrise gun, with its hollow roar,
The drum-beat repeated o'er and o'er,
   And the bugle wild and shrill.
      And the music of that old song
      Throbs in my memory still:
      " A boy's will is the wind's will,
And the thoughts of youth are long, long thoughts."

I remember the sea-fight far away,
   How it thundered o'er the tide!
And the dead captains, as they lay
In their graves, o'erlooking the tranquil bay
   Where they in battle died.
      And the sound of that mournful song
      Goes through me with a thrill:
      " A boy's will is the wind's will,
And the thoughts of youth are long, long thoughts."

I can see the breezy dome of groves,
   The shadows of Deering's Woods;
And the friendships old and the early loves
Come back with a Sabbath sound, as of doves
   In quiet neighborhoods.
      And the verse of that sweet old song,
      It flutters and murmurs still:
      " A boy's will is the wind's will,
And the thoughts of youth are long, long thoughts."

I remember the gleams and glooms that dart
   Across the school-boy's brain;
The song and the silence in the heart,

That in part are prophecies, and in part
    Are longings wild and vain.
        And the voice of that fitful song
        Sings on, and is never still:
        " A boy's will is the wind's will,
And the thoughts of youth are long, long thoughts."

There are things of which I may not speak;
    There are dreams that cannot die;
There are thoughts that make the strong heart weak,
And bring a pallor into the cheek,
    And a mist before the eye.
        And the words of that fatal song
        Come over me like a chill:
        " A boy's will is the wind's will,
And the thoughts of youth are long, long thoughts."

Strange to me now are the forms I meet
    When I visit the dear old town;
But the native air is pure and sweet,
And the trees that o'ershadow each well-known street,
    As they balance up and down,
        Are singing the beautiful song,
        Are sighing and whispering still:
        " A boy's will is the wind's will,
And the thoughts of youth are long, long thoughts."

And Deering's Woods are fresh and fair,
    And with joy that is almost pain
My heart goes back to wander there,
And among the dreams of the days that were,
    I find my lost youth again.

94

And the strange and beautiful song,
The groves are repeating it still:
" A boy's will is the wind's will,
And the thoughts of youth are long, long thoughts."

60.   *Hymn to the Night*

I HEARD the trailing garments of the Night
Sweep through her marble halls!
I saw her sable skirts all fringed with light
From the celestial walls!

I felt her presence, by its spell of might,
Stoop o'er me from above;
The calm, majestic presence of the Night,
As of the one I love.

I heard the sounds of sorrow and delight,
The manifold, soft chimes,
That fill the haunted chambers of the Night,
Like some old poet's rhymes.

From the cool cisterns of the midnight air
My spirit drank repose;
The fountain of perpetual peace flows there, —
From those deep cisterns flows.

O holy Night! from thee I learn to bear
What man has borne before!
Thou layest thy finger on the lips of Care,
And they complain no more.

95

Peace! Peace! Orestes-like I breathe this prayer!
  Descend with broad-winged flight,
The welcome, the thrice-prayed for, the most fair,
  The best-beloved Night!

61. *The Arrow and the Song*

I SHOT an arrow into the air,
  It fell to earth, I knew not where;
For, so swiftly it flew, the sight
Could not follow it in its flight.

I breathed a song into the air,
It fell to earth, I knew not where;
For who has sight so keen and strong,
That it can follow the flight of song?

Long, long afterward, in an oak
I found the arrow, still unbroke;
And the song, from beginning to end,
I found again in the heart of a friend.

62. *Paul Revere's Ride*

L ISTEN, my children, and you shall hear
  Of the midnight ride of Paul Revere,
On the eighteenth of April, in Seventy-five;
Hardly a man is now alive
Who remembers that famous day and year.

HENRY WADSWORTH LONGFELLOW

He said to his friend, " If the British march
By land or sea from the town tonight,
Hang a lantern aloft in the belfry arch
Of the North Church tower as a signal light, —
One, if by land, and two, if by sea;
And I on the opposite shore will be,
Ready to ride and spread the alarm
Through every Middlesex village and farm,
   For the country folk to be up and to arm."

Then he said, " Good night! " and with muffled oar
Silently rowed to the Charlestown shore,
Just as the moon rose over the bay,
Where swinging wide at her moorings lay
The Somerset, British man-of-war;
A phantom ship, with each mast and spar
Across the moon like a prison bar,
And a huge black hulk, that was magnified
By its own reflection in the tide.
Meanwhile, his friend, through alley and street,
Wanders and watches with eager ears,
Till in the silence around him he hears
The muster of men at the barrack door,
The sound of arms, and the tramp of feet,
And the measured tread of the grenadiers,
Marching down to their boats on the shore.

Then he climbed the tower of the Old North Church,
By the wooden stairs, with stealthy tread,
To the belfry-chamber overhead,
And startled the pigeons from their perch
On the sombre rafters, that round him made

HENRY WADSWORTH LONGFELLOW

Masses and moving shapes of shade, —
By the trembling ladder, steep and tall,
To the highest window in the wall,
Where he paused to listen and look down
A moment on the roofs of the town,
And the moonlight flowing over all.

Beneath, in the churchyard, lay the dead,
In their night-encampment on the hill,
Wrapped in silence so deep and still
That he could hear, like a sentinel's tread,
The watchful night-wind, as it went
Creeping along from tent to tent,
And seeming to whisper, "All is well!"
A moment only he feels the spell
Of the place and the hour, and the secret dread
Of the lonely belfry and the dead;
For suddenly all his thoughts are bent
On a shadowy something far away,
Where the river widens to meet the bay, —
A line of black that bends and floats
On the rising tide, like a bridge of boats.

Meanwhile, impatient to mount and ride,
Booted and spurred, with a heavy stride
On the opposite shore walked Paul Revere.
Now he patted his horse's side,
Now gazed at the landscape far and near,
Then, impetuous, stamped the earth,
And turned and tightened his saddle-girth;
But mostly he watched with eager search
The belfry-tower of the Old North Church,

HENRY WADSWORTH LONGFELLOW

As it rose above the graves on the hill,
Lonely and spectral and sombre and still.
And lo! as he looks, on the belfry's height
A glimmer, and then a stream of light!
He springs to the saddle, the bridle he turns,
But lingers and gazes, till full on his sight
A second lamp in the belfry burns!

A hurry of hoofs in a village street,
A shape in the moonlight, a bulk in the dark,
And beneath, from the pebbles, in passing, a spark
Struck out by a steed flying fearless and fleet:
That was all! And yet, through the gloom and the
    light,
The fate of a nation was riding that night;
And the spark struck out by that steed, in his flight,
Kindled the land into flame with its heat.

He has left the village and mounted the steep,
And beneath him, tranquil and broad and deep,
Is the Mystic, meeting the ocean tides;
And under the alders that skirt its edge,
Now soft on the sand, now loud on the ledge,
Is heard the tramp of his steed as he rides.

It was twelve by the village clock,
When he crossed the bridge into Medford town.
He heard the crowing of the cock,
And the barking of the farmer's dog,
And felt the damp of the river fog,
That rises after the sun goes down.

It was one by the village clock,
When he galloped into Lexington.
He saw the gilded weathercock
Swim in the moonlight as he passed,
And the meeting-house windows, blank and bare,
Gaze at him with a spectral glare,
As if they already stood aghast
At the bloody work they would look upon.

It was two by the village clock,
When he came to the bridge in Concord town.
He heard the bleating of the flock,
And the twitter of birds among the trees,
And felt the breath of the morning breeze
Blowing over the meadows brown.
And one was safe and asleep in his bed
Who at the bridge would be first to fall,
Who that day would be lying dead,
Pierced by a British musket-ball.

You know the rest. In the books you have read,
How the British Regulars fired and fled, —
How the farmers gave them ball for ball,
From behind each fence and farmyard wall,
Chasing the red-coats down the lane,
Then crossing the fields to emerge again
Under the trees at the turn of the road,
And only pausing to fire and load.

So through the night rode Paul Revere;
And so through the night went his cry of alarm
To every Middlesex village and farm, —

A cry of defiance and not of fear,
A voice in the darkness, a knock at the door,
And a word that shall echo forevermore!
For, borne on the night-wind of the Past,
Through all our history, to the last,
In the hour of darkness and peril and need,
The people will waken and listen to hear
The hurrying hoof-beats of that steed,
And the midnight message of Paul Revere.

JOHN GREENLEAF WHITTIER

1807–1892

63. *Proem*

I LOVE the old melodious lays
    Which softly melt the ages through,
The songs of Spenser's golden days,
Arcadian Sidney's silvery phrase,
Sprinkling our noon of time with freshest morning dew.

Yet, vainly in my quiet hours
To breathe their marvellous notes I try;
    I feel them, as the leaves and flowers
    In silence feel the dewy showers,
And drink with glad, still lips the blessing of the sky.

The rigor of a frozen clime,
The harshness of an untaught ear,
    The jarring words of one whose rhyme
    Beat often Labor's hurried time,
Or Duty's rugged march through storm and strife, are
here.

Of mystic beauty, dreamy grace,
No rounded art the lack supplies;
Unskilled the subtle lines to trace,
Or softer shades of Nature's face,
I view her common forms with unanointed eyes.

Nor mine the seer-like power to show
The secrets of the heart and mind;
To drop the plummet-line below
Our common world of joy and woe,
A more intense despair or brighter hope to find.

Yet here at least an earnest sense
Of human right and weal is shown;
A hate of tyranny intense,
And hearty in its vehemence,
As if my brother's pain and sorrow were my own.

O freedom! if to me belong
Nor mighty Milton's gift divine,
Nor Marvell's wit and graceful song,
Still with a love as deep and strong
As theirs, I lay, like them, my best gifts on thy shrine!

64.   *The Barefoot Boy*

Blessings on thee, little man,
Barefoot boy, with cheek of tan!
With thy turned-up pantaloons,
And thy merry whistled tunes;
With thy red lip, redder still
Kissed by strawberries on the hill;

With the sunshine on thy face,
Through thy torn brim's jaunty grace;
From my heart I give thee joy, —
I was once a barefoot boy!
Prince thou art, — the grown-up man
Only is republican.
Let the million-dollared ride!
Barefoot, trudging at his side,
Thou hast more than he can buy
In the reach of ear and eye, —
Outward sunshine, inward joy:
Blessings on thee, barefoot boy!

Oh for boyhood's painless play,
Sleep that wakes in laughing day,
Health that mocks the doctor's rules
Knowledge never learned of schools,
Of the wild bee's morning chase,
Of the wild-flower's time and place,
Flight of fowl and habitude
Of the tenants of the wood;
How the tortoise bears his shell,
How the woodchuck digs his cell,
And the ground-mole sinks his well;
How the robin feeds her young,
How the oriole's nest is hung;
Where the whitest lilies blow,
Where the freshest berries grow,
Where the ground-nut trails its vine,
Where the wood-grape's clusters shine;
Of the black wasp's cunning way,
Mason of his walls of clay,

And the architectural plans
Of gray hornet artisans!
For, eschewing books and tasks,
Nature answers all he asks;
Hand in hand with her he walks,
Face to face with her he talks,
Part and parcel of her joy, —
Blessings on the barefoot boy!

Oh for boyhood's time of June,
Crowding years in one brief moon,
When all things I heard or saw,
Me, their master, waited for.
I was rich in flowers and trees,
Humming-birds and honey-bees;
For my sport the squirrel played,
Plied the snouted mole his spade;
For my taste the blackberry cone
Purpled over hedge and stone;
Laughed the brook for my delight
Through the day and through the night,
Whispering at the garden wall,
Talked with me from fall to fall;
Mine the sand-rimmed pickerel pond,
Mine the walnut slopes beyond,
Mine, on bending orchard trees,
Apples of Hesperides!
Still as my horizon grew,
Larger grew my riches too;
All the world I saw or knew
Seemed a complex Chinese toy,
Fashioned for a barefoot boy!

Oh for festal dainties spread,
Like my bowl of milk and bread;
Pewter spoon and bowl of wood,
On the door-stone, gray and rude!
O'er me, like a regal tent,
Cloudy-ribbed, the sunset bent,
Purple-curtained, fringed with gold,
Looped in many a wind-swung fold;
While for music came the play
Of the pied frogs' orchestra;
And, to light the noisy choir,
Lit the fly his lamp of fire.
I was monarch: pomp and joy
Waited on the barefoot boy!

Cheerily, then, my little man,
Live and laugh, as boyhood can!
Though the flinty slopes be hard,
Stubble-speared the new-mown sward,
Every morn shall lead thee through
Fresh baptisms of the dew;
Every evening from thy feet
Shall the cool wind kiss the heat:
All too soon these feet must hide
In the prison cells of pride,
Lose the freedom of the sod,
Like a colt's for work be shod,
Made to tread the mills of toil,
Up and down in ceaseless moil:
Happy if their track be found
Never on forbidden ground;

Happy if they sink not in
Quick and treacherous sands of sin.
Ah! that thou couldst know thy joy,
Ere it passes, barefoot boy!

65.   *Maud Muller*

MAUD MULLER on a summer's day
Raked the meadow sweet with hay.

Beneath her torn hat glowed the wealth
Of simple beauty and rustic health.

Singing, she wrought, and her merry glee
The mock-bird echoed from his tree.

But when she glanced to the far-off town,
White from its hill-slope looking down,

The sweet song died, and a vague unrest
And a nameless longing filled her breast, —

A wish that she hardly dared to own,
For something better than she had known.

The Judge rode slowly down the lane,
Smoothing his horse's chestnut mane.

He drew his bridle in the shade
Of the apple-trees, to greet the maid,

And asked a draught from the spring that flowed
Through the meadow across the road.

She stooped where the cool spring bubbled up,
And filled for him her small tin cup,

And blushed as she gave it, looking down
On her feet so bare, and her tattered gown.

"Thanks!" said the Judge; "a sweeter draught
From a fairer hand was never quaffed."

He spoke of the grass and flowers and trees,
Of the singing birds and the humming bees;

Then talked of the haying, and wondered whether
The cloud in the west would bring foul weather,

And Maud forgot her brier-torn gown,
And her graceful ankles bare and brown;

And listened, while a pleased surprise
Looked from her long-lashed hazel eyes.

At last, like one who for delay
Seeks a vain excuse, he rode away.

Maud Muller looked and sighed: "Ah me!
That I the Judge's bride might be!

"He would dress me up in silks so fine,
And praise and toast me at his wine.

JOHN GREENLEAF WHITTIER

" My father should wear a broadcloth coat;
My brother should sail a painted boat.

" I'd dress my mother so grand and gay,
And the baby should have a new toy each day.

" And I'd feed the hungry and clothe the poor,
And all should bless me who left our door."

The Judge looked back as he climbed the hill,
And saw Maud Muller standing still.

" A form more fair, a face more sweet,
Ne'er hath it been my lot to meet.

" And her modest answer and graceful air
Show her wise and good as she is fair.

" Would she were mine, and I to-day,
Like her, a harvester of hay;

" No doubtful balance of rights and wrongs,
Nor weary lawyers with endless tongues,

" But low of cattle and song of birds,
And health and quiet and loving words."

But he thought of his sisters, proud and cold,
And his mother, vain of her rank and gold.

So, closing his heart, the Judge rode on,
And Maud was left in the field alone.

But the lawyers smiled that afternoon,
When he hummed in court an old love-tune;

And the young girl mused beside the well
Till the rain on the unraked clover fell.

He wedded a wife of richest dower,
Who lived for fashion, as he for power.

Yet oft, in his marble hearth's bright glow,
He watched a picture come and go;

And sweet Maud Muller's hazel eyes
Looked out in their innocent surprise.

Oft, when the wine in his glass was red,
He longed for the wayside well instead;

And closed his eyes on his garnished rooms
To dream of meadows and clover-blooms.

And the proud man sighed, with a secret pain,
"Ah, that I were free again!

"Free as when I rode that day,
Where the barefoot maiden raked her hay."

She wedded a man unlearned and poor,
And many children played round her door.

But care and sorrow, and childbirth pain,
Left their traces on heart and brain.

And oft, when the summer sun shone hot
On the new-mown hay in the meadow lot,

And she heard the little spring brook fall
Over the roadside, through the wall,

In the shade of the apple-tree again
She saw a rider draw his rein;

And, gazing down with timid grace,
She felt his pleased eyes read her face.

Sometimes her narrow kitchen walls
Stretched away into stately halls;

The weary wheel to a spinnet turned,
The tallow candle an astral burned,

And for him who sat by the chimney lug,
Dozing and grumbling o'er pipe and mug,

A manly form at her side she saw,
And joy was duty and love was law.

Then she took up her burden of life again,
Saying only, " It might have been."

Alas for maiden, alas for Judge,
For rich repiner and household drudge!

God pity them both; and pity us all,
Who vainly the dreams of youth recall.

For of all sad words of tongue or pen,
The saddest are these: " It might have been! "

Ah, well! for us all some sweet hope lies
Deeply buried from human eyes;

And, in the hereafter, angels may
Roll the stone from its grave away!

66. *Barbara Frietchie*

UP from the meadows rich with corn,
Clear in the cool September morn,

The clustered spires of Frederick stand
Green-walled by the hills of Maryland.

Round about them orchards sweep,
Apple and peach tree fruited deep,

Fair as the garden of the Lord
To the eyes of the famished rebel horde,

On that pleasant morn of the early fall
When Lee marched over the mountain-wall;

Over the mountains winding down,
Horse and foot, into Frederick town.

Forty flags with their silver stars,
Forty flags with their crimson bars,

Flapped in the morning wind: the sun
Of noon looked down, and saw not one.

JOHN GREENLEAF WHITTIER

Up rose old Barbara Frietchie then,
Bowed with her fourscore years and ten;

Bravest of all in Frederick town,
She took up the flag the men hauled down;

In her attic window the staff she set,
To show that one heart was loyal yet.

Up the street came the rebel tread,
Stonewall Jackson riding ahead.

Under his slouched hat left and right
He glanced; the old flag met his sight.

" Halt! " — the dust-brown ranks stood fast.
" Fire! " — out blazed the rifle-blast.

It shivered the window, pane and sash;
It rent the banner with seam and gash.

Quick, as it fell, from the broken staff
Dame Barbara snatched the silken scarf.

She leaned far out on the window-sill,
And shook it forth with a royal will.

" Shoot, if you must, this old gray head,
But spare your country's flag," she said.

A shade of sadness, a blush of shame,
Over the face of the leader came;

JOHN GREENLEAF WHITTIER

The nobler nature within him stirred
To life at that woman's deed and word;

"Who touches a hair of yon gray head
Dies like a dog! March on!" he said.

All day long through Frederick street
Sounded the tread of marching feet:

All day long that free flag tost
Over the heads of the rebel host.

Ever its torn folds rose and fell
On the loyal winds that loved it well;

And through the hill-gaps sunset light
Shone over it with a warm good-night.

Barbara Frietchie's work is o'er,
And the Rebel rides on his raids no more.

Honor to her! and let a tear
Fall, for her sake, on Stonewall's bier.

Over Barbara Frietchie's grave,
Flag of Freedom and Union, wave!

Peace and order and beauty draw
Round thy symbol of light and law;

And ever the stars above look down
On thy stars below in Frederick town!

67. *Abraham Davenport*

IN the old days (a custom laid aside
  With breeches and cocked hats) the people sent
Their wisest men to make the public laws.
And so, from a brown homestead, where the Sound
Drinks the small tribute of the Mianas,
Waved over by the woods of Rippowam,
And hallowed by pure lives and tranquil deaths,
Stamford sent up to the councils of the State
Wisdom and grace in Abraham Davenport.

  'Twas on a May-day of the far old year
Seventeen hundred eighty, that there fell
Over the bloom and sweet life of the Spring,
Over the fresh earth and the heaven of noon,
A horror of great darkness, like the night
In day of which the Norland sagas tell, —
The Twilight of the Gods. The low-hung sky
Was black with ominous clouds, save where its rim
Was fringed with a dull glow, like that which climbs
The crater's sides from the red hell below.
Birds ceased to sing, and all the barnyard fowls
Roosted; the cattle at the pasture bars
Lowed, and looked homeward; bats on leathern wings
Flitted abroad; the sounds of labor died;
Men prayed, and women wept; all ears grew sharp
To hear the doom-blast of the trumpet shatter
The black sky, that the dreadful face of Christ
Might look from the rent clouds, not as he looked
A loving guest at Bethany, but stern
As Justice and inexorable Law.

Meanwhile in the old State House, dim as ghosts,
Sat the lawgivers of Connecticut,
Trembling beneath their legislative robes.
" It is the Lord's Great Day! Let us adjourn,"
Some said; and then, as if with one accord,
All eyes were turned to Abraham Davenport.
He rose, slow cleaving with his steady voice
The intolerable hush. " This well may be
The Day of Judgment which the world awaits;
But be it so or not, I only know
My present duty, and my Lord's command
To occupy till He come. So at the post
Where He hath set me in His providence,
I choose, for one, to meet Him face to face, —
No faithless servant frightened from my task,
But ready when the Lord of the harvest calls;
And therefore, with all reverence, I would say,
Let God do His work, we will see to ours.
Bring in the candles." And they brought them in.
   Then by the flaring lights the Speaker read,
Albeit with husky voice and shaking hands,
An act to amend an act to regulate
The shad and alewive fisheries. Whereupon
Wisely and well spake Abraham Davenport,
Straight to the question, with no figures of speech
Save the ten Arab signs, yet not without
The shrewd dry humor natural to the man:
His awe-struck colleagues listening all the while,
Between the pauses of his argument,
To hear the thunder of the wrath of God
Break from the hollow trumpet of the cloud.
   And there he stands in memory to this day,

Against the background of unnatural dark,
Erect, self-poised, a rugged face, half seen
A witness to the ages as they pass,
That simple duty hath no place for fear.

68.   *From "Snow-Bound"*

UNWARMED by any sunset light
    The gray day darkened into night,
A night made hoary with the swarm
And whirl-dance of the blinding storm,
As zigzag, wavering to and fro,
Crossed and recrossed the wingèd snow:
And ere the early bedtime came
The white drift piled the window-frame,
And through the glass the clothes-line posts
Looked in like tall and sheeted ghosts.

So all night long the storm roared on:
The morning broke without a sun;
In tiny spherule traced with lines
Of Nature's geometric signs,
In starry flake, and pellicle,
All day the hoary meteor fell;
And, when the second morning shone,
We looked upon a world unknown,
On nothing we could call our own.
Around the glistening wonder bent
The blue walls of the firmament,
No cloud above, no earth below, —
A universe of sky and snow!

116

The old familiar sights of ours
Took marvellous shapes; strange domes and towers
Rose up where sty or corn-crib stood,
Or garden-wall, or belt of wood;
A smooth white mound the brush-pile showed,
A fenceless drift what once was road;
The bridle-post an old man sat
With loose-flung coat and high cocked hat;
The well-curb had a Chinese roof;
And even the long sweep, high aloof,
In its slant splendor, seemed to tell
Of Pisa's leaning miracle.

69.   *Skipper Ireson's Ride*

OF all the rides since the birth of time,
   Told in story or sung in rhyme,—
On Apuleius's Golden Ass,
Or one-eyed Calender's horse of brass,
Witch astride of a human back,
Islam's prophet on Al-Borák,—
The strangest ride that ever was sped
Was Ireson's, out from Marblehead!
   Old Floyd Ireson, for his hard heart,
    Tarred and feathered and carried in a cart
     By the women of Marblehead!

Body of turkey, head of owl,
Wings a-droop like a rained-on fowl,
Feathered and ruffled in every part,
Skipper Ireson stood in the cart.

Scores of women, old and young,
Strong of muscle, and glib of tongue,
Pushed and pulled up the rocky lane,
Shouting and singing the shrill refrain:
    " Here's Flud Oirson, fur his harrd horrt,
      Torr'd an' futherr'd an' corr'd in a corrt
      By the women o' Morble'ead! "

Wrinkled scolds with hands on hips,
Girls in bloom of cheek and lips,
Wild-eyed, free-limbed, such as chase
Bacchus round some antique vase,
Brief of skirt, with ankles bare,
Loose of kerchief and loose of hair,
With conch-shells blowing and fish-horns' twang,
Over and over the Mænads sang:
    " Here's Flud Oirson, fur his horrd horrt,
      Torr'd an' futherr'd an' corr'd in a corrt
      By the women o' Morble'ead! "

Small pity for him! — He sailed away
From a leaking ship in Chaleur Bay, —
Sailed away from a sinking wreck,
With his own town's-people on her deck!
" Lay by! lay by! " they called to him.
Back he answered, " Sink or swim!
Brag of your catch of fish again! "
And off he sailed through the fog and rain!
    Old Floyd Ireson, for his hard heart,
      Tarred and feathered and carried in a cart
      By the women of Marblehead!

JOHN GREENLEAF WHITTIER

Fathoms deep in dark Chaleur
That wreck shall lie forevermore.
Mother and sister, wife and maid,
Looked from the rocks of Marblehead
Over the moaning and rainy sea, —
Looked for the coming that might not be!
What did the winds and the sea-birds say
Of the cruel captain who sailed away? —
   Old Floyd Ireson, for his hard heart,
    Tarred and feathered and carried in a cart
      By the women of Marblehead!

Through the street, on either side,
Up flew windows, doors swung wide;
Sharp-tongued spinsters, old wives gray,
Treble lent the fish-horn's bray.
Sea-worn grandsires, cripple-bound,
Hulks of old sailors run aground,
Shook head, and fist, and hat, and cane,
And cracked with curses the hoarse refrain:
   "Here's Flud Oirson, fur his horrd horrt,
    Torr'd an' futherr'd an' corr'd in a corrt
      By the women o' Morble'ead!"

Sweetly along the Salem road
Bloom of orchard and lilac showed.
Little the wicked skipper knew
Of the fields so green and the sky so blue.
Riding there in his sorry trim,
Like an Indian idol glum and grim,
Scarcely he seemed the sound to hear
Of voices shouting, far and near:

"Here's Flud Oirson, fur his horrd horrt,
Torr'd an' futherr'd an' corr'd in a corrt
  By the women o' Morble'ead!"

"Hear me, neighbors!" at last he cried, —
"What to me is this noisy ride?
What is the shame that clothes the skin
To the nameless horror that lives within?
Waking or sleeping, I see a wreck,
And hear a cry from a reeling deck!
Hate me and curse me, — I only dread
The hand of God and the face of the dead!"
  Said old Floyd Ireson, for his hard heart,
  Tarred and feathered and carried in a cart
    By the women of Marblehead!

Then the wife of the skipper lost at sea
Said, "God has touched him! why should we!"
Said an old wife mourning her only son,
"Cut the rogue's tether and let him run!"
So with soft relentings and rude excuse,
Half scorn, half pity, they cut him loose,
And gave him a cloak to hide him in,
And left him alone with his shame and sin.
  Poor Floyd Ireson, for his hard heart,
  Tarred and feathered and carried in a cart
    By the women of Marblehead!

70.   *The Eternal Goodness*

O FRIENDS! with whom my feet have trod
    The quiet aisles of prayer,
Glad witness to your zeal for God
    And love of man I bear.

I trace your lines of argument;
    Your logic linked and strong
I weigh as one who dreads dissent,
    And fears a doubt as wrong.

But still my human hands are weak
    To hold your iron creeds:
Against the words ye bid me speak
    My heart within me pleads.

Who fathoms the Eternal Thought?
    Who talks of scheme and plan?
The Lord is God! He needeth not
    The poor device of man.

I walk with bare, hushed feet the ground
    Ye tread with boldness shod;
I dare not fix with mete and bound
    The love and power of God.

Ye praise His justice; even such
    His pitying love I deem:
Ye seek a king; I fain would touch
    The robe that hath no seam.

Ye see the curse which overbroods
    A world of pain and loss;
I hear our Lord's beatitudes
    And prayer upon the cross.

More than your schoolmen teach, within
    Myself, alas! I know:
Too dark ye cannot paint the sin,
    Too small the merit show.

I bow my forehead to the dust,
    I veil mine eyes for shame,
And urge, in trembling self-distrust,
    A prayer without a claim.

I see the wrong that round me lies,
    I feel the guilt within;
I hear, with groan and travail-cries,
    The world confess its sin.

Yet, in the maddening maze of things,
    And tossed by storm and flood,
To one fixed trust my spirit clings;
    I know that God is good!

Not mine to look where cherubim
    And seraphs may not see,
But nothing can be good in Him
    Which evil is in me.

The wrong that pains my soul below
    I dare not throne above,
I know not of His hate, — I know
    His goodness and His love.

JOHN GREENLEAF WHITTIER

I dimly guess from blessings known
   Of greater out of sight,
And, with the chastened Psalmist, own
   His judgments too are right.

I long for household voices gone,
   For vanished smiles I long,
But God hath led my dear ones on,
   And He can do no wrong.

I know not what the future hath
   Of marvel or surprise,
Assured alone that life and death
   His mercy underlies.

And if my heart and flesh are weak
   To bear an untried pain,
The bruisëd reed He will not break,
   But strengthen and sustain.

No offering of my own I have,
   Nor works my faith to prove;
I can but give the gifts He gave,
   And plead His love for love.

And so beside the Silent Sea
   I wait the muffled oar;
No harm from Him can come to me
   On ocean or on shore.

I know not where His islands lift
   Their fronded palms in air;
I only know I cannot drift
   Beyond His love and care.

O brothers! if my faith is vain,
    If hopes like these betray,
Pray for me that my feet may gain
    The sure and safer way.

And Thou, O Lord! by whom are seen
    Thy creatures as they be,
Forgive me if too close I lean
    My human heart on Thee!

NATHANIEL PARKER WILLIS

1807–1867

71.   *Unseen Spirits*

THE shadows lay along Broadway,
    'Twas near the twilight-tide,
And slowly there a lady fair
    Was walking in her pride.
Alone walked she; but, viewlessly,
    Walked spirits at her side.

Peace charmed the street beneath her feet,
    And Honor charmed the air;
And all astir looked kind on her,
    And called her good as fair,
For all God ever gave to her
    She kept with chary care.

She kept with care her beauties rare
    From lovers warm and true,
For her heart was cold to all but gold,
    And the rich came not to woo —
But honored well are charms to sell
    If priests the selling do.

Now walking there was one more fair —
    A slight girl, lily-pale;
And she had unseen company
    To make the spirit quail:
'Twixt Want and Scorn she walked forlorn,
    And nothing could avail.

No mercy now can clear her brow
    For this world's peace to pray;
For, as love's wild prayer dissolved in air,
    Her woman's heart gave way! —
But the sin forgiven by Christ in heaven
    By man is cursed alway!

EDGAR ALLAN POE

1809–1849

72.   *The Raven*

ONCE upon a midnight dreary, while I pondered, weak
    and weary,
Over many a quaint and curious volume of forgotten
    lore, —
While I nodded, nearly napping, suddenly there came a
    tapping,
As of some one gently rapping, rapping at my chamber
    door.
" 'Tis some visitor," I muttered, " tapping at my chamber
    door:
        Only this and nothing more."

Ah, distinctly I remember it was in the bleak December,
And each separate dying ember wrought its ghost upon the
floor.
Eagerly I wished the morrow; — vainly I had sought to
borrow
From my books surcease of sorrow — sorrow for the lost
Lenore,
For the rare and radiant maiden whom the angels name
Lenore:
Nameless here for evermore.

And the silken sad uncertain rustling of each purple cur-
tain
Thrilled me — filled me with fantastic terrors never felt
before;
So that now, to still the beating of my heart, I stood re-
peating
" 'Tis some visitor entreating entrance at my chamber
door,
Some late visitor entreating entrance at my chamber door:
This it is and nothing more."

Presently my soul grew stronger; hesitating then no
longer,
" Sir," said I, " or Madam, truly your forgiveness I implore;
But the fact is I was napping, and so gently you came
rapping,
And so faintly you came tapping, tapping at my chamber
door,
That I scarce was sure I heard you " — here I opened wide
the door: —
Darkness there and nothing more.

Deep into that darkness peering, long I stood there won-
    dering, fearing,
Doubting, dreaming dreams no mortals ever dared to
    dream before;
But the silence was unbroken, and the stillness gave no
    token,
And the only word there spoken was the whispered word,
    "Lenore?"
This I whispered, and an echo murmured back the word,
    "Lenore:"
        Merely this and nothing more.

Back into the chamber turning, all my soul within me
    burning,
Soon again I heard a tapping somewhat louder than be-
    fore.
"Surely," said I, "surely that is something at my window
    lattice;
Let me see, then, what thereat is, and this mystery ex-
    plore;
Let my heart be still a moment and this mystery explore:
    'Tis the wind and nothing more."

Open here I flung the shutter, when, with many a flirt and
    flutter,
In there stepped a stately Raven of the saintly days of yore.
Not the least obeisance made he; not a minute stopped or
    stayed he;
But, with mien of lord or lady, perched above my chamber
    door,
Perched upon a bust of Pallas just above my chamber door:
    Perched, and sat, and nothing more.

Then this ebony bird beguiling my sad fancy into smiling
By the grave and stern decorum of the countenance it
    wore, ——
"Though thy crest be shorn and shaven, thou," I said,
    "art sure no craven,
Ghastly grim and ancient Raven wandering from the
    Nightly shore:
Tell me what thy lordly name is on the Night's Plutonian
    shore! "
        Quoth the Raven, "Nevermore."

Much I marvelled this ungainly fowl to hear discourse
    so plainly,
Though its answer little meaning — little relevancy bore;
For we cannot help agreeing that no living human
    being
Ever yet was blessed with seeing bird above his chamber
    door,
Bird or beast upon the sculptured bust above his chamber
    door,
        With such name as "Nevermore."

But the Raven, sitting lonely on the placid bust, spoke only
That one word, as if his soul in that one word he did
    outpour.
Nothing further then he uttered, not a feather then he
    fluttered,
Till I scarcely more than muttered, — "Other friends
    have flown before;
On the morrow *he* will leave me, as my Hopes have flown
    before."
        Then the bird said, "Nevermore."

Startled at the stillness broken by reply so aptly spoken,
"Doubtless," said I, "what it utters is its only stock and
    store,
Caught from some unhappy master whom unmerciful Dis-
    aster
Followed fast and followed faster till his songs one burden
    bore:
Till the dirges of his Hope that melancholy burden bore
        Of 'Never — nevermore.'"

But the Raven still beguiling all my fancy into smil-
    ing,
Straight I wheeled a cushioned seat in front of bird and
    bust and door;
Then, upon the velvet sinking, I betook myself to linking
Fancy unto fancy, thinking what this ominous bird of
    yore,
What this grim, ungainly, ghastly, gaunt, and ominous bird
    of yore
        Meant in croaking "Nevermore."

This I sat engaged in guessing, but no syllable expressing
To the fowl whose fiery eyes now burned into my bosom's
    core;
This and more I sat divining, with my head at ease reclin-
    ing
On the cushion's velvet lining that the lamp-light gloated
    o'er,
But whose velvet violet lining with the lamp-light gloat-
    ing o'er
        She shall press, ah, nevermore!

Then, methought, the air grew denser, perfumed from an
    unseen censer
Swung by seraphim whose foot-falls tinkled on the tufted
    floor.
"Wretch," I cried, "thy God hath lent thee — by these
    angels he hath sent thee
Respite — respite and nepenthe from thy memories of
    Lenore!
Quaff, oh quaff this kind nepenthe, and forget this lost
    Lenore!"
        Quoth the Raven, "Nevermore."

"Prophet!" said I, "thing of evil! prophet still, if bird
    or devil!
Whether Tempter sent, or whether tempest tossed thee
    here ashore,
Desolate yet all undaunted, on this desert land en-
    chanted —
On this home by Horror haunted — tell me truly, I im-
    plore:
Is there — is there balm in Gilead? — tell me — tell me,
    I implore!"
        Quoth the Raven, "Nevermore."

"Prophet!" said I, "thing of evil — prophet still, if bird
    or devil!
By that Heaven that bends above us, by that God we both
    adore,
Tell this soul with sorrow laden if, within the distant
    Aidenn,
It shall clasp a sainted maiden whom the angels name
    Lenore:

Clasp a rare and radiant maiden whom the angels name
    Lenore! ”
        Quoth the Raven, “ Nevermore.”

“ Be that word our sign of parting, bird or fiend! ” I
    shrieked, upstarting:
“ Get thee back into the tempest and the Night's Plutonian
    shore!
Leave no black plume as a token of that lie thy soul hath
    spoken!
Leave my loneliness unbroken! quit the bust above my
    door!
Take thy beak from out my heart, and take thy form from
    off my door! ”
        Quoth the Raven, “ Nevermore.”

And the Raven, never flitting, still is sitting, still is sitting
On the pallid bust of Pallas just above my chamber door;
And his eyes have all the seeming of a demon's that is
    dreaming,
And the lamp-light o'er him streaming throws his shadow
    on the floor:
And my soul from out that shadow that lies floating on the
    floor
        Shall be lifted — nevermore!

73. *The Bells*

I

HEAR the sledges with the bells,
Silver bells!
What a world of merriment their melody foretells!
How they tinkle, tinkle, tinkle,
In the icy air of night!
While the stars, that oversprinkle
All the heavens, seem to twinkle
With a crystalline delight;
Keeping time, time, time,
In a sort of Runic rhyme,
To the tintinnabulation that so musically wells
From the bells, bells, bells, bells,
Bells, bells, bells —
From the jingling and the tinkling of the bells.

II

Hear the mellow wedding bells,
Golden bells!
What a world of happiness their harmony foretells!
Through the balmy air of night
How they ring out their delight!
From the molten-golden notes,
And all in tune,
What a liquid ditty floats
To the turtle-dove that listens, while she gloats
On the moon!
Oh, from out the sounding cells,

What a gush of euphony voluminously wells!
How it swells!
How it dwells
On the Future! how it tells
Of the rapture that impels
To the swinging and the ringing
Of the bells, bells, bells,
Of the bells, bells, bells, bells,
Bells, bells, bells ——
To the rhyming and the chiming of the bells!

III

Hear the loud alarum bells,
Brazen bells!
What a tale of terror, now, their turbulency tells!
In the startled ear of night
How they scream out their affright!
Too much horrified to speak,
They can only shriek, shriek,
Out of tune,
In a clamorous appealing to the mercy of the fire,
In a mad expostulation with the deaf and frantic fire,
Leaping higher, higher, higher,
With a desperate desire,
And a resolute endeavor
Now —— now to sit or never,
By the side of the pale-faced moon.
Oh, the bells, bells, bells!
What a tale their terror tells
Of Despair!
How they clang, and clash, and roar!
What a horror they outpour

On the bosom of the palpitating air!
Yet the ear it fully knows,
By the twanging
And the clanging,
How the danger ebbs and flows;
Yet the ear distinctly tells,
In the jangling
And the wrangling,
How the danger sinks and swells, —
By the sinking or the swelling in the anger of the bells,
Of the bells,
Of the bells, bells, bells, bells,
Bells, bells, bells —
In the clamor and the clangor of the bells!

IV

Hear the tolling of the bells,
Iron bells!
What a world of solemn thought their monody compels!
In the silence of the night
How we shiver with affright
At the melancholy menace of their tone!
For every sound that floats
From the rust within their throats
Is a groan.
And the people — ah, the people,
They that dwell up in the steeple,
All alone,
And who tolling, tolling, tolling,
In that muffled monotone,
Feel a glory in so rolling
On the human heart a stone —

They are neither man nor woman,
They are neither brute nor human,
They are Ghouls:
And their king it is who tolls;
And he rolls, rolls, rolls,
Rolls
A pæan from the bells;
And his merry bosom swells
With the pæan of the bells,
And he dances, and he yells:
Keeping time, time, time,
In a sort of Runic rhyme,
To the pæan of the bells,
Of the bells:
Keeping time, time, time,
In a sort of Runic rhyme,
To the throbbing of the bells,
Of the bells, bells, bells —
To the sobbing of the bells;
Keeping time, time, time,
As he knells, knells, knells,
In a happy Runic rhyme,
To the rolling of the bells,
Of the bells, bells, bells:
To the tolling of the bells,
Of the bells, bells, bells, bells,
Bells, bells, bells —
To the moaning and the groaning of the bells.

EDGAR ALLAN POE

74.   *Ulalume*

THE skies they were ashen and sober;
    The leaves they were crispëd and sere,
  The leaves they were withering and sere;
It was night in the lonesome October
    Of my most immemorial year;
It was hard by the dim lake of Auber,
    In the misty mid region of Weir:
It was down by the dank tarn of Auber,
    In the ghoul-haunted woodland of Weir.

Here once, through an alley Titanic
    Of cypress, I roamed with my Soul —
    Of cypress, with Psyche, my Soul.
These were days when my heart was volcanic
    As the scoriac rivers that roll,
    As the lavas that restlessly roll
Their sulphurous currents down Yaanek
    In the ultimate climes of the pole,
That groan as they roll down Mount Yaanek
    In the realms of the boreal pole.

Our talk had been serious and sober,
    But our thoughts they were palsied and sere,
    Our memories were treacherous and sere,
For we knew not the month was October,
    And we marked not the night of the year,
    (Ah, night of all nights in the year!)
We noted not the dim lake of Auber
    (Though once we had journeyed down here),
Remembered not the dank tarn of Auber
    Nor the ghoul-haunted woodland of Weir.

EDGAR ALLAN POE

And now, as the night was senescent
  And star-dials pointed to morn,
  As the star-dials hinted of morn,
At the end of our path a liquescent
  And nebulous lustre was born,
Out of which a miraculous crescent
  Arose with a duplicate horn,
Astarte's bediamonded crescent
  Distinct with its duplicate horn.

And I said — " She is warmer than Dian:
  She rolls through an ether of sighs,
  She revels in a region of sighs:
She has seen that the tears are not dry on
  These cheeks, where the worm never dies,
And has come past the stars of the Lion
  To point us the path to the skies,
  To the Lethean peace of the skies:
Come up, in despite of the Lion,
  To shine on us with her bright eyes:
Come up through the lair of the Lion,
  With love in her luminous eyes."

But Psyche, uplifting her finger,
  Said — " Sadly this star I mistrust,
  Her pallor I strangely mistrust:
Oh, hasten! — oh, let us not linger!
  Oh, fly! — let us fly! — for we must."
In terror she spoke, letting sink her
  Wings until they trailed in the dust;
In agony sobbed, letting sink her
  Plumes till they trailed in the dust,
  Till they sorrowfully trailed in the dust.

I replied —— " This is nothing but dreaming:
 Let us on by this tremulous light!
 Let us bathe in this crystalline light!
Its sibyllic splendor is beaming
 With hope and in beauty to-night:
 See, it flickers up the sky through the night!
Ah, we safely may trust to its gleaming,
 And be sure it will lead us aright:
We safely may trust to a gleaming
 That cannot but guide us aright,
 Since it flickers up to Heaven through the night."

Thus I pacified Psyche and kissed her,
 And tempted her out of her gloom,
 And conquered her scruples and gloom;
And we passed to the end of the vista,
 But were stopped by the door of a tomb,
 By the door of a legended tomb;
And I said —— " What is written, sweet sister,
 On the door of this legended tomb? "
She replied —— " Ulalume —— Ulalume ——
 'Tis the vault of thy lost Ulalume! "

Then my heart it grew ashen and sober
 As the leaves that were crispëd and sere,
 As the leaves that were withering and sere,
And I cried —— " It was surely October
 On this very night of last year
 That I journey —— I journey down here,
 That I brought a dread burden down here:
 On this night of all nights in the year,
 Ah, what demon has tempted me here?

Well I know, now, this dim lake of Auber,
  This misty mid region of Weir:
Well I know, now, this dank tarn of Auber,
  This ghoul-haunted woodland of Weir."

75.   *The Haunted Palace*

IN the greenest of our valleys
    By good angels tenanted,
Once a fair and stately palace —
    Radiant palace — reared its head.
In the monarch Thought's dominion,
    It stood there;
Never seraph spread a pinion
    Over fabric half so fair.

Banners yellow, glorious, golden,
    On its roof did float and flow
(This — all this — was in the olden
    Time long ago),
And every gentle air that dallied,
    In that sweet day,
Along the ramparts plumed and pallid,
    A wingèd odor went away.

Wanderers in that happy valley
    Through two luminous windows saw
Spirits moving musically,
    To a lute's well-tunèd law,
Round about a throne where, sitting,
    Porphyrogene,
In state his glory well befitting,
    The ruler of the realm was seen.

Not the gayly-jewelled dead,
Tempt the waters from their bed;
For no ripples curl, alas,
Along that wilderness of glass;
No swellings tell that winds may be
Upon some far-off happier sea;
No heavings hint that winds have been
On seas less hideously serene!

But lo, a stir is in the air!
The wave — there is a movement there!
As if the towers had thrust aside,
In slightly sinking, the dull tide;
As if their tops had feebly given
A void within the filmy Heaven!
The waves have now a redder glow,
The hours are breathing faint and low;
And when, amid no earthly moans,
Down, down that town shall settle hence,
Hell, rising from a thousand thrones,
Shall do it reverence.

77. *The Sleeper*

AT midnight, in the month of June,
I stand beneath the mystic moon.
An opiate vapor, dewy, dim,
Exhales from out her golden rim,
And, softly dripping, drop by drop,
Upon the quiet mountain-top,
Steals drowsily and musically
Into the universal valley.

EDGAR ALLAN POE

The rosemary nods upon the grave;
The lily lolls upon the wave;
Wrapping the fog about its breast,
The ruin moulders into rest;
Looking like Lethe, see! the lake
A conscious slumber seems to take,
And would not, for the world, awake.
All beauty sleeps! — and lo! where lies
Irene, with her destinies!

O lady bright! can it be right,
This window open to the night?
The wanton airs, from the tree-top,
Laughingly through the lattice drop;
The bodiless airs, a wizard rout,
Flit through thy chamber in and out,
And wave the curtain canopy
So fitfully, so fearfully,
Above the closed and fringëd lid
'Neath which thy slumb'ring soul lies hid,
That, o'er the floor and down the wall,
Like ghosts the shadows rise and fall.
O lady dear, hast thou no fear?
Why and what art thou dreaming here?
Sure thou art come o'er far-off seas,
A wonder to these garden trees!
Strange is thy pallor: strange thy dress:
Strange, above all, thy length of tress,
And this all solemn silentness!

The lady sleeps. Oh, may her sleep,
Which is enduring, so be deep!
Heaven have her in its sacred keep!

This chamber changed for one more holy,
This bed for one more melancholy,
I pray to God that she may lie
Forever with unopened eye,
While the pale sheeted ghosts go by.
My love, she sleeps. Oh, may her sleep,
As it is lasting, so be deep!
Soft may the worms about her creep!
Far in the forest, dim and old,
For her may some tall vault unfold:
Some vault that oft hath flung its black
And wingèd panels fluttering back,
Triumphant, o'er the crested palls
Of her grand family funerals:
Some sepulchre, remote, alone,
Against whose portal she hath thrown,
In childhood, many an idle stone:
Some tomb from out whose sounding door
She ne'er shall force an echo more,
Thrilling to think, poor child of sin,
It was the dead who groaned within!

78.   *Annabel Lee*

IT was many and many a year ago,
  In a kingdom by the sea,
That a maiden there lived whom you may know
  By the name of Annabel Lee;
And this maiden she lived with no other thought
  Than to love and be loved by me.

I was a child and she was a child,
  In this kingdom by the sea,
But we loved with a love that was more than love,
  I and my Annabel Lee;
With a love that the wingèd seraphs of heaven
  Coveted her and me.

And this was the reason that, long ago,
  In this kingdom by the sea,
A wind blew out of a cloud, chilling
  My beautiful Annabel Lee;
So that her highborn kinsmen came
  And bore her away from me,
To shut her up in a sepulchre
  In this kingdom by the sea.

The angels, not half so happy in heaven,
  Went envying her and me;
Yes, that was the reason (as all men know,
  In this kingdom by the sea)
That the wind came out of the cloud by night,
  Chilling and killing my Annabel Lee.

But our love it was stronger by far than the love
  Of those who were older than we,
  Of many far wiser than we;
And neither the angels in heaven above,
  Nor the demons down under the sea,
Can ever dissever my soul from the soul
  Of the beautiful Annabel Lee.

For the moon never beams, without bringing me dreams
　　Of the beautiful Annabel Lee;
And the stars never rise, but I feel the bright eyes
　　Of the beautiful Annabel Lee;
And so, all the night-tide, I lie down by the side
Of my darling, — my darling, — my life and my bride,
　　In her sepulchre there by the sea,
　　In her tomb by the sounding sea.

79.　　　　　　*To Helen*

HELEN, thy beauty is to me
　　Like those Nicæan barks of yore,
That gently, o'er a perfumed sea,
　　The weary, wayworn wanderer bore
　　To his own native shore.

On desperate seas long wont to roam,
　　Thy hyacinth hair, thy classic face,
Thy Naiad airs, have brought me home
　　To the glory that was Greece
And the grandeur that was Rome.

Lo! in yon brilliant window-niche
　　How statue-like I see thee stand,
　　The agate lamp within thy hand!
Ah, Psyche, from the regions which
　　Are Holy Land!

146

EDGAR ALLAN POE

80.   *To One in Paradise*

THOU wast all that to me, love,
    For which my soul did pine:
A green isle in the sea, love,
    A fountain and a shrine
All wreathed with fairy fruits and flowers,
    And all the flowers were mine.

Ah, dream too bright to last!
    Ah, starry Hope, that didst arise
But to be overcast!
    A voice from out the Future cries,
"On! on!"—but o'er the Past
    (Dim gulf!) my spirit hovering lies
Mute, motionless, aghast.

For, alas! alas! with me
    The light of Life is o'er!
No more—no more—no more—
(Such language holds the solemn sea
    To the sands upon the shore)
Shall bloom the thunder-blasted tree,
    Or the stricken eagle soar.

And all my days are trances,
    And all my nightly dreams
Are where thy gray eye glances,
    And where thy footstep gleams—
In what ethereal dances,
    By what eternal streams.

Eighteen hundred increased by ten; —
" Hahnsum kerridge " they called it then.
Eighteen hundred and twenty came; —
Running as usual; much the same.
Thirty and forty at last arrive,
And then come fifty, and FIFTY-FIVE.

Little of all we value here
Wakes on the morn of its hundredth year
Without both feeling and looking queer.
In fact, there's nothing that keeps its youth,
So far as I know, but a tree and truth.
(This is a moral that runs at large;
Take it. — You 're welcome. — No extra charge.)

FIRST OF NOVEMBER, — the Earthquake-day —
There are traces of age in the one-hoss shay,
A general flavor of mild decay,
But nothing local, as one may say.
There couldn't be, — for the Deacon's art
Had made it so like in every part
That there wasn't a chance for one to start.
For the wheels were just as strong as the thills,
And the floor was just as strong as the sills,
And the panels just as strong as the floor,
And the whipple-tree neither less nor more,
And the back-crossbar as strong as the fore,
And spring and axle and hub *encore*.
And yet, *as a whole*, it is past a doubt
In another hour it will be *worn out!*

OLIVER WENDELL HOLMES

First of November, 'Fifty-five!
This morning the parson takes a drive.
Now, small boys, get out of the way!
Here comes the wonderful one-hoss shay,
Drawn by a rat-tailed, ewe-necked bay.
" Huddup! " said the parson. — Off went they.
The parson was working his Sunday's text, —
Had got to *fifthly*, and stopped perplexed
At what the — Moses — was coming next.
All at once the horse stood still,
Close by the meet'n'-house on the hill.
— First a shiver, and then a thrill,
Then something decidedly like a spill, —
And the parson was sitting upon a rock,
At half past nine by the meet'n'-house clock, —
Just the hour of the Earthquake shock!

— What do you think the parson found,
When he got up and stared around?
The poor old chaise in a heap or mound,
As if it had been to the mill and ground!
You see, of course, if you're not a dunce,
How it went to pieces all at once, —
All at once, and nothing first, —
Just as bubbles do when they burst.

End of the wonderful one-hoss shay.
Logic is logic. That's all I say.

HENRY DAVID THOREAU

1817–1862

86. *Inspiration*

IF with light head erect I sing,
  Though all the Muses lend their force,
From my poor love of anything,
The verse is weak and shallow as its source.

But if with bended neck I grope
Listening behind me for my wit,
With faith superior to hope,
More anxious to keep back than forward it, —

Making my soul accomplice there
Unto the flame my heart hath lit,
Then will the verse forever wear, —
Time cannot bend the line which God has writ.

I hearing get, who had but ears,
And sight, who had but eyes before;
I moments live, who lived but years,
And truth discern, who knew but learning's lore.

Now chiefly is my natal hour,
And only now my prime of life;
Of manhood's strength it is the flower,
'Tis peace's end, and war's beginning strife.

It comes in summer's broadest noon,
By a gray wall, or some chance place,
Unseasoning time, insulting June,
And vexing day with its presuming face.

I will not doubt the love untold
Which not my worth nor want hath bought,
Which wooed me young, and woos me old,
And to this evening hath me brought.

87. *The Fisher's Boy*

MY life is like a stroll upon the beach,
  As near the ocean's edge as I can go;
My tardy steps its waves sometimes o'erreach,
  Sometimes I stay to let them overflow.

My sole employment is, and scrupulous care,
  To place my gains beyond the reach of tides, —
Each smoother pebble, and each shell more rare,
  Which Ocean kindly to my hand confides.

I have but few companions on the shore:
  They scorn the strand who sail upon the sea;
Yet oft I think the ocean they've sailed o'er
  Is deeper known upon the strand to me.

The middle sea contains no crimson dulse,
  Its deeper waves cast up no pearls to view;
Along the shore my hand is on its pulse,
  And I converse with many a shipwrecked crew.

WALT WHITMAN

1819–1892

88. *From " Song of Myself "*

I

I CELEBRATE myself, and sing myself,
   And what I assume you shall assume,
For every atom belonging to me as good belongs to you,
I loaf and invite my soul,
I lean and loaf at my ease observing a spear of summer
   grass.

My tongue, every atom of my blood, formed from this
   soil, this air,
Born here of parents born here from parents the same, and
   their parents the same,
I, now thirty-seven years old in perfect health begin,
Hoping to cease not till death.

Creeds and schools in abeyance,
Retiring back awhile sufficed at what they are, but never
   forgotten,
I harbor for good or bad, I permit to speak at every hazard,
Nature without check with original energy.

A child said *What is the grass?* fetching it to me with full
   hands;
How could I answer the child? I do not know what it is
   any more than he.

I guess it must be the flag of my disposition, out of hope-
   ful green stuff woven.

162

Or I guess it is the handkerchief of the Lord,
A scented gift and remembrancer designedly dropped,
Bearing the owner's name someway in the corners, that we
    may see and remark, and say *Whose?*

Or I guess the grass is itself a child, the produced babe of
    the vegetation.

Or I guess it is a uniform hieroglyphic,
And it means, Sprouting alike in broad zones and narrow
    zones,
Growing among black folks as among white,
Kanuck, Tuckahoe, Congressman, Cuff, I gave them the
    same, I receive them the same.

And now it seems to me the beautiful uncut hair of graves.

Tenderly will I use you curling grass,
It may be you transpire from the breasts of young men,
It may be if I had known them I would have loved them,
It may be you are from old people, or from offspring taken
    soon out of their mothers' laps,
And here you are the mothers' laps.

This grass is very dark to be from the white heads of old
    mothers,
Darker than the colorless beards of old men,
Dark to come from under the faint red roofs of mouths.

O I perceive after all so many uttering tongues,
And I perceive they do not come from the roofs of mouths
    for nothing.

I wish I could translate the hints about the dead young
 men and women,
And the hints about old men and mothers, and the offspring taken soon out of their laps.

What do you think has become of the young and old men?
And what do you think has become of the women and
 children?

They are alive and well somewhere,
The smallest sprout shows there is really no death,
And if ever there was it led forward life, and does not
 wait at the end to arrest it,
And ceased the moment life appeared.
All goes onward and outward, nothing collapses,
And to die is different from what any one supposed, and
 luckier.

89. *When I Heard at the Close of the Day*

WHEN I heard at the close of the day how my name
 had been receiv'd with plaudits in the capitol, still
 it was not a happy night for me that follow'd,
And else when I carous'd, or when my plans were ac-
 complish'd, still I was not happy,
But the day when I rose at dawn from the bed of perfect
 health, refresh'd, singing, inhaling the ripe breath
 of autumn,
When I saw the full moon in the west grow pale and disappear in the morning light,

When I wander'd alone over the beach, and undressing
  bathed, laughing with the cool waters, and saw the
  sun rise,
And when I thought how my dear friend my lover was
  on his way coming, O then I was happy,
O then each breath tasted sweeter, and all that day my
  food nourish'd me more, and the beautiful day pass'd
  well,
And the next came with equal joy, and with the next at
  evening came my friend,
And that night while all was still I heard the waters roll
  slowly continually up the shores,
I heard the hissing rustle of the liquid and sands as di-
  rected to me whispering to congratulate me,
For the one I love most lay sleeping by me under the
  same cover in the cool night,
In the stillness in the autumn moonbeams his face was inclined toward me,
And his arm lay lightly around my breast — and that night
  I was happy.

I am the poet of the Body and I am the poet of the Soul,
The pleasures of heaven are with me and the pains of
  hell are with me,
The first I graft and increase upon myself, the latter I
  translate into a new tongue.

I am the poet of the woman the same as the man,
And I say it is as great to be a woman as to be a man,
And I say there is nothing greater than the mother of
  men.

WALT WHITMAN

I chant the chant of dilation or pride,
We have had ducking and deprecating about enough,
I show that size is only development.

Have you outstript the rest? are you the President?
It is a trifle, they will more than arrive there every one,
and still pass on.

I am he that walks with the tender and growing night,
I call to the earth and sea half-held by the night.

Press close bare-bosom'd night — press close magnetic
nourishing night!
Night of south winds — night of the large few stars!
Still nodding night — mad naked summer night.

Smile O voluptuous cool-breath'd earth!
Earth of the slumbering and liquid trees!
Earth of departed sunset — earth of the mountains misty-
topt!
Earth of the vitreous pour of the full moon just tinged
with blue!
Earth of shine and dark mottling the tide of the river!
Earth of the limpid gray of clouds brighter and clearer
for my sake!
Far-swooping elbow'd earth — rich apple-blossom'd earth!
Smile, for your lover comes.

Prodigal, you have given me love — therefore I to you
give love!
O unspeakable passionate love.

I have said that the soul is not more than the body,
And I have said that the body is not more than the soul,
And nothing, not God, is greater to one than one's self is,
And whoever walks a furlong without sympathy walks to
    his own funeral drest in his shroud,
And I or you pocketless of a dime may purchase the pick
    of the earth,
And to glance with an eye or show a beam in its pod con-
    founds the learning of all times,
And there is no trade or employment but the young man
    following it may become a hero,
And there is no object so soft but it makes a hub for the
    wheel'd universe,
And I say to any man or woman, Let your soul stand cool
    and composed before a million universes.

And I say to mankind, Be not curious about God,
For I who am curious about each am not curious about
    God,
(No array of terms can say how much I am at peace about
    God and about death.)

I hear and behold God in every object, yet understand God
    not in the least,
Nor do I understand who there can be more wonderful
    than myself.

Why should I wish to see God better than this day?
I see something of God each hour of the twenty-four, and
    each moment then,
In the faces of men and women I see God, and in my
    own face in the glass,

I find letters from God dropt in the street, and every
    one is sign'd by God's name,
And I leave them where they are, for I know that where-
    soe'er I go,
Others will punctually come for ever and ever.

90. *Out of the Cradle Endlessly Rocking*

OUT of the cradle endlessly rocking,
    Out of the mocking-bird's throat, the musical shuttle,
Out of the Ninth-month midnight,
Over the sterile sands and the fields beyond, where the
    child leaving his bed wandered alone, bareheaded,
    barefoot,
Down from the showered halo,
Up from the mystic play of shadows twining and twisting
    as if they were alive,
Out from the patches of briers and blackberries,
From the memories of the bird that chanted to me,
From your memories, sad brother, from the fitful risings
    and fallings I heard,
From under that yellow half-moon late-risen and swollen
    as if with tears,
From those beginning notes of yearning and love there
    in the mist,
From the thousand responses of my heart never to cease,
From the myriad thence-aroused words,
From the word stronger and more delicious than any,
From such as now they start the scene revisiting,
As a flock, twittering, rising, or overhead passing,

WALT WHITMAN

Borne hither, ere all eludes me, hurriedly,
A man, yet by these tears a little boy again,
Throwing myself on the sand, confronting the waves,
I, chanter of pains and joys, uniter of here and hereafter,
Taking all hints to use them, but swiftly leaping beyond
    them,
A reminiscence sing.

Once Paumanok,
When the lilac-scent was in the air and Fifth-month grass
    was growing,
Up this seashore in some briers,
Two feathered guests from Alabama, two together,
And their nest, and four light-green eggs spotted with
    brown,
And every day the he-bird to and fro near at hand,
And every day the she-bird crouched on her nest, silent,
    with bright eyes,
And every day I, a curious boy, never too close, never dis-
    turbing them,
Cautiously peering, absorbing, translating.

Shine! shine! shine!
Pour down your warmth, great sun!
While we bask, we two together.

Two together!
Winds blow south, or winds blow north,
Day come white, or night come black,
Home, or rivers and mountains from home,
Singing all time, minding no time,
While we bask, we two together.

Till of a sudden,
Maybe killed, unknown to her mate,
One forenoon the she-bird crouched not on the nest,
Nor returned that afternoon, nor the next,
Nor ever appeared again.

And thenceforward all summer in the sound of the sea,
And at night under the full of the moon in calmer
    weather,
Over the hoarse surging of the sea,
Or flitting from brier to brier by day,
I saw, I heard at intervals the remaining one, the he-bird,
The solitary guest from Alabama.

Blow! blow! blow!
Blow up sea-winds along Paumanok's shore;
I wait and I wait till you blow my mate to me.

Yes, when the stars glistened,
All night long on the prong of a moss-scalloped stake,
Down almost amid the slapping waves,
Sat the lone singer wonderful causing tears.

He called on his mate,
He poured forth the meanings which I of all men know.

Yes, my brother, I know, —
The rest might not, but I have treasured every note,
For more than once dimly down to the beach gliding,
Silent, avoiding the moonbeams, blending myself with the
    shadows,

WALT WHITMAN

Recalling now the obscure shapes, the echoes, the sounds
     and sights after their sorts,
The white arms out in the breakers tirelessly tossing,
I, with bare feet, a child, the wind wafting my hair,
Listened long and long.

Listened to keep, to sing, now translating the notes,
Following you, my brother.

Soothe! soothe! soothe!
Close on its wave soothes the wave behind,
And again another behind embracing and lapping, every
    one close,
But my love soothes not me, not me.

Low hangs the moon, it rose late,
It is lagging — O I think it is heavy with love, with love.

O madly the sea pushes upon the land,
With love, with love.

O night! do I not see my love fluttering out among the
    breakers?
What is that little black thing I see there in the white?

Loud! loud! loud!
Loud I call to you, my love!

High and clear I shoot my voice over the waves,
Surely you must know who is here, is here,
You must know who I am, my love.

171

WALT WHITMAN

Low-hanging moon!
What is that dusty spot in your brown yellow?
O it is the shape, the shape of my mate!
O moon, do not keep her from me any longer.

Land! land! O land!
Whichever way I turn, O, I think you could give me my
*   mate back again if you only would,*
For I am almost sure I see her dimly whichever way I look.

O rising stars!
Perhaps the one I want so much will rise, will rise with
*   some of you.*

O throat! O trembling throat!
Sound clearer through the atmosphere!
Pierce the woods, the earth,
Somewhere listening to catch you must be the one I want.

Shake out carols!
Solitary here, the night's carols!
Carols of lonesome love! death's carols!
Carols under that lagging, yellow, waning moon!
O under that moon where she droops almost down into the
*   sea!*
O reckless despairing carols!

But soft! sink low!
Soft! let me just murmur,
And do you wait a moment, you husky-noised sea,
For somewhere I believe I heard my mate responding to
*   me,*

WALT WHITMAN

So faint, I must be still, be still to listen,
But not altogether still, for then she might not come
immediately to me.

Hither, my love!
Here I am! here!
With this just-sustained note I announce myself to you,
This gentle call is for you my love, for you.

Do not be decoyed elsewhere:
That is the whistle of the wind, it is not my voice,
That is the fluttering, the fluttering of the spray,
Those are the shadows of leaves.

O darkness! O in vain!
O I am very sick and sorrowful.

O brown halo in the sky near the moon, drooping upon the
sea!
O troubled reflection in the sea!
O throat! O throbbing heart!
And I singing uselessly, uselessly all the night.

O past! O happy life! O songs of joy!
In the air, in the woods, over fields,
Loved! loved! loved! loved! loved!
But my mate no more, no more with me!
We two together no more.

The aria sinking,
All else continuing, the stars shining,
The winds blowing, the notes of the bird continuous echo-
ing,

With angry moans the fierce old mother incessantly moan-
  ing,
On the sands of Paumanok's shore gray and rustling,
The yellow half-moon enlarged, sagging down, drooping,
  the face of the sea almost touching,
The boy ecstatic, with his bare feet the waves, with his hair
  the atmosphere dallying,
The love in the heart long pent, now loose, now at last
  tumultuously bursting,
The aria's meaning, the ears, the soul, swiftly depositing,
The strange tears down the cheeks coursing,
The colloquy there, the trio, each uttering,
The undertone, the savage old mother incessantly crying,
To the boy's soul's questions sullenly timing, some drown'd
  secret hissing,
To the outsetting bard.

Demon or bird (said the boy's soul)
Is it indeed toward your mate you sing? or is it really to
  me?
For I, that was a child, my tongue's use sleeping, now I
  have heard you,
Now in a moment I know what I am for, I awake,
And already a thousand singers, a thousand songs, clearer,
  louder and more sorrowful than yours,
A thousand warbling echoes have started to life within me,
  never to die.

O you singers solitary, singing by yourself, projecting me,
O solitary me listening, never more shall I cease perpetu-
  ating you,
Never more shall I escape, never more the reverberations,

WALT WHITMAN

Never more the cries of unsatisfied love be absent from me,
Never again leave me to be the peaceful child I was before
     what there in the night,
By the sea under the yellow and sagging moon,
The messenger there aroused, the fire, the sweet hell
     within,
The unknown want, the destiny of me.
O give me the clew! (it lurks in the night here some-
     where)
O if I am to have so much, let me have more!

A word then, (for I will conquer it)
The word final, superior to all,
Subtle, sent up — what is it? — I listen;
Are you whispering it, and have been all the time, you
     sea-waves?
Is that it from your liquid rims and wet sands?

Whereto answering, the sea,
Delaying not, hurrying not,
Whispered me through the night, and very plainly before
     daybreak,
Lisped to me the low and delicious word death,
And again death, death, death, death,
Hissing melodious, neither like the bird nor like my
     aroused child's heart,
But edging near as privately for me, rustling at my feet,
Creeping thence steadily up to my ears and laving me
     softly all over,
Death, death, death, death, death.
Which I do not forget,
But fuse the song of my dusky demon and brother,

That he sang to me in the moonlight on Paumanok's gray
 beach,
With the thousand responsive songs at random,
My own songs awaked from that hour,
And with them the key, the word up from the waves,
The word of the sweetest song and all songs,
That strong and delicious word which, creeping to my
 feet,
(Or like some old crone rocking the cradle, swathed in
 sweet garments, bending aside)
The sea whispered me.

91. *To the Man-of-War-Bird*

THOU who hast slept all night upon the storm,
 Waking renewed on thy prodigious pinions,
(Burst the wild storm? above it thou ascendedst,
And rested on the sky, thy slave that cradled thee)
Now a blue point, far, far in heaven floating,
As to the light emerging here on deck I watch thee,
(Myself a speck, a point on the world's floating vast.)

Far, far at sea,
After the night's fierce drifts have strewn the shore with
 wrecks,
With re-appearing day as now so happy and serene,
The rosy and elastic dawn, the flashing sun,
The limpid spread of air cerulean,
Thou also re-appearest.

Thou born to match the gale, (thou art all wings)
To cope with heaven and earth and sea and hurricane,

Thou ship of air that never furl'st thy sails,
Days, even weeks untired and onward, through spaces,
  realms gyrating,
At dusk that look'st on Senegal, at morn America,
That sport'st amid the lightning-flash and thunder-cloud,
In them, in thy experiences, hadst thou my soul,
What joys! what joys were thine!

92. Give Me the Splendid Silent Sun

GIVE me the splendid silent sun with all his beams full-
  dazzling,
Give me juicy autumnal fruit ripe and red from the
  orchard,
Give me a field where the unmowed grass grows,
Give me an arbor, give me the trellised grape,
Give me fresh corn and wheat, give me serene-moving
  animals teaching content,
Give me nights perfectly quiet as on high plateaus west of
  the Mississippi, and I looking up at the stars,
Give me odorous at sunrise a garden of beautiful flowers
  where I can walk undisturbed,
Give me for marriage a sweet-breathed woman of whom
  I should never tire,
Give me a perfect child, give me, away aside from the
  noise of the world, a rural domestic life,
Give me to warble spontaneous songs recluse by myself,
  for my own ears only,
Give me solitude, give me Nature, give me again O Na-
  ture your primal sanities!

These demanding to have them, (tired with ceaseless excitement, and racked by the war-strife)
These to procure incessantly asking, rising in cries from my heart,
While yet incessantly asking still I adhere to my city,
Day upon day and year upon year, O city, walking your streets,
Where you hold me enchained a certain time refusing to give me up,
Yet giving to make me glutted, enriched of soul, you give me forever faces;
(O I see what I sought to escape, confronting, reversing my cries,
I see my own soul trampling down what it asked for.)

Keep your splendid silent sun,
Keep your woods, O Nature, and the quiet places by the woods,
Keep your fields of clover and timothy, and your corn-fields and orchards,
Keep the blossoming buckwheat fields where the Ninth-month bees hum;
Give me faces and streets — give me these phantoms incessant and endless along the trottoirs!
Give me interminable eyes — give me women — give me comrades and lovers by the thousand!
Let me see new ones every day — let me hold new ones by the hand every day!
Give me such shows — give me the streets of Manhattan!
Give me Broadway, with the soldiers marching — give me the sound of the trumpets and drums!

(The soldiers in companies or regiments — some starting
away flushed and reckless,
Some, their time up, returning with thinned ranks, young,
yet very old, worn, marching, noticing nothing;)
Give me the shores and wharves heavy-fringed with black
ships!
O such for me! O an intense life, full of repletion and
varied!
The life of the theatre, bar-room, huge hotel, for me!
The saloon of the steamer! The crowded excursion for
me! The torchlight procession!
The dense brigade bound for the war, with high-piled
military wagons following;
People, endless, streaming, with strong voices, passions,
pageants,
Manhattan streets with their powerful throbs, with beating
drums as now,
The endless and noisy chorus, the rustle and clank of
muskets (even the sight of the wounded),
Manhattan crowds, with their turbulent musical chorus!
Manhattan faces and eyes forever for me.

93.   *O Captain! My Captain!*

O CAPTAIN! my Captain! our fearful trip is done,
The ship has weathered every rack, the prize we
sought is won,
The port is near, the bells I hear, the people all exulting,
While follow eyes the steady keel, the vessel grim and
daring;

But O heart! heart! heart!
  O the bleeding drops of red,
    Where on the deck my Captain lies,
    Fallen cold and dead.

O Captain! my Captain! rise up and hear the bells;
Rise up — for you the flag is flung — for you the bugle
    trills,
For you bouquets and ribboned wreaths — for you the
    shores acrowding,
For you they call, the swaying mass, their eager faces
    turning;
  Here Captain! dear father!
    This arm beneath your head!
      It is some dream that on the deck
      You 've fallen cold and dead.

My Captain does not answer, his lips are pale and still,
My father does not feel my arm, he has no pulse nor will,
The ship is anchored safe and sound, its voyage closed and
    done,
From fearful trip the victor ship comes in with object
    won;
  Exult O shores, and ring O bells!
    But I, with mournful tread,
      Walk the deck my Captain lies,
      Fallen cold and dead.

94.   *When Lilacs Last in the Dooryard Bloom'd*

I

WHEN lilacs last in the dooryard bloom'd,
    And the great star early droop'd in the western sky
        in the night,
I mourn'd, and yet shall mourn with ever-returning spring.

Ever-returning spring, trinity sure to me you bring,
Lilac blooming perennial and drooping star in the west,
And thought of him I love.

II

O powerful western fallen star!
O shades of night — O moody, tearful night!
O great star disappear'd — O the black murk that hides
    the star!
O cruel hands that hold me powerless — O helpless soul
    of me!
O harsh surrounding cloud that will not free my soul.

III

In the doorway fronting an old farm-house near the white-
    wash'd palings,
Stands the lilac-bush tall-growing with heart-shaped leaves
    of rich green,
With many a pointed blossom rising delicate, with the
    perfume strong I love,

With every leaf a miracle — and from this bush in the
dooryard,
With delicate-color'd blossoms and heart-shaped leaves of
rich green,
A sprig with its flower I break.

IV

In the swamp in secluded recesses,
A shy and hidden bird is warbling a song.

Solitary the thrush,
The hermit withdrawn to himself, avoiding the settle-
ments,
Sings by himself a song.

Song of the bleeding throat,
Death's outlet song of life, (for well dear brother I know,
If thou wast not granted to sing thou would'st surely die.)

And I in the middle as with companions, and as holding
the hands of companions,
I fled forth to the hiding receiving night that talks not,
Down to the shores of the water, the path by the swamp in
the dimness,
To the solemn shadowy cedars and ghostly pines so still.

And the singer so shy to the rest receiv'd me,
The gray-brown bird I know receiv'd us comrades three,
And he sang the carol of death, and a verse for him I
love.

WALT WHITMAN

From deep secluded recesses,
From the fragrant cedars and the ghostly pines so still,
Came the carol of the bird.

And the charm of the carol rapt me,
As I held as if by their hands my comrades in the night,
And the voice of my spirit tallied the song of the bird.

Come lovely and soothing death,
Undulate round the world, serenely arriving, arriving,
In the day, in the night, to all, to each,
Sooner or later delicate death.

Prais'd be the fathomless universe,
For life and joy, and for objects and knowledge curious,
And for love, sweet love — but praise! praise! praise!
For the sure-enwinding arms of cool-enfolding death.

Dark mother always gliding near with soft feet,
Have none chanted for thee a chant of fullest welcome?
Then I chant it for thee, I glorify thee above all,
I bring thee a song that when thou must indeed come,
come unfalteringly.

Approach, strong deliveress,
When it is so, when thou hast taken them I joyously sing
the dead,
Lost in the loving floating ocean of thee,
Laved in the flood of thy bliss, O death.

183

From me to thee glad serenades,
Dances for thee I propose saluting thee, adornments and
feastings for thee,
And the sights of the open landscape and the high-spread
sky are fitting,
And life and the fields, and the huge and thoughtful
night.

The night in silence under many a star,
The ocean shore and the husky whispering wave whose
voice I know,
And the soul turning to thee, O vast and well-veil'd death,
And the body gratefully nestling close to thee.

Over the tree-tops I float thee a song,
Over the rising and sinking waves, over the myriad fields
and the prairies wide,
Over the dense-pack'd cities all and the teeming wharves
and ways,
I float this carol with joy, with joy to thee, O death.

95. *Darest Thou Now, O Soul*

DAREST thou now, O soul,
  Walk out with me toward the unknown region,
Where neither ground is for the feet nor any path to
  follow?

No map there, nor guide,
Nor voice sounding, nor touch of human hand,
Nor face with blooming flesh, nor lips, nor eyes, are in
  that land.

I know it not, O soul!
Nor dost thou, all is a blank before us, —
All waits undreamed of in that region, that inaccessible
    land.

Till when the tie is loosened,
All but the ties eternal, Time and Space,
Nor darkness, gravitation, sense, nor any bounds bounding
    us.

Then we burst forth, we float,
In Time and Space, O soul! prepared for them,
Equal, equipped at last, (O joy! O fruit of all!) them to
    fulfil, O soul!

96. *Good-bye My Fancy!*

GOOD–BYE my Fancy!
    Farewell dear mate, dear love!
I'm going away, I know not where,
Or to what fortune, or whether I may ever see you again,
So good-bye my Fancy.

Now for my last — let me look back a moment;
The slower fainter ticking of the clock is in me,
Exit, nightfall, and soon the heart-thud stopping.

Long have we lived, joy'd, caress'd together;
Delightful! — now separation — Good-bye my Fancy.

Then I roused, and roared in answer,
  And unsheathed from my cushioned feet
My curving claws, and stretched me,
  And wandered my mate to greet.
We toyed in the amber moonlight,
  Upon the warm flat sand,
And struck at each other our massive arms —
  How powerful he was and grand!
His yellow eyes flashed fiercely
  As he crouched and gazed at me,
And his quivering tail, like a serpent,
  Twitched curving nervously.
Then like a storm he seized me,
  With a wild triumphant cry,
And we met, as two clouds in heaven
  When the thunders before them fly.
We grappled and struggled together,
  For his love like his rage was rude;
And his teeth in the swelling folds of my neck
  At times, in our play, drew blood.

Often another suitor —
  For I was flexile and fair —
Fought for me in the moonlight,
  While I lay couching there,
Till his blood was drained by the desert;
And, ruffled with triumph and power,
He licked me and lay beside me
  To breathe him a vast half-hour.

Then down to the fountain we loitered,
  Where the antelopes came to drink;

Like a bolt we sprang upon them,
   Ere they had time to shrink.
We drank their blood and crushed them,
   And tore them limb from limb,
And the hungriest lion doubted
   Ere he disputed with him.

That was a life to live for!
   Not this weak human life,
With its frivolous bloodless passions,
   Its poor and petty strife!

Come to my arms, my hero!
   The shadows of twilight grow,
And the tiger's ancient fierceness
   In my veins begins to flow.
Come not cringing to sue me!
   Take me with triumph and power,
As a warrior storms a fortress!
   I will not shrink or cower.
Come, as you came in the desert,
   Ere we were women and men,
When the tiger passions were in us,
   And love as you loved me then!

98.   *Praxiteles and Phryne*

A THOUSAND silent years ago,
   The twilight faint and pale
Was drawing o'er the sunset glow
   Its soft and shadowy veil;

WILLIAM WETMORE STORY

When from his work the Sculptor stayed
  His hand, and, turned to one
Who stood beside him, half in shade,
  Said, with a sigh, " 'Tis done.

" Thus much is saved from chance and change,
  That waits for me and thee;
Thus much — how little! — from the range
  Of Death and Destiny.

" Phryne, thy human lips shall pale,
  Thy rounded limbs decay, —
Nor love nor prayers can aught avail
  To bid thy beauty stay;

" But there thy smile for centuries
  On marble lips shall live, —
For Art can grant what Love denies,
  And fix the fugitive.

" Sad thought! nor age nor death shall fade
  The youth of this cold bust;
When this quick brain and hand that made,
  And thou and I are dust!

" When all our hopes and fears are dead,
  And both our hearts are cold,
And love is like a tune that's played,
  And life a tale that's told,

" This senseless stone, so coldly fair,
  That love nor life can warm,
The same enchanting look shall wear,
  The same enchanting form.

WILLIAM WETMORE STORY

"Its peace no sorrow shall destroy;
   Its beauty age shall spare
The bitterness of vanished joy,
   The wearing waste of care.

"And there upon that silent face
   Shall unborn ages see
Perennial youth, perennial grace,
   And sealed serenity.

"And strangers, when we sleep in peace,
   Shall say, not quite unmoved,
'So smiled upon Praxiteles
   The Phryne whom he loved!'"

THOMAS DUNN ENGLISH

1819–1902

99.   *Ben Bolt*

Don't you remember sweet Alice, Ben Bolt, —
   Sweet Alice whose hair was so brown,
Who wept with delight when you gave her a smile,
   And trembled with fear at your frown?
In the old church-yard in the valley, Ben Bolt,
   In a corner obscure and alone,
They have fitted a slab of the granite so gray,
   And Alice lies under the stone.

Under the hickory tree, Ben Bolt,
   Which stood at the foot of the hill,
Together we've lain in the noonday shade,
   And listened to Appleton's mill.

The mill-wheel has fallen to pieces, Ben Bolt,
  The rafters have tumbled in,
And a quiet which crawls round the walls as you gaze
  Has followed the olden din.

Do you mind of the cabin of logs, Ben Bolt,
  At the edge of the pathless wood,
And the button-ball tree with its motley limbs,
  Which nigh by the doorstep stood?
The cabin to ruin has gone, Ben Bolt,
  The tree you would seek for in vain;
And where once the lords of the forest waved
  Are grass and the golden grain.

And don't you remember the school, Ben Bolt,
  With the master so cruel and grim,
And the shaded nook in the running brook
  Where the children went to swim?
Grass grows on the master's grave, Ben Bolt,
  The spring of the brook is dry,
And of all the boys who were schoolmates then
  There are only you and I.

There is change in the things I loved, Ben Bolt,
  They have changed from the old to the new;
But I feel in the deeps of my spirit the truth,
  There never was change in you.
Twelvemonths twenty have past, Ben Bolt,
  Since first we were friends — yet I hail
Your presence a blessing, your friendship a truth,
  Ben Bolt of the salt-sea gale.

THOMAS WILLIAM PARSONS
1819–1892

100.　　*On A Bust of Dante*

SEE, from this counterfeit of him
　　Whom Arno shall remember long,
　How stern of lineament, how grim,
The father was of Tuscan song:
There but the burning sense of wrong,
　Perpetual care and scorn, abide;
Small friendship for the lordly throng;
　Distrust of all the world beside.

　Faithful if this wan image be,
No dream his life was, — but a fight!
　Could any Beatrice see
A lover in that anchorite?
To that cold Ghibelline's gloomy sight
　Who could have guessed the visions came
Of Beauty, veiled with heavenly light,
　In circles of eternal flame?

　The lips of Cumæ's cavern close,
The cheeks with fast and sorrow thin,
　The rigid front, almost morose,
But for the patient hope within,
Declare a life whose course hath been
　Unsullied still, though still severe,
Which, through the wavering days of sin,
　Kept itself icy-chaste and clear.

　Not wholly such his haggard look
When wandering once, forlorn, he strayed,
　With no companion save his book,

THOMAS WILLIAM PARSONS

To Corvo's hushed monastic shade;
Where, as the Benedictine laid
   His palm upon the convent's guest,
The single boon for which he prayed
   Was peace, that pilgrim's one request.

   Peace dwells not here, — this rugged face
Betrays no spirit of repose;
   The sullen warrior sole we trace,
The marble man of many woes.
Such was his mien when first arose
   The thought of that strange tale divine,
When hell he peopled with his foes,
   Dread scourge of many a guilty line.

   War to the last he waged with all
The tyrant canker-worms of earth;
   Baron and duke, in hold and hall,
Cursed the dark hour that gave him birth;
He used Rome's harlot for his mirth;
   Plucked bare hypocrisy and crime;
But valiant souls of knightly worth
   Transmitted to the rolls of Time.

   O Time! whose verdicts mock our own,
The only righteous judge art thou;
   That poor old exile, sad and lone,
Is Latium's other Virgil now:
Before his name the nations bow;
   His words are parcel of mankind,
Deep in whose hearts, as on his brow,
   The marks have sunk of Dante's mind.

THOMAS WILLIAM PARSONS

Dirge

For One Who Fell in Battle

ROOM for a soldier! lay him in the clover;
   He loved the fields, and they shall be his cover;
Make his mound with hers who called him once her lover:
   Where the rain may rain upon it,
   Where the sun may shine upon it,
   Where the lamb hath lain upon it,
   And the bee will dine upon it.

Bear him to no dismal tomb under city churches;
Take him to the fragrant fields, by the silver birches,
Where the whip-poor-will shall mourn, where the oriole
      perches:
   Make his mound with sunshine on it.
   Where the bee will dine upon it,
   Where the lamb hath lain upon it,
   And the rain will rain upon it.
Busy as the bee was he, and his rest should be the clover;
Gentle as the lamb was he, and the fern should be his
      cover;
Fern and rosemary shall grow my soldier's pillow over:
   Where the rain may rain upon it,
   Where the sun may shine upon it,
   Where the lamb hath lain upon it,
   And the bee will dine upon it.

Sunshine in his heart, the rain would come full often
Out of those tender eyes which evermore did soften:
He never could look cold till we saw him in his coffin.

Make his mound with sunshine on it,
Plant the lordly pine upon it,
Where the moon may stream upon it,
And memory shall dream upon it.

" Captain or Colonel," — whatever invocation
Suit our hymn the best, no matter for thy station, —
On thy grave the rain shall fall from the eyes of a
    mighty nation!
Long as the sun doth shine upon it
Shall glow the goodly pine upon it,
Long as the stars do gleam upon it
Shall memory come to dream upon it.

102.   *Mary Booth*

WHAT shall we do now, Mary being dead,
    Or say or write that shall express the half?
What can we do but pillow that fair head,
    And let the Spring-time write her epitaph! —

As it will soon, in snowdrop, violet,
    Wind-flower and columbine and maiden's tear;
Each letter of that pretty alphabet,
    That spells in flowers the pageant of the year.

She was a maiden for a man to love;
    She was a woman for a husband's life;
One that has learned to value, far above
    The name of love, the sacred name of wife.

Her little life-dream, rounded so with sleep,
  Had all there is of life, except gray hairs, —
Hope, love, trust, passion, and devotion deep;
  And that mysterious tie a mother bears.

She hath fulfilled her promise and hath passed;
  Set her down gently at the iron door!
Eyes look on that loved image for the last:
  Now cover it in earth, — her earth no more.

103.   *Paradisi Gloria*

        "O frate mio! ciascuna e cittadina
          D' una vera città" . . .

THERE is a city, builded by no hand,
    And unapproachable by sea or shore,
And unassailable by any band
    Of storming soldiery for evermore.

There we no longer shall divide our time
  By acts or pleasures, — doing petty things
Of work or warfare, merchandise or rhyme;
  But we shall sit beside the silver springs

That flow from God's own footstool, and behold
  Sages and martyrs, and those blessed few
Who loved us once and were beloved of old;
  To dwell with them and walk with them anew,

In alternations of sublime repose,
　　Musical motion, the perpetual play
Of every faculty that Heaven bestows
　　Through the bright, busy, and eternal day.

JULIA WARD HOWE

1819–1910

104. Battle-Hymn of the Republic

MINE eyes have seen the glory of the coming of the
　　Lord:
He is trampling out the vintage where the grapes of wrath
　　are stored;
He hath loosed the fateful lightning of his terrible swift
　　sword:
　　　　His truth is marching on.

I have seen Him in the watch-fires of a hundred circling
　　camps;
They have builded Him an altar in the evening dews
　　and damps;
I can read His righteous sentence by the dim and flaring
　　lamps.
　　　　His day is marching on.

I have read a fiery gospel, writ in burnished rows of steel:
" As ye deal with my contemners, so with you my grace
　　shall deal;
Let the Hero, born of woman, crush the serpent with his
　　heel,
　　　　Since God is marching on."

JULIA WARD HOWE

He has sounded forth the trumpet that shall never call
    retreat;
He is sifting out the hearts of men before his judgment-
    seat:
Oh! be swift, my soul, to answer Him! be jubilant, my
    feet!
        Our God is marching on.

In the beauty of the lilies Christ was born across the sea,
With a glory in his bosom that transfigures you and me:
As he died to make men holy, let us die to make men free,
        While God is marching on.

JAMES RUSSELL LOWELL
1819–1891

105. St. Michael the Weigher

STOOD the tall Archangel weighing
    All man's dreaming, doing, saying,
All the failure and the pain,
All the triumph and the gain,
In the unimagined years,
Full of hopes, more full of tears,
Since old Adam's hopeless eyes
Backward searched for Paradise,
And, instead, the flame-blade saw
Of inexorable Law.
Waking, I beheld him there,
With his fire-gold, flickering hair,
In his blinding armor stand,
And the scales were in his hand:
Mighty were they, and full well
They could poise both heaven and hell.

" Angel," asked I humbly then,
" Weighest thou the souls of men?
That thine office is, I know."
" Nay," he answered me, " not so;
But I weigh the hope of Man
Since the power of choice began,
In the world, of good or ill."
Then I waited and was still.

In one scale I saw him place
All the glories of our race,
Cups that lit Belshazzar's feast,
Gems, the lightning of the East,
Kublai's sceptre, Cæsar's sword,
Many a poet's golden word,
Many a skill of science, vain
To make men as gods again.

In the other scale he threw
Things regardless, outcast, few,
Martyr-ash, arena sand,
Of St. Francis' cord a strand,
Beechen cups of men whose need
Fasted that the poor might feed,
Disillusions and despairs
Of young saints with grief-grayed hairs,
Broken hearts that brake for Man.

Marvel through my pulses ran
Seeing then the beam divine
Swiftly on this hand decline,
While Earth's splendor and renown
Mounted light as thistle-down.

106.   *Aladdin*

WHEN I was a beggarly boy
    And lived in a cellar damp,
I had not a friend nor a toy,
    But I had Aladdin's lamp;
When I could not sleep for the cold,
    I had fire enough in my brain,
And builded, with roofs of gold,
    My beautiful castles in Spain!

Since then I have toiled day and night,
    I have money and power good store,
But I'd give all my lamps of silver bright
    For the one that is mine no more;
Take, Fortune, whatever you choose,
    You gave, and may snatch again;
I have nothing 'twould pain me to lose,
    For I own no more castles in Spain!

107.   *The Courtin'*

GOD makes sech nights, all white an' still
    Fur 'z you can look or listen,
Moonshine an' snow on field an' hill,
    All silence an' all glisten.

Zekle crep' up quite unbeknown
    An' peeked in thru' the winder,
An' there sot Huldy all alone,
    'ith no one nigh to hender.

"You want to see my Pa, I s'pose? "
  "Wal . . . no . . . I come dasignin' " —
"To see my Ma? She's sprinklin' clo'es
  Agin to-morrer's i'nin'."

To say why gals act so or so,
  Or don't, 'ould be persumin';
Mebby to mean *yes* an' say *no*
  Comes nateral to women.

He stood a spell on one foot fust,
  Then stood a spell on t'other,
An' on which one he felt the wust
  He couldn't ha' told ye nuther.

Says he, " I'd better call agin: "
  Says she, " Think likely, Mister: "
Thet last word pricked him like a pin,
  An' . . . Wal, he up an' kist her.

When Ma bimeby upon 'em slips,
  Huldy sot pale ez ashes,
All kin' o' smily roun' the lips
  An' teary roun' the lashes.

For she was jes' the quiet kind
  Whose naturs never vary,
Like streams that keep a summer mind
  Snowhid in Jenooary.

The blood clost roun' her heart felt glued
  Too tight for all expressin',
Tell mother see how metters stood,
  An' gin 'em both her blessin'.

Then her red come back like the tide
    Down to the Bay o' Fundy,
An' all I know is they cried
    In meetin' come nex' Sunday.

108. From " The Vision of Sir Launfal "

AND what is so rare as a day in June?
    Then, if ever, come perfect days;
Then Heaven tries earth if it be in tune,
    And over it softly her warm ear lays;
Whether we look, or whether we listen,
We hear life murmur, or see it glisten;
Every clod feels a stir of might,
    An instinct within it that reaches and towers,
And, groping blindly above it for light,
    Climbs to a soul in grass and flowers;
The flush of life may well be seen
    Thrilling back over hills and valleys;
The cowslip startles in meadows green,
    The buttercup catches the sun in its chalice,
And there's never a leaf nor a blade too mean
    To be some happy creature's palace;
The little bird sits at his door in the sun,
    Atilt like a blossom among the leaves,
And lets his illumined being o'errun
    With the deluge of summer it receives;
His mate feels the eggs beneath her wings,
And the heart in her dumb breast flutters and sings;
He sings to the wide world, and she to her nest, —
In the nice ear of Nature which song is the best?

JAMES RUSSELL LOWELL

109.   *To the Dandelion*

DEAR common flower, that grow'st beside the way
    Fringing the dusty road with harmless gold,
  First pledge of blithesome May,
Which children pluck, and, full of pride uphold,
    High-hearted buccaneers, o'erjoyed that they
An Eldorado in the grass have found,
Which not the rich earth's ample round
May match in wealth, thou art more dear to me
Than all the prouder summer-blooms may be.

  Gold such as thine ne'er drew the Spanish prow
Through the primeval hush of Indian seas,
    Nor wrinkled the lean brow
Of age, to rob the lover's heart of ease;
    'Tis the Spring's largess, which she scatters now.
To rich and poor alike, with lavish hand,
Though most hearts never understand
To take it at God's value, but pass by
The offered wealth with unrewarded eye.

  Thou art my tropics and mine Italy;
To look at thee unlocks a warmer clime;
    The eyes thou givest me
Are in the heart, and heed not space or time:
    Not in mid June the golden-cuirassed bee
Feels a more summer-like warm ravishment
In the white lily's breezy tent,
His fragrant Sybaris, than I, when first
From the dark green thy yellow circles burst.

208

JAMES RUSSELL LOWELL

Then think I of deep shadows on the grass,
Of meadows where in sun the cattle graze,
　Where, as the breezes pass,
The gleaming rushes lean a thousand ways,
　Of leaves that slumber in a cloudy mass,
Or whiten in the wind, of waters blue
That from the distance sparkle through
Some woodland gap, and of a sky above,
Where one white cloud like a stray lamb doth move.

My childhood's earliest thoughts are linked with thee;
The sight of thee calls back the robin's song,
　Who, from the dark old tree
Beside the door, sang clearly all day long,
　And I, secure in childish piety,
Listened as if I heard an angel sing
With news from heaven, which he could bring
Fresh every day to my untainted ears
When birds and flowers and I were happy peers.

How like a prodigal doth nature seem,
When thou, for all thy gold, so common art!
　Thou teachest me to deem
More sacredly of every human heart,
　Since each reflects in joy its scanty gleam
Of heaven, and could some wondrous secret show,
Did we but pay the love we owe,
And with a child's undoubting wisdom look
On all these living pages of God's book.

ALICE CARY

By the fork of a tall red mulberry tree,
Which close to the edge of our flax-field grew, —
Dead at the top, — just one branch full
Of leaves, notched round and lined with wool,
From which it tenderly shook the dew
Over our heads, when we came to play
In its hand-breadth of shadow day after day —
Afraid to go home, sir; for one of us bare
A nest full of speckled and thin-shelled eggs, —
The other, a bird held fast by the legs,
Not so big as a straw of wheat.
The berries we gave her she wouldn't eat,
But cried and cried, till we held her bill
So slim and shining, to keep her still.

At last we stood at our mother's knee.
Do you think, sir, if you try,
You can paint the look of a lie?
If you can, pray have the grace
To put it solely in the face
Of the urchin that is likest me:
I think 'twas sole'y mine, indeed:
But that's no matter, — paint it so;
The eyes of our mother (take good heed)
Looking not on the nestful of eggs,
Nor the fluttering bird held so fast by the legs,
But straight through our faces down to our lies,
And, oh, with such injured, reproachful surprise!
I felt my heart bleed where that glance went, as though
A sharp blade went through it.

ALICE CARY

                    You, sir, know
That you on the canvas are to repeat
Things that are fairest, things most sweet, —
Woods and corn fields and mulberry tree, —
The mother, — the lads with their bird at her knee:
But oh, that look of reproachful woe!
High as the heavens your name I'll shout,
If you paint me the picture and leave that out.

THOMAS BUCHANAN READ

115.   *Drifting*   1822–1872

M^Y soul to-day
            Is far away,
Sailing the Vesuvian Bay;
      My wingëd boat,
      A bird afloat,
Swings round the purple peaks remote: —

      Round purple peaks
      It sails, and seeks
Blue inlets and their crystal creeks,
      Where high rocks throw,
      Through deeps below,
A duplicated golden glow.

      Far, vague, and dim,
      The mountains swim;
While on Vesuvius' misty brim,

THOMAS BUCHANAN READ

With outstretched hands,
The gray smoke stands
O'erlooking the volcanic lands.

Here Ischia smiles
O'er liquid miles;
And yonder, bluest of the isles,
Calm Capri waits,
Her sapphire gates
Beguiling to her bright estates.

I heed not, if
My rippling skiff
Float swift or slow from cliff to cliff;
With dreamful eyes
My spirit lies
Under the walls of Paradise.

Under the walls
Where swells and falls
The Bay's deep breast at intervals
At peace I lie,
Blown softly by,
A cloud upon this liquid sky.

The day, so mild,
Is Heaven's own child,
With Earth and Ocean reconciled;
The airs I feel
Around me steal
Are murmuring to the murmuring keel.

THOMAS BUCHANAN READ

Over the rail
My hand I trail
Within the shadow of the sail,
A joy intense,
The cooling sense
Glides down my drowsy indolence.

With dreamful eyes
My spirit lies
Where Summer sings and never dies, —
O'erveiled with vines
She glows and shines
Among her future oil and wines.

Her children, hid
The cliffs amid,
Are gambolling with the gambolling kid;
Or down the walls,
With tipsy calls,
Laugh on the rocks like waterfalls.

The fisher's child,
With tresses wild,
Unto the smooth, bright sand beguiled,
With glowing lips
Sings as she skips,
Or gazes at the far-off ships.

Yon deep bark goes
Where traffic blows,
From lands of sun to lands of snows;

This happier one, —
Its course is run
From lands of snow to lands of sun.

O happy ship,
To rise and dip,
With the blue crystal at your lip!
O happy crew,
My heart with you
Sails, and sails, and sings anew!

No more, no more
The worldly shore
Upbraids me with its loud uproar:
With dreamful eyes
My spirit lies
Under the walls of Paradise!

116.   *Sheridan's Ride*

UP from the South at break of day,
　　Bringing to Winchester fresh dismay,
The affrighted air with a shudder bore,
Like a herald in haste, to the chieftain's door,
The terrible grumble, and rumble, and roar,
Telling the battle was on once more,
And Sheridan twenty miles away.

And wider still those billows of war,
Thundered along the horizon's bar;
And louder yet into Winchester rolled

THOMAS BUCHANAN READ

The roar of that red sea uncontrolled,
Making the blood of the listener cold,
As he thought of the stake in that fiery fray,
And Sheridan twenty miles away.

But there is a road from Winchester town,
A good, broad highway leading down;
And there, through the flush of the morning light,
A steed as black as the steeds of night,
Was seen to pass, as with eagle flight,
As if he knew the terrible need;
He stretched away with his utmost speed;
Hills rose and fell; but his heart was gay,
With Sheridan fifteen miles away.

Still sprung from those swift hoofs, thundering South,
The dust, like smoke from the cannon's mouth;
Or the trail of a comet, sweeping faster and faster,
Foreboding to traitors the doom of disaster.
The heart of the steed, and the heart of the master
Were beating like prisoners assaulting their walls,
Impatient to be where the battle-field calls;
Every nerve of the charger was strained to full play,
With Sheridan only ten miles away.

Under his spurning feet the road
Like an arrowy Alpine river flowed,
And the landscape sped away behind
Like an ocean flying before the wind,
And the steed, like a barque fed with furnace ire,

Swept on, with his wild eyes full of fire.
But lo! he is nearing his heart's desire;
He is snuffing the smoke of the roaring fray,
With Sheridan only five miles away.

The first that the general saw were the groups
Of stragglers, and then the retreating troops;
What was done? what to do? a glance told him both,
Then, striking his spurs, with a terrible oath,
He dashed down the line 'mid a storm of huzzas,
And the wave of retreat checked its course there, because
The sight of the master compelled it to pause.
With foam and with dust the black charger was gray;
By the flash of his eye, and the red nostril's play,
He seemed to the whole great army to say,
" I have brought you Sheridan all the way
From Winchester, down to save the day! "

Hurrah! hurrah for Sheridan!
Hurrah! hurrah for horse and man!
And when their statues are placed on high,
Under the dome of the Union sky,
The American soldier's Temple of Fame;
There with the glorious general's name,
Be it said, in letters both bold and bright,
   " Here is the steed that saved the day,
By carrying Sheridan into the fight,
   From Winchester, twenty miles away! "

FRANCIS ORRERY TICKNOR

1822–1874

117.   *Little Giffen*

OUT of the focal and foremost fire,
    Out of the hospital walls as dire;
Smitten of grape-shot and gangrene,
(Eighteenth battle, and *he* sixteen!)
Spectre! such as you seldom see,
Little Giffen, of Tennessee!

" Take him and welcome! " the surgeons said;
Little the doctor can help the dead!
So we took him; and brought him where
The balm was sweet in the summer air;
And we laid him down on a wholesome bed, —
Utter Lazarus, heel to head!

And we watched the war with abated breath, —
Skeleton Boy against skeleton Death.
Months of torture, how many such?
Weary weeks of the stick and crutch;
And still a glint of the steel-blue eye
Told of a spirit that wouldn't die,

And didn't. Nay, more! in death's despite
The crippled skeleton " learned to write."
" Dear mother," at first, of course; and then
" Dear captain," inquiring about the men.
Captain's answer: " Of eighty-and-five,
Giffen and I are left alive."

FRANCIS ORRERY TICKNOR

Word of gloom from the war, one day;
Johnson pressed at the front, they say.
Little Giffen was up and away;
A tear — his first — as he bade good-by,
Dimmed the glint of his steel-blue eye.
"I'll write, if spared!" There was news of the fight;
But none of Giffen. — He did not write.

I sometimes fancy that, were I king
Of the princely Knights of the Golden Ring,
With the song of the minstrel in mine ear,
And the tender legend that trembles here,
I'd give the best on his bended knee,
The whitest soul of my chivalry,
For "Little Giffen," of Tennessee.

GEORGE HENRY BOKER

1823–1890

118.   *Dirge for a Soldier*

CLOSE his eyes; his work is done!
    What to him is friend or foeman,
Rise of moon, or set of sun,
    Hand of man, or kiss of woman?
      Lay him low, lay him low,
      In the clover or the snow!
      What cares he? he cannot know:
        Lay him low!

As man may, he fought his fight,
    Proved his truth by his endeavor;
Let him sleep in solemn night,
    Sleep forever and forever.
        Lay him low, lay him low,
        In the clover or the snow!
        What cares he? he cannot know:
            Lay him low!

Fold him in his country's stars,
    Roll the drum and fire the volley!
What to him are all our wars,
    What but death bemocking folly?
        Lay him low, lay him low,
        In the clover or the snow!
        What cares he? he cannot know:
            Lay him low!

Leave him to God's watching eye,
    Trust him to the hand that made him.
Mortal love weeps idly by:
    God alone has power to aid him.
        Lay him low, lay him low,
        In the clover or the snow!
        What cares he? he cannot know:
            Lay him low!

119.   *The Ferry*

THERE was a gay maiden lived down by the mill, —
    Ferry me over the ferry, —
Her hair was as bright as the waves of a rill,
When the sun on the brink of his setting stands still,
    Her lips were as full as a cherry.

BAYARD TAYLOR

Sleep, soldiers! still in honored rest
Your truth and valor wearing:
The bravest are the tenderest, —
The loving are the daring.

RICHARD HENRY STODDARD

1825–1903

125.   *Songs*

HOW are songs begot and bred?
How do golden measures flow?
From the heart, or from the head?
Happy Poet, let me know.

Tell me first how folded flowers
Bud and bloom in vernal bowers;
How the south wind shapes its tune,
The harper, he, of June.

None may answer, none may know,
Winds and flowers come and go,
And the selfsame canons bind
Nature and the Poet's mind.

126.   *The Sky*

THE sky is a drinking-cup,
That was overturned of old,
And it pours in the eyes of men
Its wine of airy gold.

We drink that wine all day,
    Till the last drop is drained up,
And are lighted off to bed
    By the jewels in the cup!

127.   *The Flight of Youth*

THERE are gains for all our losses,
    There are balms for all our pain:
But when youth, the dream, departs,
It takes something from our hearts,
    And it never comes again.

We are stronger, and are better,
    Under manhood's sterner reign:
Still we feel that something sweet
Followed youth, with flying feet,
    And will never come again.

Something beautiful is vanished,
    And we sigh for it in vain:
We behold it everywhere,
On the earth, and in the air,
    But it never comes again.

128.   *Arab Song*

BREAK thou my heart, ah, break it,
    If such thy pleasure be;
Thy will is mine, what say I?
    'Tis more than mine to me.

And if my life offend thee,
　My passion and my pain,
Take thou my life, ah, take it,
　But spare me thy disdain!

129.　　　　　*The Jar*

DAY and night my thoughts incline
　To the blandishments of wine:
Jars were made to drain, I think,
Wine, I know, was made to drink.

When I die, (the day be far!)
Should the potters make a jar
Out of this poor clay of mine,
Let the jar be filled with wine!

WILLIAM HAINES LYTLE

1826–1863

130.　　*Antony to Cleopatra*

I AM dying, Egypt, dying!
　Ebbs the crimson life-tide fast,
And the dark Plutonian shadows
　Gather on the evening blast;
Let thine arm, O Queen, enfold me,
　Hush thy sobs and bow thine ear,
Listen to the great heart secrets
　Thou, and thou alone, must hear.

WILLIAM HAINES LYTLE

Though my scarred and veteran legions
    Bear their eagles high no more,
And my wrecked and scattered galleys
    Strew dark Actium's fatal shore;
Though no glittering guards surround me,
    Prompt to do their master's will,
I must perish like a Roman,
    Die the great Triumvir still.

Let not Cæsar's servile minions
    Mock the lion thus laid low;
'Twas no foeman's arm that felled him,
    'Twas his own that struck the blow:
His who, pillowed on thy bosom,
    Turned aside from glory's ray —
His who, drunk with thy caresses,
    Madly threw a world away.

Should the base plebeian rabble
    Dare assail my name at Rome,
Where the noble spouse Octavia
    Weeps within her widowed home,
Seek her; say the gods bear witness, —
    Altars, augurs, circling wings, —
That her blood, with mine commingled,
    Yet shall mount the thrones of kings.

And for thee, star-eyed Egyptian —
    Glorious sorceress of the Nile!
Light the path to Stygian horrors,
    With the splendor of thy smile;

WILLIAM HAINES LYTLE

Give the Cæsar crowns and arches,
    Let his brow the laurel twine:
I can scorn the senate's triumphs,
    Triumphing in love like thine.

I am dying, Egypt, dying!
    Hark! the insulting foeman's cry;
They are coming — quick, my falchion!
    Let me front them ere I die.
Ah, no more amid the battle
    Shall my heart exulting swell;
Isis and Osiris guard thee —
    Cleopatra — Rome — farewell!

WALTER MITCHELL

1826–1908

131.   *Tacking Ship Off Shore*

THE weather-leech of the topsail shivers,
    The bowlines strain, and the lee-shrouds slacken,
The braces are taut, the lithe boom quivers,
    And the waves with the coming squall-cloud blacken.

Open one point on the weather-brow,
    Is the light-house tall on Fire Island Head.
There's a shade of doubt on the captain's brow,
    And the pilot watches the heaving lead.

I stand at the wheel, and with eager eye
    To sea and to sky and to shore I gaze,
Till the muttered order of " Full and by! "
    Is suddenly changed for " Full for stays! "

242

WALTER MITCHELL

The ship bends lower before the breeze,
  As her broadside fair to the blast she lays;
And she swifter springs to the rising seas,
  As the pilot calls, " Stand by for stays! "

It is silence all, as each in his place,
  With the gathered coil in his hardened hands,
By tack and bowline, by sheet and brace,
  Waiting the watchword impatient stands.

And the light on Fire Island Head draws near,
  As, trumpet-winged, the pilot's shout
From his post on the bowsprit's heel I hear,
  With the welcome call of " Ready! About! "

No time to spare! It is touch and go;
  And the captain growls, " Down helm! hard down! "
As my weight on the whirling spokes I throw,
  While heaven grows black with the storm-cloud's frown.

High o'er the knight-heads flies the spray,
  As we meet the shock of the plunging sea;
And my shoulder stiff to the wheel I lay,
  As I answer, " Ay, ay, sir! Ha-a-rd a-lee! "

With the swerving leap of a startled steed
  The ship flies fast in the eye of the wind,
The dangerous shoals on the lee recede,
  And the headland white we have left behind.

The topsails flutter, the jibs collapse,
  And belly and tug at the groaning cleats;
The spanker slats, and the mainsail flaps;
  And thunders the order, " Tacks and sheets! "

STEPHEN COLLINS FOSTER

Old Folks at Home

WAY down upon de Swanee Ribber,
    Far, far away,
Dere's wha my heart is turning ebber,
    Dere's wha de old folks stay.
All up and down de whole creation
    Sadly I roam,
Still longing for de old plantation,
    And for de old folks at home.

        All de world am sad and dreary,
            Eberywhere I roam;
        Oh, darkeys, how my heart grows weary,
            Far from de old folks at home!

All round de little farm I wandered
    When I was young,
Den many happy days I squandered,
    Many de songs I sung.
When I was playing wid my brudder
    Happy was I;
Oh, take me to my kind old mudder!
    Dere let me live and die.

One little hut among de bushes,
    One dat I love,
Still sadly to my memory rushes,
    No matter where I rove.
When will I see de bees a-humming
    All round de comb?
When will I hear de banjo tumming,
    Down in my good old home?

All de world am sad and dreary,
    Eberywhere I roam,
Oh, darkeys, how my heart grows weary,
    Far from de old folks at home!

134. *Massa's in de Cold Ground*

ROUND de meadows am a-ringing
    De darkeys' mournful song,
While de mocking-bird am singing,
    Happy as de day am long.
Where de ivy am a-creeping,
    O'er de grassy mound,
Dere old massa am a-sleeping,
    Sleeping in de cold, cold ground.

Down in de corn-field
    Hear dat mournful sound:
All de darkeys am a-weeping, —
    Massa's in de cold, cold ground.

When de autumn leaves were falling,
    When de days were cold,
'Twas hard to hear old massa calling,
    Cayse he was so weak and old.
Now de orange tree am blooming
    On de sandy shore,
Now de summer days am coming, —
    Massa nebber calls no more.

247

Massa make de darkeys love him,
   Cayse he was so kind;
Now dey sadly weep above him,
   Mourning cayse he leave dem behind.
I cannot work before to-morrow,
   Cayse de tear-drop flow;
I try to drive away my sorrow,
   Pickin' on de old banjo.

    Down in de corn-field
      Hear dat mournful sound:
    All de darkeys am a-weeping, —
      Massa's in de cold, cold ground.

LUCY LARCOM

1826–1893

135.   *A Strip of Blue*

I DO not own an inch of land,
   But all I see is mine, —
The orchard and the mowing-fields,
   The lawns and gardens fine.
The winds my tax-collectors are,
   They bring me tithes divine, —
Wild scents and subtle essences,
   A tribute rare and free;
And, more magnificent than all,
   My window keeps for me
A glimpse of blue immensity, —
   A little strip of sea.

LUCY LARCOM

Richer am I than he who owns
   Great fleets and argosies;
I have a share in every ship
   Won by the inland breeze,
To loiter on yon airy road
   Above the apple-trees.
I freight them with my untold dreams;
   Each bears my own picked crew;
And nobler cargoes wait for them
   Than ever India knew, —
My ships that sail into the East
   Across that outlet blue.

Sometimes they seem like living shapes, —
   The people of the sky, —
Guests in white raiment coming down
   From heaven, which is close by;
I call them by familiar names,
   As one by one draws nigh.
So white, so light, so spirit-like,
   From violet mists they bloom!
The aching wastes of the unknown
   Are half reclaimed from gloom,
Since on life's hospitable sea
   All souls find sailing-room.

The ocean grows a weariness
   With nothing else in sight;
Its east and west, its north and south,
   Spread out from morn till night;
We miss the warm, caressing shore,
   Its brooding shade and light.

249

LUCY LARCOM

A part is greater than the whole;
    By hints are mysteries told.
The fringes of eternity, —
    God's sweeping garment-fold,
In that bright shred of glittering sea,
    I reach out for and hold.

The sails, like flakes of roseate pearl,
    Float in upon the mist;
The waves are broken precious stones, —
    Sapphire and amethyst
Washed from celestial basement walls,
    By suns unsetting kist.
Out through the utmost gates of space,
    Past where the gray stars drift,
To the widening Infinite, my soul
    Glides on, a vessel swift,
Yet loses not her anchorage
    In yonder azure rift.

Here sit I, as a little child;
    The threshold of God's door
Is that clear band of chrysoprase;
    Now the vast temple floor,
The binding glory of the dome
    I bow my head before.
Thy universe, O God, is home,
    In height or depth, to me;
Yet here upon thy footstool green
    Content am I to be;
Glad when is oped unto by need
    Some sea-like glimpse of Thee.

FRANCIS MILES FINCH

136.   *The Blue and the Gray*

BY the flow of the inland river,
   Whence the fleets of iron have fled,
Where the blades of the grave-grass quiver,
   Asleep are the ranks of the dead:
     Under the sod and the dew,
       Waiting the judgment-day;
     Under the one, the Blue,
       Under the other, the Gray.

These in the robings of glory,
   Those in the gloom of defeat,
All with the battle-blood gory,
   In the dusk of eternity meet:
     Under the sod and the dew,
       Waiting the judgment-day;
     Under the laurel, the Blue,
       Under the willow, the Gray.

From the silence of sorrowful hours
   The desolate mourners go,
Lovingly laden with flowers
   Alike for the friend and the foe:
     Under the sod and the dew,
       Waiting the judgment-day;
     Under the roses, the Blue,
       Under the lilies, the Gray.

FRANCIS MILES FINCH

So with an equal splendor,
  The morning sun-rays fall,
With a touch impartially tender,
  On the blossoms blooming for all:
    Under the sod and the dew,
      Waiting the judgment-day;
    Broidered with gold, the Blue,
      Mellowed with gold, the Gray.

So, when the summer calleth,
  On forest and field of grain,
With an equal murmur falleth
  The cooling drip of the rain:
    Under the sod and the dew,
      Waiting the judgment-day;
    Wet with the rain, the Blue,
      Wet with the rain, the Gray.

Sadly, but not with upbraiding,
  The generous deed was done,
In the storm of the years that are fading
  No braver battle was won:
    Under the sod and the dew,
      Waiting the judgment-day;
    Under the blossoms, the Blue,
      Under the garlands, the Gray.

No more shall the war cry sever,
  Or the winding rivers be red;
They banish our anger forever
  When they laurel the graves of our dead!

Under the sod and the dew,
  Waiting the judgment-day;
Love and tears for the Blue,
  Tears and love for the Gray.

JOHN TOWNSEND TROWBRIDGE

1827–1916

137.   *Midwinter*

THE speckled sky is dim with snow,
  The light flakes falter and fall slow;
Athwart the hill-top, rapt and pale,
Silently drops a silvery veil;
And all the valley is shut in
By flickering curtains gray and thin.

But cheerily the chickadee
Singeth to me on fence and tree;
The snow sails round him as he sings,
White as the down of angels' wings.

I watch the slow flakes as they fall
On bank and brier and broken wall;
Over the orchard, waste and brown,
All noiselessly they settle down,
Tipping the apple-boughs, and each
Light quivering twig of plum and peach.

On turf and curb and bower-roof
The snow-storm spreads its ivory woof;

It paves with pearl the garden-walk;
And lovingly round tattered stalk
And shivering stem its magic weaves
A mantle fair as lily-leaves.

The hooded beehive, small and low,
Stands like a maiden in the snow;
And the old door-slab is half hid
Under an alabaster lid.

All day it snows: the sheeted post
Gleams in the dimness like a ghost;
All day the blasted oak has stood
A muffled wizard of the wood;
Garland and airy cap adorn
The sumach and the wayside thorn,
And clustering spangles lodge and shine
In the dark tresses of the pine.

The ragged bramble, dwarfed and old,
Shrinks like a beggar in the cold;
In surplice white the cedar stands,
And blesses him with priestly hands.

Still cheerily the chickadee
Singeth to me on fence and tree:
But in my inmost ear is heard
The music of a holier bird;
And heavenly thoughts as soft and white
As snow-flakes, on my soul alight,
Clothing with love my lonely heart,
Healing with peace each bruisèd part,
Till all my being seems to be
Transfigured by their purity.

JOHN TOWNSEND TROWBRIDGE

138.　　　*The Vagabonds*

WE are two travellers, Roger and I.
　　Roger's my dog. — Come here, you scamp!
Jump for the gentleman, — mind your eye!
　　Over the table, — look out for the lamp!
The rogue is growing a little old;
　　Five years we've tramped through wind and weather,
And slept out-doors when nights were cold,
　　And ate and drank — and starved — together.

We've learned what comfort is, I tell you!
　　A bed on the floor, a bit of rosin,
A fire to thaw our thumbs (poor fellow!
　　The paw he holds up there's been frozen),
Plenty of catgut for my fiddle
　　(This out-door business is bad for strings),
Then a few nice buckwheats hot from the griddle,
　　And Roger and I set up for kings!

No, thank ye, Sir, — I never drink;
　　Roger and I are exceedingly moral, —
Aren't we, Roger? — See him wink! —
　　Well, something hot, then, — we won't quarrel.
He's thirsty, too, — see him nod his head?
　　What a pity, Sir, that dogs can't talk!
He understands every word that's said, —
　　And he knows good milk from water-and-chalk.

The truth is, Sir, now I reflect,
　　I've been so sadly given to grog,
I wonder I've not lost the respect
　　(Here's to you, Sir!) even of my dog.

But he sticks by, through thick and thin;
  And this old coat, with its empty pockets,
And rags that smell of tobacco and gin,
  He'll follow while he has eyes in his sockets.

There isn't another creature living
  Would do it, and prove, through every disaster,
So fond, so faithful, and so forgiving,
  To such a miserable, thankless master!
No, Sir! — see him wag his tail and grin!
  By George! it makes my old eyes water!
That is, there's something in this gin
  That chokes a fellow. But no matter!

We'll have some music, if you're willing,
  And Roger (hem! what a plague a cough is, Sir!)
Shall march a little — Start, you villain!
  Paws up! Eyes front! Salute your officer!
'Bout face! Attention! Take your rifle!
  (Some dogs have arms, you see!) Now hold your
Cap while the gentlemen give a trifle,
  To aid a poor old patriot soldier!

March! Halt! Now show how the rebel shakes
  When he stands up to hear his sentence.
Now tell us how many drams it takes
  To honour a jolly new acquaintance.
Five yelps, — that's five; he's mighty knowing!
  The night's before us, fill the glasses! —
Quick, Sir! I'm ill, — my brain is going! —
  Some brandy, — thank you, — there! — it passes!

JOHN TOWNSEND TROWBRIDGE

Why not reform? That's easily said;
 But I've gone through such wretched treatment,
Sometimes forgetting the taste of bread,
 And scarce remembering what meat meant,
That my poor stomach's past reform;
 And there are times when, mad with thinking,
I'd sell out heaven for something warm
 To prop a horrible inward sinking.

Is there a way to forget to think?
 At your age, Sir, home, fortune, friends,
A dear girl's love, — but I took to drink, —
 The same old story; you know how it ends.
If you could have seen these classic features, —
 You needn't laugh, Sir; they were not then
Such a burning libel on God's creatures:
 I was one of your handsome men!

If you had seen *her*, so fair and young,
 Whose head was happy on this breast!
If you could have heard the songs I sung
 When the wine went round, you wouldn't have guessed
That ever I, Sir, should be straying
 From door to door, with fiddle and dog,
Ragged and penniless, and playing
 To you to-night for a glass of grog!

She's married since, — a parson's wife:
 'Twas better for her that we should part, —
Better the soberest, prosiest life
 Than a blasted home and a broken heart.

JOHN TOWNSEND TROWBRIDGE

I have seen her? Once: I was weak and spent
　　On the dusty road: a carriage stopped:
But little she dreamed, as on she went,
　　Who kissed the coin that her fingers dropped!

You've set me talking, Sir; I'm sorry;
　　It makes me wild to think of the change!
What do you care for a beggar's story?
　　Is it amusing? You find it strange?
I had a mother so proud of me!
　　'Twas well she died before. Do you know
If the happy spirits in heaven can see
　　The ruin and wretchedness here below?

Another glass, and strong, to deaden
　　This pain; then Roger and I will start.
I wonder, has he such a lumpish, leaden
　　Aching thing in place of a heart?
He is sad sometimes, and would weep, if he could,
　　No doubt remembering things that were, —
A virtuous kennel with plenty of food,
　　And himself a sober, respectable cur.

I'm better now; that glass was warming. —
　　You rascal! limber your lazy feet!
We must be fiddling and performing
　　For supper and bed, or starve in the street.
Not a very gay life we lead, you think?
　　But soon we shall go where lodgings are free,
And the sleepers need neither victuals nor drink: —
　　The sooner the better for Roger and me!

JOHN TOWNSEND TROWBRIDGE

139. *Midsummer*

AROUND this lovely valley rise
  The purple hills of Paradise —

O, softly on yon banks of haze
Her rosy face the Summer lays!

Becalmed along the azure sky,
The argosies of cloudland lie,
Whose shores, with many a shining rift,
Far off their pearl-white pearls uplift.

Through all the long midsummer-day
The meadow-sides are sweet with hay.
I seek the coolest sheltered seat,
Just where the field and forest meet, —
Where grow the pine-trees tall and bland,
The ancient oaks austere and grand,
And fringy roots and pebbles fret
The ripples of the rivulet.

I watch the mowers, as they go
Through the tall grass, a white-sleeved row.
With even stroke their scythes they swing,
In tune their merry whetstones ring.
Behind the nimble youngsters run,
And toss the thick swarths in the sun.
The cattle graze, while, warm and still,
Slopes the broad pasture, basks the hill,
And bright, where summer breezes break,
The green wheat crinkles like a lake.

The butterfly and humblebee
Come to the pleasant woods with me;
Quickly before me runs the quail,
Her chickens skulk behind the rail;
High up the lone wood-pigeon sits,
And the woodpecker pecks and flits.
Sweet woodland music sinks and swells,
The brooklet rings its tinkling bells,
The swarming insects drone and hum,
The partridge beats its throbbing drum.
The squirrel leaps among the boughs,
And chatters in his leafy house.
The oriole flashes by; and, look!
Into the mirror of the brook,
Where the vain bluebird trims his coat,
Two tiny feathers fall and float.

As silently, as tenderly,
The down of peace descends on me.
O, this is peace! I have no need
Of friend to talk, of book to read:
A dear Companion here abides;
Close to my thrilling heart He hides;
The holy silence in His Voice:
I lie and listen, and rejoice.

ROSE TERRY COOKE

1827–1892

140.   *Bluebeard's Closet*

FASTEN the chamber!
  Hide the red key;
Cover the portal,
That eyes may not see.
Get thee to market,
To wedding and prayer;
Labor or revel,
The chamber is there!

In comes a stranger —
"Thy pictures how fine,
Titian or Guido,
Whose is the sign?"
Looks he behind them?
Ah! have a care!
"Here is a finer."
The chamber is there!

Fair spreads the banquet,
Rich the array;
See the bright torches
Mimicking day;
When harp and viol
Thrill the soft air,
Comes a light whisper:
The chamber is there!

ROSE TERRY COOKE

The lift of angry billows
Through which a swift keel slid;
For my body is in Segovia,
But my soul is in Madrid.

O fair-haired little darlings
Who bore my heart away!
A wide and woful ocean
Between us roars to-day;
Yet am I close beside you
Though time and space forbid;
My body is in Segovia,
But my soul is in Madrid.

If I were once in heaven,
There would be no more sea;
My heart would cease to wander,
My sorrows cease to be;
My sad eyes sleep forever,
In dust and daisies hid,
And my body leave Segovia.
— Would my soul forget Madrid?

GEORGE PERRY

1828–1888

142.   *Siva, Destroyer*

WHOSE voice shall say him nay?
Whose arm shall bar the way?
Lord of unbounded sway! —
Siva, Destroyer.

ROSE TERRY COOKE

Proud kings, whose lightest breath
To men is life or death,
Heeds he your ruth or wrath? —
        Siva, Destroyer.

Mother with bleeding breast
Bowed o'er thy birdling's nest,
Shall thy last woe arrest
        Siva, Destroyer?

Maiden with eyes of love
Fixed on the heaven above,
Hast thou a prayer to move
        Siva, Destroyer?

Youth of the lion heart,
Brave for life's noblest act,
Shall fame's fair glory thwart
        Siva, Destroyer?

Earth in thy sweet array,
Bride of celestial day,
Hast thou one bloom to stay
        Siva, Destroyer?

Stars on the dome of night,
Climbing to your far height,
Do ye escape his night? —
        Siva, Destroyer.

What voice shall say him nay,
What arm shall bar his way,
Lord of unbounded sway! —
        Siva, Destroyer.

JEREMIAH EAMES RANKIN
1828–1904

143. *The Word of God to Leyden Came*

THE word of God to Leyden came,
   Dutch town by Zuyder-Zee;
Rise up, my children of no name,
   My kings and priests to be.
There is an empire in the West,
   Which I will soon unfold;
A thousand harvests in her breast,
   Rocks ribbed with iron and gold.

Rise up, my children, time is ripe!
   Old things are passed away.
Bishops and kings from earth I wipe:
   Too long they've had their day.
A little ship have I prepared
   To bear you o'er the seas;
And in your souls, my will declared,
   Shall grow by slow degrees.

Beneath my throne the martyrs cry:
   I hear their voice, How long?
It mingles with their praises high,
   And with their victor song.
The thing they longed and waited for,
   But died without the sight;
So, this shall be! I wrong abhor,
   The world I'll now set right.

JEREMIAH EAMES RANKIN

Leave, then, the hammer and the loom,
  You've other work to do;
For Freedom's commonwealth there's room,
  And you shall build it too.
I'm tired of bishops and their pride,
  I'm tired of kings as well;
Henceforth I take the people's side,
  And with the people dwell.

Tear off the mitre from the priest,
  And from the king, his crown;
Let all my captives be released;
  Lift up, who men cast down.
Their pastors let the people choose,
  And choose their rulers too;
Whom they select, I'll not refuse,
  But bless the work they do.

The Pilgrims rose, at this God's word,
  And sailed the wintry seas:
With their own flesh nor blood conferred,
  Nor thought of wealth or ease.
They left the towers of Leyden town,
  They left the Zuyder-Zee;
And where they cast their anchor down,
  Rose Freedom's realm to be.

GUY HUMPHREYS McMASTER

1829–1887

144. *Carmen Bellicosum*

IN their ragged regimentals,
 Stood the old Continentals,
  Yielding not,
While the grenadiers were lunging,
And like hail fell the plunging
  Cannon-shot;
  When the files
  Of the isles,
From the smoky night-encampment, bore the banner of
 the rampant
  Unicorn;
And grummer, grummer, grummer, rolled the roll of the
 drummer
  Through the morn!

Then with eyes to the front all,
And with guns horizontal,
  Stood our sires;
While the balls whistled deadly,
And in streams flashing redly
  Blazed the fires:
  As the roar
  On the shore
Swept the strong battle-breakers o'er the green-sodded
 acres
  Of the plain;
And louder, louder, louder, cracked the black gunpowder,
  Cracking amain!

GUY HUMPHREYS McMASTER

Now like smiths at their forges
Worked the red St. George's
    Cannoneers,
And the villainous saltpetre
Rang a fierce, discordant metre
    Round our ears:
    As the swift
    Storm-drift,
With hot sweeping anger, came the horse-guards' clangor
    On our flanks.
Then higher, higher, higher, burned the old-fashioned fire
    Through the ranks!

Then the bare-headed Colonel
Galloped through the white infernal
    Powder-cloud;
And his broadsword was swinging,
And his brazen throat was ringing
    Trumpet-loud;
    Then the blue
    Bullets flew,
And the trooper-jackets redden at the touch of the leaden
    Rifle-breath;
And rounder, rounder, rounder, roared the iron six-pounder,
    Hurling death!

HENRY TIMROD

145.   *Quatorzain*

MOST men know love but as a part of life;
   They hide it in some corner of the breast,
Even from themselves; and only when they rest
In the brief pauses of that daily strife,
Wherewith the world might else be not so rife,
They draw it forth (as one draws forth a toy
To soothe some ardent, kiss-exacting boy)
And hold it up to sister, child, or wife.
Ah me! why may not love and life be one?
Why walk we thus alone, when by our side,
Love, like a visible god, might be our guide?
How would the marts grow noble! and the street,
Worn like a dungeon-floor by weary feet,
Seem then a golden court-way of the Sun!

146.   *At Magnolia Cemetery*

SLEEP sweetly in your humble graves,
   Sleep, martyrs of a fallen cause;
Though yet no marble column craves
   The pilgrim here to pause.

In seeds of laurel in the earth
   The blossom of your fame is blown,
And somewhere, waiting for its birth,
   The shaft is in the stone!

Meanwhile, behalf the tardy years
  Which keep in trust your storied tombs,
Behold! your sisters bring their tears,
  And these memorial blooms.

Small tributes! but your shades will smile
  More proudly on these wreaths to-day,
Than when some cannon-moulded pile
  Shall overlook this bay.

Stoop, angels, hither from the skies!
  There is no holier spot of ground
Than where defeated valor lies,
  By mourning beauty crowned.

147.   *Charleston*

CALM as that second summer which precedes
  The first fall of the snow,
In the broad sunlight of heroic deeds,
  The city bides the foe.

As yet, behind their ramparts, stern and proud,
  Her bolted thunders sleep, ——
Dark Sumter, like a battlemented cloud,
  Looms o'er the solemn deep.

No Calpe frowns from lofty cliff or scaur
  To guard the holy strand;
But Moultrie holds in leash her dogs of war
  Above the level sand.

S. WEIR MITCHELL

If for companionship of purity
    The equal pallor of the risen moon
Disturb thy dreams, dost know to read aright
    Her silver tracery on the dark lagoon?

The mischief-making fruitfulness of May
    Stirs all the garden folk with vague desires:
Doth there not reach thine apprehensive ear
    The faded longing of these dark-robed friars,

When, in the evening hour to memories given,
    Some gray-haired man amid the gathering gloom
For one delirious moment sees again
    The gleam of eyes and white-walled Erzeroum?

Hast thou not loved him for this human dream?
    Or sighed with him who yester-evening sat
Upon the low sea-wall, and saw through tears
    His ruined home, and snow-clad Ararat?

If thou art dowered with some refinëd sense
    That shares the counsels of the nesting bird,
Canst hear the mighty laughter of the earth,
    And all that ear of man hath never heard,

If the abysmal stillness of the night
    Be eloquent for thee, if thou canst read
The glowing rubric of the morning song,
    Doth each new day no gentle warning breed?

Shall not the gossip of the maudlin bee,
    The fragrant history of the fallen rose,
Unto the prescience of instinctive love
    Some humbler prophecy of joy disclose?

S. WEIR MITCHELL

Cold vestal of the leafy convent cell,
  The traitor days have thy calm trust betrayed;
The sea-wind boldly parts thy shining leaves
  To let the angel in. Be not afraid!

The gold-winged sun, divinely penetrant,
  The pure annunciation of the morn
Breathes o'er thy chastity, and to thy soul
  The tender thrill of motherhood is borne.

Set wide the glory of thy perfect bloom!
  Call every wind to share thy scented breaths!
No life is brief that doth perfection win.
  To-day is thine — to-morrow thou art death's!

149. Of One Who Seemed to Have Failed

DEATH'S but once more to-morrow. Thou art gray
  With many a death of many a yesterday.
O yearning heart that lacked the athlete's force
And, stumbling, fell upon the beaten course,
And looked, and saw with ever glazing eyes
Some lower soul that seemed to win the prize!
Lo, Death, the just, who comes to all alike,
Life's sorry scales of right anew shall strike.
Forth, through the night, on unknown shores to win
The peace of God unstirred by sense of sin!
There love without desire shall, like a mist
At evening precious to the drooping flower,
Possess thy soul in ownership, and kissed
By viewless lips, whose touch shall be a dower

S. WEIR MITCHELL

Of genius and of winged serenity,
Thou shalt abide in realms of poesy.
There soul hath touch of soul, and there the great
Cast wide to welcome thee joy's golden gate.
Freeborn to untold thoughts that age on age
Caressed sweet singers in their sacred sleep,
Thy soul shall enter on its heritage
Of God's unuttered wisdom. Thou shalt sweep
With hand assured the ringing lyre of life,
Till the fierce anguish of its bitter strife,
Its pain, death, discord, sorrow, and despair,
Break into rhythmic music. Thou shalt share
The prophet-joy that kept forever glad
God's poet-souls when all a world was sad.
Enter and live! Thou hast not lived before;
We were but soul-cast shadows. Ah, no more
The heart shall bear the burdens of the brain;
Now shall the strong heart think, nor think in vain.
In the dear company of peace, and those
Who bore for man life's utmost agony,
Thy soul shall climb to cliffs of still repose,
And see before thee lie Time's mystery,
And that which is God's time, Eternity;
Whence sweeping over thee dim myriad things,
The awful centuries yet to be, in hosts
That stir the vast of heaven with formless wings,
Shall cast for thee their shrouds, and, like to ghosts,
Unriddle all the past, till, awed and still,
Thy soul the secret hath of good and ill.

S. WEIR MITCHELL

150. *The Quaker Graveyard*

FOUR straight brick walls, severely plain,
　A quiet city square surround;
A level space of nameless graves, —
　The Quakers' burial-ground.

In gown of gray, or coat of drab,
　They trod the common ways of life,
With passions held in sternest leash,
　And hearts that knew not strife.

To yon grim meeting-house they fared,
　With thoughts as sober as their speech,
To voiceless prayer, to songless praise,
　To hear the elders preach.

Through quiet lengths of days they came,
　With scarce a change to this repose;
Of all life's loveliness they took
　The thorn without the rose.

But in the porch and o'er the graves,
　Glad rings the southward robin's glee,
And sparrows fill the autumn air
　With merry mutiny;

While on the graves of drab and gray
　The red and gold of autumn lie,
And wilful Nature decks the sod
　In gentlest mockery.

151.　　　*Idleness*

THERE is no dearer lover of lost hours
　　　　　　Than I.
I can be idler than the idlest flowers;
　　　　　　More idly lie
Than noonday lilies languidly afloat,
And water pillowed in a windless moat.
　　And I can be
Stiller than some gray stone
That hath no motion known.
　It seems to me
　　　　That my still idleness doth make my own
　　All magic gifts of joy's simplicity.

*152.　A Decanter of Madeira, Aged 86, to
George Bancroft, Aged 86, Greeting*

GOOD Master, you and I were born
　　In " Teacup days " of hoop and hood,
And when the silver cue hung down,
And toasts were drunk, and wine was good;

When kin of mine (a jolly brood)
From sideboards looked, and knew full well
What courage they had given the beau,
How generous made the blushing belle.

Ah me! what gossip could I prate
Of days when doors were locked at dinners!
Believe me, I have kissed the lips
Of many pretty saints — or sinners.

S. WEIR MITCHELL

Lip service have I done, alack!
I don't repent, but come what may,
What ready lips, sir, I have kissed,
Be sure at least I shall not say.

Two honest gentlemen are we, —
I Demi John, whole George are you;
When Nature grew us one in years
She meant to make a generous brew.

She bade me store for festal hours
The sun our south-side vineyard knew;
To sterner tasks she set your life,
As statesman, writer, scholar, grew.

Years eighty-six have come and gone;
At last we meet. Your health to-night.
Take from this board of friendly hearts
The memory of a proud delight.

The days that went have made you wise,
There's wisdom in my rare bouquet.
I'm rather paler than I was;
And, on my soul, you're growing gray.

I like to think, when Toper Time
Has drained the last of me and you,
Some here shall say, They both were good, —
The wine we drank, the man we knew.

PAUL HAMILTON HAYNE

1830–1886

153. *A Little While I Fain Would*
Linger Yet

A LITTLE while (my life is almost set!)
   I fain would pause along the downward way,
  Musing an hour in this sad sunset-ray,
While, Sweet! our eyes with tender tears are wet:
A little hour I fain would linger yet.

A little while I fain would linger yet,
   All for love's sake, for love that cannot tire;
  Though fervid youth be dead, with youth's desire,
And hope has faded to a vague regret,
A little while I fain would linger yet.

A little while I fain would linger here:
   Behold! who knows what strange, mysterious bars
  'Twixt souls that love may rise in other stars?
Nor can love deem the face of death is fair:
A little while I still would linger here.

A little while I yearn to hold thee fast,
   Hand locked in hand, and loyal heart to heart;
  (O pitying Christ! those woeful words, " We part! ")
So ere the darkness fall, the light be past,
A little while I fain would hold thee fast.

A little while, when light and twilight meet, —
   Behind, our broken years; before, the deep
  Weird wonder of the last unfathomed sleep, —
A little while I still would clasp thee, Sweet,
A little while, when night and twilight meet.

280

A little while I fain would linger here;
  Behold! who knows what soul-dividing bars
  Earth's faithful loves may part in other stars?
Nor can love deem the face of death is fair:
A little while I still would linger here.

154.   *A Storm in the Distance*

I SEE the cloud-born squadrons of the gale,
  Their lines of rain like glittering spears deprest,
While all the affrighted land grows darkly pale
  In flashing change on earth's half-shielded breast.

Sounds like the rush of trampling columns float
  From that fierce conflict; volleyed thunders peal,
Blent with the maddened wind's wild bugle-note;
  The lightnings flash, the solid woodlands reel!

Ha! many a foliaged guardian of the height,
  Majestic pine or chestnut, riven and bare,
Falls in the rage of that aerial flight,
  Led by the Prince of all the Powers of air!

Vast boughs like shattered banners hurtling fly
  Down the thick tumult: while, like emerald snow,
Millions of orphaned leaves make wild the sky,
  Or drift in shuddering helplessness below.

Still, still, the levelled lances of the rain
  At earth's half-shielded breast take glittering aim;
All space is life with fury, racked with pain,
  Earth bathed in vapor, and heaven rent by flame!

281

At last the cloud-battalions through long rifts
   Of luminous mists retire: — the strife is done,
And earth once more her wounded beauty lifts,
   To meet the healing kisses of the sun.

EMILY DICKINSON

1830–1886

155.   *From " Life "*

I [1]

OUR share of night to bear,
   Our share of morning,
Our blank in bliss to fill,
Our blank in scorning.

Here a star, and there a star,
Some lose their way.
Here a mist, and there a mist,
Afterwards — day!

II [1]

He ate and drank the precious words,
His spirit grew robust;
He knew no more that he was poor,
Nor that his frame was dust.
He danced along the dingy days,
And this bequest of wings
Was but a book. What liberty
A loosened spirit brings!

EMILY DICKINSON

III [1]

I found the phrase to every thought
I ever had, but one;
And that defies me, — as a hand
Did try to chalk the sun

To races nurtured in the dark: —
How would your own begin?
Can blaze be done in cochineal,
Or noon in mazarin?

IV [2]

My life closed twice before its close;
   It yet remains to see
If Immortality unveil
   A third event to me,

So huge, so hopeless to conceive,
   As these that twice befell:
Parting is all we know of heaven,
   And all we need of hell.

V [1]

Just lost when I was saved!
Just felt the world go by!
Just girt me for the onset with eternity,
When breath blew back,
And on the other side
I heard recede the disappointed tide;

Therefore, as one returned, I feel,
Odd secrets of the line to tell!
Some sailor, skirting foreign shores,
Some pale reporter from the awful doors
Before the seal!

Next time, to stay!
Next time, the things to see
By ear unheard,
Unscrutinized by eye.

Next time, to tarry,
While the ages steal, —
Slow tramp the centuries,
And the cycles wheel.

VI [1]

Of all the souls that stand create
I have elected one.
When sense from spirit files away,
And subterfuge is done;

When that which is and that which was
Apart, intrinsic, stand,
And this brief tragedy of flesh
Is shifted like a sand;

When figures show their royal front
And mists are carved away, —
Behold the atom I preferred
To all the lists of clay!

[1] Copyright, 1891, by Little, Brown & Company

EMILY DICKINSON

VII [1]

Alter? When the hills do.
Falter? When the sun
Question if his glory
Be the perfect one.

Surfeit? When the daffodil
Doth of the dew:
Even as herself, O friend!
I will of you!

VIII [2]

Heart, we will forget him!
   You and I, to-night!
You may forget the warmth he gave
   I will forget the light.

When you have done, pray tell me,
   That I my thoughts may dim;
Haste! lest while you're lagging,
   I may remember him!

IX [2]

A lady red upon the hill
   Her annual secret keeps;
A lady white within the field
   In placid lily sleeps!

[1] Copyright, 1890, by Little, Brown & Company
[2] Copyright, 1896, by Little, Brown & Company

The tidy breezes with their brooms
  Sweep vale, and hill, and tree!
Prithee, my pretty housewives!
  Who may expected be?

The neighbors do not yet suspect!
  The woods exchange a smile, —
Orchard, and buttercup, and bird,
  In such a little while!

And yet how still the landscape stands,
  How nonchalant the wood,
As if the resurrection
  Were nothing very odd!

X [1]

The morns are meeker than they were,
The nuts are getting brown;
The berry's cheek is plumper,
The rose is out of town.
The maple wears a gayer scarf,
The field a scarlet gown.
Lest I should be old-fashioned,
I'll put a trinket on.

XI [1]

The sky is low, the clouds are mean,
A travelling flake of snow
Across a barn or through a rut
Debates if it will go.

A narrow wind complains all day
How someone treated him:
Nature, like us, is sometimes caught
Without her diadem.

XII [2]

God made a little gentian;
It tried to be a rose
And failed, and all the summer laughed:
But just before the snows
There came a purple creature
That ravished all the hill;
And summer hid her forehead,
And mockery was still.
The frosts were her condition;
The Tyrian would not come
Until the North evoked it: —
"Creator! shall I bloom?"

XIII [1]

Delayed till she had ceased to know,
Delayed till in its vest of snow
    Her loving bosom lay:
An hour behind the fleeting breath,
Later by just an hour than death, —
    Oh, lagging yesterday!

Could she have guessed that it would be;
Could but a crier of the glee
    Have climbed the distant hill;

Her little figure at the gate
The angels must have spied,
Since I could never find her
Upon the mortal side.

XVIII [1]

Because I could not stop for Death,
   He kindly stopped for me;
The carriage held but just ourselves
   And Immortality.

We slowly drove, he knew no haste,
   And I had put away
My labor, and my leisure too,
   For his civility.

We passed the school where children played,
   Their lessons scarcely done;
We passed the fields of gazing grain,
   We passed the setting sun.

We paused before a house that seemed
   A swelling of the ground;
The roof was scarcely visible,
   The cornice but a mound.

Since then 'tis centuries; but each
   Feels shorter than the day
I first surmised the horses' heads
   Were toward Eternity.

[1] Copyright, 1890, by Little, Brown & Company

EMILY DICKINSON

XIX [1]

Have you got a brook in your little heart,
Where bashful flowers blow,
And blushing birds go down to drink,
And shadows tremble so?

And nobody knows, so still it flows,
That any brook is there;
And yet your little draught of life
Is daily drunken there.

Then look out for the little brook in March,
When the rivers ever flow,
And the snow comes hurrying from the hills,
And the bridges often go.

And later, in August it may be,
When the meadows parching lie,
Beware, lest this little brook of life
Some burning noon go dry!

XX [1]

I'll tell you how the sun rose, —
A ribbon at a time.
The steeples swam in amethyst,
The news like squirrels ran.

The hills untied their bonnets,
The bobolinks begun.
Then I said softly to myself,
" That must have been the Sun! "

. . . .

EMILY DICKINSON

But has he set, I know not:
There seemed a purple stile
Which little yellow boys and girls
Were climbing all the while,

Till when they reached the other side,
A dominie in gray
Put gently up the evening bars,
And led the flock away.

XXI [1]

The bustle in a house
The morning after death
Is solemnest of industries
Enacted upon earth, —

The sweeping up the heart,
And putting love away
We shall not want to use again
Until Eternity.

NORA PERRY

1833-1896

156.   *Riding Down*

OH, did you see him riding down,
    And riding down, while all the town
Came out to see, came out to see,
And all the bells rang mad with glee?

NORA PERRY

Oh, did you hear those bells ring out,
The bells ring out, the people shout,
And did you hear that cheer on cheer
That over all the bells rang clear?

And did you see the waving flags,
The fluttering flags, the tattered flags,
Red, white, and blue, shot through and through,
Baptized with battle's deadly dew?

And did you hear the drums' gay beat,
The drums' gay beat, the bugles sweet,
The cymbals' clash, the cannons' crash,
That rent the sky with sound and flash?

And did you see me waiting there,
Just waiting there and watching there,
One little lass, amid the mass
That pressed to see the hero pass?

And did you see him smiling down,
And smiling down, as riding down
With slowest pace, with stately grace,
He caught the vision of a face, —

My face uplifted red and white,
Turned red and white with sheer delight
To meet the eyes, the smiling eyes,
Outflashing in their swift surprise?

Oh, did you see how swift it came,
How swift it came, like sudden flame,
That smile to me, to only me,
The little lass who blushed to see?

On the king's gate the moss grew gray;
　　The king came not. They called him dead;
And made his eldest son one day
　　Slave in his father's stead.

158.   *Emigravit*

WITH sails full set, the ship her anchor weighs.
　　Strange names shines out beneath her figure head.
What glad farewells with eager eyes are said!
What cheer for him who goes, and him who stays!
Fair skies, rich lands, new homes, and untried days
Some go to seek: the rest but wait instead,
Watching the way wherein their comrades led,
Until the next stanch ship her flag doth raise.
Who knows what myriad colonies there are
Of fairest fields, and rich, undreamed-of gains
Thick planted in the distant shining plains
Which we call sky because they lie so far?
Oh, write of me, not " Died in bitter pains,"
But " Emigrated to another star! "

159.   *Poppies in the Wheat*

ALONG Ancona's hills the shimmering heat,
　　A tropic tide of air, with ebb and flow
Bathes all the fields of wheat until they glow
Like flashing seas of green, which toss and beat

296

Around the vines. The poppies lithe and fleet
Seem running, fiery torchmen, to and fro
To mark the shore. The farmer does not know
That they are there. He walks with heavy feet,
Counting the bread and wine by autumn's gain,
But I, — I smile to think that days remain
Perhaps to me in which, though bread be sweet
No more, and red wine warm my blood in vain,
I shall be glad remembering how the fleet,
Lithe poppies ran like torchmen with the wheat.

160.   *A Last Prayer*

FATHER, I scarcely dare to pray,
        So clear I see, now it is done,
That I have wasted half my day,
        And left my work but just begun;

So clear I see that things I thought
        Were right or harmless were a sin;
So clear I see that I have sought,
        Unconscious, selfish aims to win;

So clear I see that I have hurt
        The souls I might have helped to save;
That I have slothful been, inert,
        Deaf to the calls thy leaders gave.

In outskirts of thy kingdoms vast,
        Father, the humblest spot give me;
Set me the lowliest task thou hast;
        Let me repentant work for thee!

161.   *Habeas Corpus*

MY body, eh? Friend Death, how now?
    Why all this tedious pomp of writ?
Thou hast reclaimed it sure and slow
    For half a century, bit by bit.

In faith thou knowest more to-day
    Than I do, where it can be found!
This shriveled lump of suffering clay,
    To which I now am chained and bound,

Has not of kith or kin a trace
    To the good body once I bore;
Look at this shrunken, ghastly face:
    Didst ever see that face before?

Ah, well, friend Death, good friend thou art;
    Thy only fault thy lagging gait,
Mistaken pity in thy heart
    For timorous ones that bid thee wait.

Do quickly all thou hast to do,
    Nor I nor mine will hindrance make;
I shall be free when thou art through;
    I grudge thee naught that thou must take!

Stay! I have lied: I grudge thee one,
    Yes, two I grudge thee at this last, —
Two members which have faithful done
    My will and bidding in the past.

HELEN HUNT JACKSON

I grudge thee this right hand of mine;
    I grudge thee this quick-beating heart;
They never gave me coward sign,
    Nor played me once a traitor's part.

I see now why in olden days
    Men in barbaric love or hate
Nailed enemies' hands at wild crossways,
    Shrined leaders' hearts in costly state:

The symbol, sign, and instrument
    Of each soul's purpose, passion, strife,
Of fires in which are poured and spent
    Their all of love, their all of life.

O feeble, mighty human hand!
    O fragile, dauntless human heart!
The universe holds nothing planned
    With such sublime, transcendent art!

Yes, Death, I own I grudge thee mine
    Poor little hand, so feeble now;
Its wrinkled palm, its altered line,
    Its veins so pallid and so slow —

(*Unfinished here.*)

Ah, well, friend Death, good friend thou art:
    I shall be free when thou art through.
Take all there is — take hand and heart:
    There must be somewhere work to do.

ELIZABETH AKERS ALLEN

1832–1911

162.   *Rock Me to Sleep*

BACKWARD, turn backward, O Time, in your flight,
   Make me a child again just for to-night!
Mother, come back from the echoless shore,
Take me again to your heart as of yore;
Kiss from my forehead the furrows of care,
Smooth the few silver threads out of my hair;
Over my slumbers your loving watch keep; —
Rock me to sleep, mother, — rock me to sleep!

Backward, flow backward, O tide of the years!
I am so weary of toil and of tears, —
Toil without recompense, tears all in vain, —
Take them, and give me my childhood again!
I have grown weary of dust and decay, —
Weary of flinging my soul-wealth away;
Weary of sowing for others to reap; —
Rock me to sleep, mother, — rock me to sleep!

Tired of the hollow, the base, the untrue,
Mother, O mother, my heart calls for you!
Many a summer the grass has grown green,
Blossomed and faded, our faces between:
Yet, with strong yearning and passionate pain,
Long I to-night for your presence again.
Come from the silence so long and so deep; —
Rock me to sleep, mother, — rock me to sleep!

ELIZABETH AKERS ALLEN

Over my heart, in the days that are flown,
No love like mother-love ever has shone;
No other worship abides and endures, —
Faithful, unselfish, and patient like yours:
None like a mother can charm away pain
From the sick soul and the world-weary brain.
Slumber's soft calms o'er my heavy lids creep; —
Rock me to sleep, mother, — rock me to sleep!

Come, let your brown hair, just lighted with gold,
Fall on your shoulders again as of old;
Let it drop over my forehead to-night,
Shading my faint eyes away from the light;
For with its sunny-edged shadows once more
Haply will throng the sweet visions of yore;
Lovingly, softly, its bright billows sweep; —
Rock me to sleep, mother, — rock me to sleep!

Mother, dear mother, the years have been long
Since I last listened your lullaby song:
Sing, then, and unto my soul it shall seem
Womanhood's years have been only a dream.
Clasped to your heart in a loving embrace,
With your light lashes just sweeping my face,
Never hereafter to wake or to weep; —
Rock me to sleep, mother, — rock me to sleep!

EDMUND CLARENCE STEDMAN

1833-1908

163. How Old Brown Took Harper's Ferry

JOHN BROWN in Kansas settled, like a steadfast
    Yankee farmer,
  Brave and godly, with four sons, all stalwart men of
    might.
There he spoke aloud for freedom, and the Border-strife
    grew warmer,
  Till the Rangers fired his dwelling, in his absence, in
    the night;
          And Old Brown,
          Osawatomie Brown,
Came homeward in the morning to find his house burned
  down.

Then he grasped his trusty rifle and boldly fought for
    freedom;
  Smote from border unto border the fierce, invading
    band;
And he and his brave boys vowed — so might Heaven help
    and speed 'em! —
  They would save those grand old prairies from the
    curse that blights the land;
          And Old Brown,
          Osawatomie Brown,
Said, " Boys, the Lord will aid us! " and he shoved his
  ramrod down.

302

And the Lord *did* aid these men, and they labored day
    and even,
  Saving Kansas from its peril; and their very lives
    seemed charmed,
Till the ruffians killed one son, in the blessed light of
    Heaven, —
  In cold blood the fellows slew him, as he journeyed all
    unarmed;
                Then Old Brown,
              Osawatomie Brown,
Shed not a tear, but shut his teeth, and frowned a terrible
    frown!

Then they seized another brave boy, — not amid the heat
    of battle,
  But in peace, behind his ploughshare, — and they
    loaded him with chains,
And with pikes, before their horses, even as they goad
    their cattle,
  Drove him cruelly, for their sport, and at last blew
    out his brains;
                Then Old Brown,
              Osawatomie Brown,
Raised his right hands up to Heaven, calling Heaven's
    vengeance down.

And he swore a fearful oath, by the name of the Al-
    mighty,
  He would hunt this ravening evil that had scathed and
    torn him so;

He would seize it by the vitals; he would crush it day
    and night; he
  Would so pursue its footsteps, so return it blow for
    blow,
           That Old Brown,
           Osawatomie Brown,
Should be a name to swear by, in backwoods or in town!

Then his beard became more grizzled, and his wild blue
    eye grew wilder,
  And more sharply curved his hawk's-nose, snuffing battle
    from afar;
And he and the two boys left, though the Kansas strife
    waxed milder,
  Grew more sullen, till was over the bloody Border War,
           And Old Brown,
           Osawatomie Brown,
Had gone crazy, as they reckoned by his fearful glare
    and frown.

So he left the plains of Kansas and their bitter woes
    behind him,
  Slipt off into Virginia, where the statesmen all are
    born,
Hired a farm by Harper's Ferry, and no one knew where
    to find him,
  Or whether he'd turned parson, or was jacketed and
    shorn;
           For Old Brown,
           Osawatomie Brown,
Mad as he was, knew texts enough to wear a parson's
    gown.

He bought no ploughs and harrows, spades and shovels,
    and such trifles;
  But quietly to his rancho there came, by every train,
Boxes full of pikes and pistols, and his well-beloved Sharps
    rifles;
  And eighteen other madmen joined their leader there
    again.
               Says Old Brown,
               Osawatomie Brown,
"Boys, we've got an army large enough to march and take
    the town!

  Take the town, and seize the muskets, free the negroes
    and then arm them;
  Carry the County and the State, ay, and all the potent
    South.
On their own heads be the slaughter, if their victims rise
    to harm them —
  These Virginians! who believed not, nor would heed
    the warning mouth."
               Says Old Brown,
               Osawatomie Brown,
"The world shall see a Republic, or my name is not
    John Brown."

'Twas the sixteenth of October, on the evening of a
    Sunday:
  "This good work," declared the captain, "shall be on
    a holy night!"
It was on a Sunday evening, and before the noon of Mon-
    day,

With two sons, and Captain Stephens, fifteen privates
— black and white,

Captain Brown,

Osawatomie Brown,

Marched across the bridged Potomac, and knocked the
sentry down;

Took the guarded armory-building, and the muskets and
the cannon;
Captured all the county majors and the colonels, one
by one;
Scared to death each gallant scion of Virginia they ran on,
And before the noon of Monday, I say, the deed was
done.

Mad Old Brown,

Osawatomie Brown,

With his eighteen other crazy men, went in and took the
town.

Very little noise and bluster, little smell of powder made
he;
It was all done in the midnight, like the Emperor's *coup
d'état*.
"Cut the wires! Stop the rail-cars! Hold the streets and
bridges!" said he,
Then declared the new Republic, with himself for
guiding star, —

This Old Brown,

Osawatomie Brown;

And the bold two thousand citizens ran off and left the
town.

306

Then was riding and railroading and expressing here and
thither;
And the Martinsburg Sharpshooters and the Charles-
town Volunteers,
And the Shepherdstown and Winchester Militia hastened
whither
Old Brown was said to muster his ten thousand grena-
diers.
General Brown!
Osawatomie Brown!!
Behind whose rampant banner all the North was pouring
down.

But at last, 'tis said, some prisoners escaped from Old
Brown's durance,
And the effervescent valor of the Chivalry broke out,
When they learned that nineteen madmen had the marvel-
lous assurance —
Only nineteen — thus to seize the place and drive them
straight about;
And Old Brown,
Osawatomie Brown,
Found an army come to take him, encamped around the
town.

But to storm, with all the forces I have mentioned, was
too risky;
So they hurried off to Richmond for the Government
Marines,
Tore them from their weeping matrons, fired their souls
with Bourbon whiskey,

Till they battered down Brown's castle with their
    ladders and machines;
          And Old Brown,
          Osawatomie Brown,
Received three bayonet stabs, and a cut on his brave old
    crown.

Tallyho! the old Virginia gentry gather to the baying!
    In they rushed and killed the game, shooting lustily
       away;
And whene'er they slew a rebel, those who came too late
    for slaying,
    Not to lose a share of glory, fired their bullets in his
       clay;
          And Old Brown,
          Osawatomie Brown,
Saw his sons fall dead beside him, and between them laid
    him down.

How the conquerors wore their laurels; how they hastened
    on the trial;
    How Old Brown was placed, half dying, on the
       Charlestown court-house floor;
How he spoke his grand oration, in the scorn of all
    denial;
    What the brave old madman told them, — these are
       known the country o'er.
          " Hang Old Brown,
          Osawatomie Brown,"
Said the judge, "and all such rebels!" with his most
    judicial frown.

308

But Virginians, don't do it! for I tell you that the flagon,
   Filled with blood of Old Brown's offspring, was first
      poured by Southern hands;
And each drop from Old Brown's life-veins, like the red
   gore of the dragon,
May spring up a vengeful Fury, hissing through your
   slave-worn lands!
             And Old Brown,
            Osawatomie Brown,
May trouble you more than ever, when you've nailed his
   coffin down!

164.   *Morgan*

     O H, what a set of Vagabundos,
        Sons of Neptune, sons of Mars,
   Raked from todos otros mundos,
      Lascars, Gascons, Portsmouth tars,
   Prison mate and dock-yard fellow,
      Blades to Meg and Molly dear,
   Off to capture Porto Bello
      Sailed with Morgan the Buccaneer!

   Out they voyaged from Port Royal
      (Fathoms deep its ruins be,
   Pier and convent, fortress loyal,
      Sunk beneath the gaping sea);

   On the Spaniard's beach they landed,
      Dead to pity, void of fear,
   Round their blood-red flag embanded,
      Led by Morgan the Buccaneer.

Dawn till dusk they stormed the castle,
  Beat the gates and gratings down;
Then, with ruthless rout and wassail,
  Night and day they sacked the town,
Staved the bins its cellars boasted,
  Port and Lisbon, tier on tier,
Quaffed to heart's content, and toasted
  Harry Morgan the Buccaneer:

Stripped the church and monastery,
  Racked the prior for his gold,
With the traders' wives made merry,
  Lipped the young and mocked the old,
Diced for hapless señoritas
  (Sire and brother bound anear), —
Juanas, Lolas, Manuelitas,
  Cursing Morgan the Buccaneer.

Lust and rapine, flame and slaughter,
  Forayed with the Welshman grim:
"Take my pesos, spare my daughter!"
  "Ha! ha!" roared the devil's limb,
"These shall jingle in our pouches,
  She with us shall find good cheer."
"Lash the graybeard till he crouches!"
  Shouted Morgan the Buccaneer.

Out again through reef and breaker,
  While the Spaniard moaned his fate,
Back they voyaged to Jamaica,
  Flush with doubloons, coins of eight,

Crosses wrung from Popish varlets,
  Jewels torn from arm and ear, —
Jesu! how the Jews and harlots
  Welcomed Morgan the Buccaneer!

165.   *Falstaff's Song*

WHERE'S he that died o' Wednesday?
    What place on earth hath he?
A tailor's yard beneath, I wot,
    Where worms approaching be;
For the wight that died o' Wednesday,
    Just laid the light below,
Is dead as the varlet turned to clay
    A score of years ago.

Where's he that died o' Sabba' day?
    Good Lord, I'd not be he!
The best of days is foul enough
    From this world's fare to flee;
And the saint that died o' Sabba' day,
    With his grave turf yet to grow,
Is dead as the sinner brought to pray
    A hundred years ago.

Where's he that died o' yesterday?
    What better chance hath he
To clink the can and toss the pot
    When this night's junkets be?
For the lad that died o' yesterday
    Is just as dead — ho! ho! —
As the whoreson knave men laid away
    A thousand years ago.

EDMUND CLARENCE STEDMAN

166.   *The Dutch Patrol*

WHEN Christmas-Eve is ended,
    Just at the noon of night,
Rare things are seen by mortal een
    That have the second sight.
In St. Mark's church-yard then
    They see the shape arise
Of him who ruled Nieuw Amsterdam
    And here in slumber lies.

His face, beneath the close black cap,
    Has a martial look and grim;
On either side his locks fall wide
    To the broad collar's rim;
His sleeves are slashed; the velvet coat
    Is fashioned Hollandese
Above his fustian breeches, trimmed
    With scarf-knots at the knees.

His leg of flesh is hosed in silk;
    His wooden leg is bound,
As well befits a conqueror's,
    With silver bands around.
He reads the lines that mark
    His tablet on the wall,
Where boldly PETRUS STUYVESANT
    Stands out beyond them all.

" 'Tis well! " he says, and sternly smiles,
    " They hold our memory dear;
Nor rust nor moss hath crept across;
    'Twill last this many a year."

EDMUND CLARENCE STEDMAN

Then down the path he strides,
  And through the iron gate,
Where the sage Nine Men, his councillors,
  Their Governor await.

Here are Van der Donck and Van Cortlandt,
  A triplet more of Vans,
And Hendrick Kip of the haughty lip,
  And Govert Loockermans,
Jan Jansen Dam, and Jansen,
  Of whom our annals tell, —
All risen this night their lord to greet
  At sound of the Christmas bell.

Nine lusty forms in linsey coats,
  Puffed sleeves and ample hose!
Each burgher smokes a Flemish pipe
  To warm his ancient nose;
The smoke-wreaths rise like mist,
  The smokers all are mute,
Yet all, with pipes thrice waving slow,
  Brave Stuyvesant salute.

Then into ranks they fall,
  And step out three by three,
And he of the wooden leg and staff
  In front walks solemnly.
Along their wonted course
  The phantom troop patrol,
To see how fares Nieuw Amsterdam,
  And what the years unroll.

EDMUND CLARENCE STEDMAN

Street after street and mile on mile,
   From river bound to bound,
From old St. Mark's to Whitehall Point,
   They foot the limits round;
From Maiden Lane to Corlaer's Hook
   The Dutchmen's pijpen glow,
But never a word from their lips is heard,
   And none their passing know.

Ere the first streak of dawn
   St. Mark's again they near,
And by a vault the Nine Men halt,
   Their Governor's voice to hear.
" Mynheeren," he says, " ye see
   Each year our borders spread!
So, one by one, the landmarks gone,
   And marvels come instead!

" Not even a windmill left,
   Nor a garden-plot we knew,
And but a paling marks the spot
   Where erst my pear-tree grew.
Our walks are wearier still, —
   Perchance and it were best,
So little of worth is left on earth,
   To break no more our rest? "

Thus speaks old Petrus doubtfully
   And shakes his valiant head,
When — on the roofs a sound of hoofs,
   A rattling, pattering tread!

EDMUND CLARENCE STEDMAN

The bells of reindeer tinkle,
  The Dutchmen plainly spy
St. Nicholas, who drives his team
  Across the roof-tops nigh.

" Beshrew me for a craven! "
  Cries Petrus — " All goes well!
Our patron saint still makes his round
  At sound of the Christmas bell.
So long as staunch St. Nicholas
  Shall guard these houses tall,
There shall come no harm from hostile arm —
  No evil chance befall!

" The yongens and the meisjes
  Shall have their hosen filled;
The butcher and the baker,
  And every honest guild,
Shall merrily thrive and flourish;
  Good-night, and be of cheer;
We may safely lay us down again
  To sleep another year! "

Once more the pipes are waved,
  Stout Petrus gives the sign,
The misty smoke enfolds them round, —
  Him and his burghers nine.
All, when the cloud has lifted,
  Have vanished quite away,
And the crowing cock and steeple clock
  Proclaim 'tis Christmas-Day.

Oh, what a sight to see,
  Rigged in her best!
Wearing the famous gown
  Drawn from her chest, —
Worn, ere King George's reign
  Here chanced to cease,
Once by a forbear
  Of Cousin Lucrece.

Damask brocaded,
  Cut very low;
Short sleeves and finger-mitts
  Fit for a show;
Palsied neck shaking her
  Rust-yellow curls,
Rattling its roundabout
  String of mock pearls;

Over her noddle,
  Draggled and stark,
Two ostrich feathers —
  Brought from the ark.
Shoes of frayed satin,
  All heel and toe,
On her poor crippled feet
  Hobbled below.

My! how the Justice's
  Sons and their wives
Laughed; while the little folk
  Ran for their lives,

Asking if beldames
    Out of the past,
Old fairy godmothers,
    Always could last?

No! One Thanksgiving,
    Bitterly cold,
After they took her home
    (Ever so old),
In her great chair she sank,
    There to find peace;
Died in her ancient dress —
    Poor old Lucrece.

168.   *Toujours Amour*

PRITHEE tell me, Dimple-Chin,
    At what age does Love begin?
Your blue eyes have scarcely seen
Summers three, my fairy queen,
But a miracle of sweets,
Soft approaches, sly retreats,
Show the little archer there,
Hidden in your pretty hair;
When didst learn a heart to win?
Prithee tell me, Dimple-Chin!

    " Oh! " the rosy lips reply,
    " I can't tell you if I try.
'Tis so long I can't remember:
    Ask some younger lass than I! "

Tell, O tell me, Grizzled-Face,
Do your heart and head keep pace?
When does hoary Love expire,
When do frosts put out the fire?
Can its embers burn below
All that chill December snow?
Care you still soft hands to press,
Bonny heads to smooth and bless?
When does Love give up the chase?
Tell, O tell me, Grizzled-Face!

"Ah!" the wise old lips reply,
"Youth may pass and strength may die;
But of Love I can't foretoken:
Ask some older sage than I!"

169.   *The World Well Lost*

THAT year? Yes, doubtless I remember still, —
    Though why take count of every wind that blows!
'Twas plain, men said, that Fortune used me ill
    That year, — the selfsame year I met with Rose.

Crops failed; wealth took a flight; house, treasure, land,
    Slipped from my hold — thus plenty comes and goes.
One friend I had, but he too loosed his hand
    (Or was it I?) the year I met with Rose.

There was a war, I think; some rumor, too,
    Of famine, pestilence, fire, deluge, snows;
Things went awry. My rivals, straight in view,
    Throve, spite of all; but I, — I met with Rose.

EDMUND CLARENCE STEDMAN

That year my white-faced Alma pined and died:
　　Some trouble vexed her quiet heart, — who knows?
Not I, who scarcely missed her from my side,
　　Or aught else gone, the year I met with Rose.

Was there no more? Yes, that year life began:
　　All life before a dream, false joys, light woes, —
All after-life compressed within the span
　　Of that one year, — the year I met with Rose!

RICHARD REALF

1834-1878

170.　　　*Indirection*

FAIR are the flowers and the children, but their subtle
　　suggestion is fairer;
Rare is the roseburst of dawn, but the secret that clasps
　　it is rarer;
Sweet the exultance of song, but the strain that precedes
　　it is sweeter;
And never was poem yet writ, but the meaning outmas-
　　tered the metre.

Never a daisy that grows, but a mystery guideth the grow-
　　ing;
Never a river that flows, but a majesty sceptres the flow-
　　ing;
Never a Shakespeare that soared, but a stronger than he
　　did enfold him,
Nor ever a prophet foretells, but a mightier seer hath
　　foretold him.

RICHARD REALF

In the gardens of Life we strayed together;
　　And the luscious apples were ripe and red,
And the languid lilac and honeyed heather
　　Swooned with the fragrance which they shed.
And under the trees the angels walked,
　　And up in the air a sense of wings
Awed us tenderly while we talked
　　Softly in sacred communings.

In the meadows of Life we strayed together,
　　Watching the waving harvests grow;
And under the benison of the Father
　　Our hearts, like the lambs, skipped to and fro.
And the cowslip, hearing our low replies,
　　Broidered fairer the emerald banks,
And glad tears shone in the daisy's eyes,
　　And the timid violet glistened thanks.

Who was with us, and what was round us,
　　Neither myself nor my darling guessed;
Only we knew that something crowned us
　　Out from the heavens with crowns of rest;
Only we knew that something bright
　　Lingered lovingly where we stood,
Clothed with the incandescent light
　　Of something higher than humanhood.

O the riches Love doth inherit!
　　Ah, the alchemy which doth change
Dross of body and dregs of spirit
　　Into sanctities rare and strange!

RICHARD REALF

My flesh is feeble and dry and old,
    My darling's beautiful hair is gray;
But our elixir and precious gold
    Laugh at the footsteps of decay.

Harms of the world have come unto us,
    Cups of sorrow we yet shall drain;
But we have a secret which doth show us
    Wonderful rainbows in the rain.
And we hear the tread of the years move by,
    And the sun is setting behind the hills;
But my darling does not fear to die,
    And I am happy in what God wills.

So we sit by our household fires together,
    Dreaming the dreams of long ago:
Then it was balmy summer weather,
    And now the valleys are laid in snow.
Icicles hang from the slippery eaves;
    The wind blows cold, — 'tis growing late;
Well, well! we have garnered all our sheaves,
    I and my darling, and we wait.

JOHN JAMES PIATT

1835–1917

173.   *The Lost Genius*

A GIANT came to me when I was young,
    My instant will to ask —
My earthly Servant, from the earth he sprung
    Eager for any task!

"What wilt thou, O my Master?" he began,
  "Whatever can be," I.
"Say thy first wish — whate'er thou wilt I can,"
  The Strong Slave made reply.

"Enter the earth and bring its riches forth,
  For pearls explore the sea,"
He brought, from East and West and South and North,
  All treasures back to me!

"Build me a palace wherein I may dwell."
  "Awake and see it done,"
Spake his great voice at dawn. Oh, miracle
  That glittered in the sun!

"Find me the princess fit for my embrace,
  The vision of my breast;
For her search every clime and every race."
  My yearning arms were blessed!

"Get me all knowledge." Sages with their lore,
  And poets with their songs,
Crowded my palace halls at every door,
  In still, obedient throngs!

"Now bring me wisdom." Long ago he went;
  (The cold task harder seems:)
He did not hasten with the last content —
  The rest, meanwhile, were dreams!

Houseless and poor, on many a trackless road,
  Without a guide, I found
A white-haired phantom with the world his load,
  Bending him to the ground!

JOHN JAMES PIATT

" I bring thee wisdom, Master." Is it he,
   I marvelled then, in sooth?
" Thy palace-builder, beauty-seeker, see! "
   I saw the Ghost of Youth!

LOUISE CHANDLER MOULTON

1835–1908

174.   *To-night*

BEND low, O dusky Night,
   And give my spirit rest.
     Hold me to your deep breast,
And put old cares to flight.
Give back the lost delight
   That once my soul possest,
     When Love was loveliest.
Bend low, O dusky Night!

Enfold me in your arms —
   The sole embrace I crave
     Until the embracing grave
Shield me from life's alarms.
I dare your subtlest charms;
   Your deepest spell I brave, —
     O, strong to slay or save,
Enfold me in your arms!

I could not find him in the old-time place, —
I must pursue him, made by sorrow bold,
Through worlds unknown, in strange Celestial race,
Whose mystic round no traveller has told,
From star to star, until I see his face.

178.   *We Lay Us Down to Sleep*

WE lay us down to sleep,
    And leave to God the rest:
Whether to wake and weep
    Or wake no more be best.

Why vex our souls with care?
    The grave is cool and low, —
Have we found life so fair
    That we should dread to go?

We've kissed love's sweet, red lips,
    And left them sweet and red:
The rose the wild bee sips
    Blooms on when he is dead.

Some faithful friends we've found;
    But they who love us best,
When we are under ground,
    Will laugh on with the rest.

No task have we begun
    But other hands can take;
No work beneath the sun
    For which we need to wake.

Then hold us fast, sweet Death,
    If so it seemeth best
To Him who gave us breath
    That we should go to rest.

We lay us down to sleep;
    Our weary eyes we close:
Whether to wake and weep,
    Or wake no more, He knows.

179.   *The House of Death*

NOT a hand has lifted the latchet
    Since she went out of the door —
No footstep shall cross the threshold,
    Since she can come in no more.

There is rust upon locks and hinges,
    And mold and blight on the walls,
And silence faints in the chambers,
    And darkness waits in the halls —

Waits as all things have waited
    Since she went, that day of spring,
Borne in her pallid splendor
    To dwell in the Court of the King:

With lilies on brow and bosom,
    With robes of silken sheen,
And her wonderful, frozen beauty,
    The lilies and silk between.

THOMAS BAILEY ALDRICH

188.   *Thalia*

A middle-aged lyrical poet is supposed to be taking final
leave of the Muse of Comedy. She has brought him his hat
and gloves, and is abstractedly picking a thread of gold hair
from his coat sleeve as he begins to speak:

I SAY it under the rose —
    oh, thanks! — yes, under the laurel,
We part lovers, not foes;
    we are not going to quarrel.

We have too long been friends
    on foot and in gilded coaches,
Now that the whole thing ends,
    to spoil our kiss with reproaches.

I leave you; my soul is wrung;
    I pause, look back from the portal —
Ah, I no more am young,
    and you, child, you are immortal!

Mine is the glacier's way,
    yours is the blossom's weather —
When were December and May
    known to be happy together?

Before my kisses grow tame,
    before my moodiness grieve you,
While yet my heart is flame,
    and I all lover, I leave you.

THOMAS BAILEY ALDRICH

So, in the coming time,
>   when you count the rich years over,
Think of me in my prime,
>   and not as a white-haired lover,

Fretful, pierced with regret,
>   the wraith of a dead Desire
Thrumming a cracked spinet
>   by a slowly dying fire.

When, at last, I am cold —
>   years hence, if the gods so will it —
Say, " He was true as gold,"
>   and wear a rose in your fillet!

Others, tender as I,
>   will come and sue for caresses,
Woo you, win you, and die —
>   mind you, a rose in your tresses!

Some Melpomene woo,
>   some hold Clio the nearest;
You, sweet Comedy — you
>   were ever sweetest and dearest!

Nay, it is time to go.
>   When writing your tragic sister
Say to that child of woe
>   how sorry I was I missed her.

Really, I cannot stay,
>   though " parting is such sweet sorrow " . . .
Perhaps I will, on my way
>   down-town, look in to-morrow!

THOMAS BAILEY ALDRICH

189.   *No Songs in Winter*

THE sky is gray as gray may be,
   There is no bird upon the bough,
There is no leaf on vine or tree.

In the Neponset marshes now
Willow-stems, rosy in the wind,
Shiver with hidden sense of snow.

So too 't is winter in my mind,
No light-winged fancy comes and stays:
A season churlish and unkind.

Slow creep the hours, slow creep the days,
The black ink crusts upon the pen —
Wait till the bluebirds and the jays
And golden orioles come again!

190.   *"I'll Not Confer with Sorrow"*

I'LL not confer with Sorrow
   Till to-morrow;
But Joy shall have her way
   This very day.

Ho, eglantine and cresses
   For her tresses! —
Let Care, the beggar, wait
   Outside the gate.

342

THOMAS BAILEY ALDRICH

Tears if you will — but after
　　Mirth and laughter;
Then, folded hands on breast
　　And endless rest.

WILLIAM WINTER

1836–1917

191.   *Asleep*

HE knelt beside her pillow, in the dead watch of the
　　night,
And he heard her gentle breathing, but her face was still
　　and white,
And on her poor, wan cheek a tear told how the heart
　　can weep,
And he said, " My love was weary — God bless her! she's
　　asleep."

He knelt beside her gravestone in the shuddering autumn
　　night,
And he heard the dry grass rustle, and his face was thin
　　and white,
And through his heart the tremor ran of grief that cannot
　　weep,
And he said, " My love was weary — God bless her! she's
　　asleep."

192. I. H. B. Died, August 11, 1898

THE dirge is sung, the ritual said,
   No more the brooding organ weeps,
And, cool and green, the turf is spread
   On that lone grave where Bromley sleeps.

Gone — in his ripe, meridian hour!
   Gone — when the wave was at its crest!
And wayward Humor's perfect flower
   Is turned to darkness and to rest.

No more those honest eyes will beam
   With torrid light of proud desire;
No more those fluent lips will teem
   With Wit's gay quip or Passion's fire.

Forever gone! And with him fade
   The dreams that Youth and Friendship know —
The frolic and the glee that made
   The golden time of Long Ago.

The golden time! Ah, many a face, —
   And his the merriest of them all, —
That made this world so sweet a place,
   Is cold and still, beneath the pall.

His was the heart that over-much
   In human goodness puts its trust,
And his the keen, satiric touch
   That shrivels falsehood into dust.

WILLIAM WINTER

His love was like the liberal air, —
　　Embracing all, to cheer and bless;
And every grief that mortals share
　　Found pity in his tenderness.

His subtle vision deeply saw,
　　Through piteous webs of human fate,
The motion of the sovereign law,
　　On which all tides of being wait.

No sad recluse, no lettered drone,
　　His mirthful spirit, blithely poured,
In many a crescent frolic shone, —
　　The light of many a festal board.

No pompous pedant, did he feign,
　　With dull conceit of learning's store;
But not for him were writ in vain
　　The statesman's craft, the scholar's lore.

Fierce for the right, he bore his part
　　In strife with many a valiant foe;
But Laughter winged his polished dart,
　　And Kindness tempered every blow.

No selfish purpose marked his way;
　　Still for the common good he wrought,
And still enriched the passing day
　　With sheen of wit and sheaves of thought.

Shrine him, New-England, in thy breast!
　　With wild-flowers grace his hallowed bed,
And guard with love his laurelled rest,
　　Forever with thy holiest dead!

For not in all the teeming years
    Of thy long glory hast thou known
A being framed of smiles and tears,
    Humor and force, so like thine own!

And never did thy asters gleam,
    Or through thy pines the night-wind roll,
To soothe, in death's transcendent dream,
    A sweeter or a nobler soul!

WILLIAM DEAN HOWELLS

1837–1920

193.   *Change* [1]

SOMETIMES, when after spirited debate
    Of letters or affairs, in thought I go
Smiling unto myself, and all aglow
With some immediate purpose, and elate
As if my little, trivial scheme were great,
And what I would so were already so:
Suddenly I think of her that died, and know,
Whatever friendly or unfriendly fate
Befall me in my hope or in my pride,
It is all nothing but a mockery,
And nothing can be what it used to be,
When I could bid my happy life abide,
And build on earth for perpetuity,
Then, in the deathless days before she died.

[1] Copyright 1895 by Harper & Brothers, Copyright 1923 by Mildred Howells and J. M. Howells.

WILLIAM DEAN HOWELLS

194.   *If* [1]

YES, death is at the bottom of the cup,
    And every one that lives must drink it up;
And yet between the sparkle at the top
And the black lees where lurks that bitter drop,
There swims enough good liquor, Heaven knows,
To ease our hearts of all their other woes.

The bubbles rise in sunshine at the brim;
That drop below is very far and dim;
The quick fumes spread, and shape us such bright dreams
That in the glad delirium it seems
As though by some deft sleight, if so we willed,
That drop untasted might be somehow spilled.

195.   *Hope* [1]

WE sailed and sailed uopn the desert sea
    Where for whole days we alone seemed to be.
At last we saw a dim, vague line arise
Between the empty billows and the skies,
That grew and grew until it wore the shape
Of cove and inlet, promontory and cape;
Then hills and valleys, rivers, fields, and woods,
Steeples and roofs, and village neighborhoods.
And then I thought, "Sometime I shall embark
Upon a sea more desert and more dark
Than ever this was, and between the skies
And empty billows I shall see arise
Another world out of that waste and lapse,
Like yonder land. Perhaps — perhaps — perhaps!"

JOHN BURROUGHS

1837–1921

196.　　　　*Waiting*

SERENE, I fold my hands and wait,
　　Nor care for wind, or tide, or sea;
I rave no more 'gainst time or fate,
　　For, lo! my own shall come to me.

I stay my haste, I make delays,
　　For what avails this eager pace?
I stand amid the eternal ways,
　　And what is mine shall know my face.

Asleep, awake, by night or day,
　　The friends I seek are seeking me;
No wind can drive my bark astray,
　　Nor change the tide of destiny.

What matter if I stand alone?
　　I wait with joy the coming years;
My heart shall reap where it has sown,
　　And garner up its fruit of tears.

The waters know their own and draw
　　The brook that springs in yonder height;
So flows the good with equal law
　　Unto the soul of pure delight.

The stars come nightly to the sky;
　　The tidal wave unto the sea;
Nor time, nor space, nor deep, nor high,
　　Can keep my own away from me.

JOHN HAY

1838-1905

197.   *Jim Bludso*

WALL, no! I can't tell whar he lives,
    Becase he don't live, you see;
Leastways, he's got out of the habit
    Of livin' like you and me.
Whar have you been for the last three year
    That you haven't heard folks tell
How Jimmy Bludso passed in his checks
    The night of the Prairie Belle?

He weren't no saint, — them engineers
    Is all pretty much alike, —
One wife in Natchez-under-the-Hill
    And another one here, in Pike;
A keerless man in his talk was Jim,
    And an awkward hand in a row,
But he never flunked, and he never lied, —
    I reckon he never knowed how.

And this was all the religion he had, —
    To treat his engine well;
Never be passed on the river;
    To mind the pilot's bell;
And if ever the Prairie Belle took fire, —
    A thousand times he swore
He'd hold her nozzle agin the bank
    Till the last soul got ashore.

349

JOHN HAY

All boats has their day on the Mississip,
  And her day come at last, —
The Movastar was a better boat,
  But the Belle she *wouldn't* be passed.
And so she come tearin' along that night —
  The oldest craft on the line —
With a nigger squat on her safety-valve,
  And her furnace crammed, rosin and pine.

The fire bust out as she clared the bar,
  And burnt a hole in the night,
And quick as a flash she turned, and made
  For that willer-bank on the right.
There was runnin' and cursin', but Jim yelled out,
  Over all the infernal roar,
" I'll hold her nozzle agin the bank
  Till the last galoot's ashore."

Through the hot, black breath of the burnin' boat
  Jim Bludso's voice was heard,
And they all had trust in his cussedness,
  And knowed he would keep his word.
And, sure's you're born, they all got off
  Afore the smokestacks fell, —
And Bludso's ghost went up alone
  In the smoke of the Prairie Belle.

He weren't no saint, — but at jedgment
  I'd run my chance with Jim,
'Longside of some pious gentlemen
  That wouldn't shook hands with him.

350

He seen his duty, a dead-sure thing, —
    And went for it thar and then;
And Christ ain't a goin' to be too hard
    On a man that died for men.

198.   *Little Breeches*

I DON'T go much on religion,
    I never ain't had no show;
But I've got a middlin' tight grip, sir,
    On the handful o' things I know.
I don't pan out on the prophets
    And free-will and that sort of thing, —
But I b'lieve in God and the angels,
    Ever sence one night last spring.

I come into town with some turnips,
    And my little Gabe come along, —
No four-year-old in the county
    Could beat him for pretty and strong, —
Peart and chipper and sassy,
    Always ready to swear and fight, —
And I'd larnt him to chaw terbacker
    Jest to keep his milk-teeth white.

The snow come down like a blanket
    As I passed by Taggart's store;
I went in for a jug of molasses
    And left the team at the door.
They scared at something and started, —
    I heard one little squall,
And hell-to-split over the prairie
    Went team, Little Breeches, and all.

And made him see, who had been blind.
Their words passed by him like the wind
Which raves and howls, but cannot shock
The hundred-fathom-rooted rock.

Their threats and fury all went wide;
They could not touch his Hebrew pride;
Their sneers at Jesus and his band,
Nameless and homeless in the land,
Their boasts of Moses and his Lord,
All could not change him by one word.

I know not what this man may be,
Sinner or Saint; but as for me,
One thing I know, that I am he,
Who once was blind, and now I see.

They were all doctors of renown,
The great men of a famous town,
With deep brows, wrinkled, broad, and wise,
Beneath their wide phylacteries;
The wisdom of the East was theirs,
And honor crowned their silver hairs;
The man they jeered and laughed to scorn
Was unlearned, poor, and humbly born;
But he knew better far than they
What came to him that Sabbath day;
And what the Christ had done for him,
He knew, and not the Sanhedrim.

JAMES RYDER RANDALL

1839–1908

200. *My Maryland*

THE despot's heel is on thy shore,
   Maryland!
His torch is at thy temple door,
   Maryland!
Avenge the patriotic gore
That flecked the streets of Baltimore,
And be the battle-queen of yore,
   Maryland, My Maryland!

Hark to an exiled son's appeal,
   Maryland!
My Mother State, to thee I kneel,
   Maryland!
For life and death, for woe and weal,
Thy peerless chivalry reveal,
And gird thy beauteous limbs with steel,
   Maryland, My Maryland!

Thou wilt not cower in the dust,
   Maryland!
Thy beaming sword shall never rust,
   Maryland!
Remember Carroll's sacred trust,
Remember Howard's warlike thrust,
And all thy slumbers with the just,
   Maryland, My Maryland!

JAMES RYDER RANDALL

Come! 'tis the red dawn of the day,
    Maryland!
Come with thy panoplied array,
    Maryland!
With Ringgold's spirit for the fray,
With Watson's blood at Monterey,
With fearless Lowe and dashing May,
    Maryland, My Maryland!

Dear Mother, burst the tyrant's chain,
    Maryland!
Virginia should not call in vain,
    Maryland!
She meets her sisters on the plain, —
" *Sic semper!* " 'tis the proud refrain
That baffles minions back amain,
    Maryland!
Arise in majesty again,
    Maryland, My Maryland!

Come! for thy shield is bright and strong,
    Maryland!
Come! for thy dalliance does thee wrong,
    Maryland!
Come to thine own heroic throng
Stalking with Liberty along,
And chant thy dauntless slogan-song,
    Maryland, My Maryland!

I see the blush upon thy cheek,
    Maryland!
For thou wast ever bravely meek,
    Maryland!

But lo! there surges forth a shriek,
From hill to hill, from creek to creek,
Potomac calls to Chesapeake,
       Maryland, My Maryland!

Thou wilt not yield the Vandal toll,
       Maryland!
Thou wilt not crook to his control,
       Maryland!
Better the fire upon thee roll,
Better the shot, the blade, the bowl,
Than crucifixion of the soul,
       Maryland, My Maryland!

I hear the distant thunder hum,
       Maryland!
The Old Line's bugle, fife, and drum,
       Maryland!
She is not dead, nor deaf, nor dumb;
Huzza! she spurns the Northern scum!
She breathes! She burns! She'll come! She'll come!
       Maryland, My Maryland!

ABRAM JOSEPH RYAN
1839–1886

201. *The Conquered Banner*

FURL that Banner, for 'tis weary;
  Round its staff 'tis drooping dreary:
    Furl it, fold it, — it is best;
For there's not a man to wave it,

And there's not a sword to save it,
And there's not one left to lave it
In the blood which heroes gave it,
And its foes now scorn and brave it:
   Furl it, hide it, — let it rest!

Take that Banner down! 'tis tattered;
Broken is its staff and shattered;
And the valiant hosts are scattered,
   Over whom it floated high.
Oh, 'tis hard for us to fold it,
Hard to think there's none to hold it,
Hard that those who once unrolled it
   Now must furl it with a sigh!
Furl that Banner — furl it sadly!
Once ten thousands hailed it gladly,
And ten thousands wildly, madly,
   Swore it should forever wave;
Swore that foeman's sword should never
Hearts like theirs entwined dissever,
Till that flag should float forever
   O'er their freedom or their grave!

Furl it! for the hands that grasped it,
And the hearts that fondly clasped it,
   Cold and dead are lying low;
And that Banner — it is trailing,
While around it sounds the wailing
   Of its people in their woe.

For, though conquered, they adore it, —
Love the cold, dead hands that bore it,

ABRAM JOSEPH RYAN

Weep for those who fell before it,
Pardon those who trailed and tore it;
And oh, wildly they deplore it,
    Now to furl and fold it so!

Furl that Banner! True, 'tis gory,
Yet 'tis wreathed around with glory,
And 'twill live in song and story
    Though its folds are in the dust!
For its fame on brightest pages,
Penned by poets and by sages,
Shall go sounding down the ages —
    Furl its folds though now we must.

Furl that Banner, softly, slowly!
Treat it gently — it is holy,
    For it droops above the dead.
Touch it not — unfold it never;
Let it droop there, furled forever, —
    For its people's hopes are fled!

BRET HARTE

1839–1902

202.   *At the Hacienda*

KNOW I not who thou mayst be
    Carved upon this olive-tree, —
    " Manuela of La Torre," —
For around on broken walls
Summer sun and spring rain falls,
And in vain the low wind calls
    " Manuela of La Torre."

Of that song no words remain
But the musical refrain, —
    " Manuela of La Torre."
Yet at night, when winds are still,
Tinkles on the distant hill
A guitar, and words that thrill
    Tell to me the old, old story, —
Old when first thy charms were sung,
Old when these old walls were young,
    " Manuela of La Torre."

203.   *Grizzly*

COWARD, — of heroic size,
    In whose lazy muscles lies
Strength we fear and yet despise;
Savage, — whose relentless tusks
Are content with acorn husks;
Robber, — whose exploits ne'er soared
O'er the bee's or squirrel's hoard;
Whiskered chin, and feeble nose,
Claws of steel on baby toes, —
Here, in solitude and shade,
Shambling, shuffling plantigrade,
Be thy courses undismayed!

Here, where Nature makes thy bed,
Let thy rude, half-human tread
    Point to hidden Indian springs,
Lost in ferns and fragrant grasses,
    Hovered o'er by timid wings,
Where the wood-duck lightly passes,

Where the wild bee holds her sweets,
Epicurean retreats,
Fit for thee, and better than
Fearful spoils of dangerous man.
In thy fat-jowled deviltry
Friar Tuck shall live in thee;
Thou mayest levy tithe and dole;
    Thou shalt spread the woodland cheer,
From the pilgrim taking toll;
    Match thy cunning with his fear;
Eat, and drink, and have thy fill;
Yet remain an outlaw still!

204. *Plain Language from Truthful James*

Table Mountain, 1870.

WHICH I wish to remark,
    And my language is plain,
That for ways that are dark
    And for tricks that are vain,
The heathen Chinee is peculiar,
    Which the same I would rise to explain.

Ah Sin was his name;
    And I shall not deny,
In regard to the same,
    What that name might imply;
But his smile it was pensive and childlike,
    As I frequent remarked to Bill Nye.

It was August the third,
  And quite soft was the skies;
Which it might be inferred
  That Ah Sin was likewise;
Yet he played it that day upon William
  And me in a way I despise.

Which we had a small game,
  And Ah Sin took a hand:
It was Euchre. The same
  He did not understand;
But he smiled as he sat by the table,
  With the smile that was childlike and bland.

Yet the cards they were stocked
  In a way that I grieve,
And my feelings were shocked
  At the state of Nye's sleeve,
Which was stuffed full of aces and bowers,
  And the same with intent to deceive.

But the hands that were played
  By that heathen Chinee,
And the points that he made,
  Were quite frightful to see, —
Till at last he put down a right bower,
  Which the same Nye had dealt unto me.

Then I looked up at Nye,
  And he gazed upon me;
And he rose with a sigh,
  And said, " Can this be?
We are ruined by Chinese cheap labor, — "
  And he went for that heathen Chinee.

In the scene that ensued
  I did not take a hand,
But the floor it was strewed
  Like the leaves on the strand
With the cards that Ah Sin had been hiding,
  In the game " he did not understand."

In his sleeves, which were long,
  He had twenty-four jacks —
Which was coming it strong,
  Yet I state but the facts;
And we found on his nails, which were taper,
  What is frequent in tapers, — that's wax.

Which is why I remark,
  And my language is plain,
That for ways that are dark
  And for tricks that are vain,
The heathen Chinee is peculiar, —
  Which the same I am free to maintain.

205.   *Madroño*

CAPTAIN of the Western wood,
    Thou that apest Robin Hood!
Green above thy scarlet hose,
How thy velvet mantle shows!
Never tree like thee arrayed,
O thou gallant of the glade!

BRET HARTE

When the fervid August sun
Scorches all it looks upon,
And the balsam of the pine
Drips from stem to needle fine,
Round thy compact shade arranged,
Not a leaf of thee is changed!

When the yellow autumn sun
Saddens all it looks upon,
Spreads its sackcloth on the hills,
Strews its ashes in the rills,
Thou thy scarlet hose dost doff,
And in limbs of purest buff
Challengest the sombre glade
For a sylvan masquerade.

Where, oh, where, shall he begin
Who would paint thee, Harlequin?
With thy waxen burnished leaf,
With thy branches' red relief,
With thy polytinted fruit, —
In thy spring or autumn suit, —
Where begin, and, oh, where end,
Thou whose charms all art transcend!

ROBERT KELLEY WEEKS

1840-

206.   *A Song for Lexington*

THE spring came earlier on
   Than usual that year;
The shadiest snow was gone,
The slowest brook was clear,
And warming in the sun
Shy flowers began to peer.

'Twas more like middle May,
The earth so seemed to thrive,
That Nineteenth April day
Of Seventeen Seventy-Five;
Winter was well away,
New England was alive!

Alive and sternly glad!
Her doubts were with the snow;
Her courage, long forbade,
Ran full to overflow;
And every hope she had
Began to bud and grow.

She rose betimes that morn,
For there was work to do;
A planting, not of corn,
Of what she hardly knew, —
Blessings for men unborn;
And well she did it too!

ROBERT KELLEY WEEKS

With open hand she stood,
And sowed for all the years,
And watered it with blood,
And watered it with tears,
The seed of quickening food
For both the hemispheres.

This was the planting done
That April morn of fame;
Honor to every one
To that seed-field that came!
Honor to Lexington,
Our first immortal name!

JOAQUIN MILLER

1841–1913

207. *Columbus*

BEHIND him lay the gray Azores,
    Behind the Gates of Hercules;
Before him not the ghost of shores,
    Before him only shoreless seas.
The good mate said: " Now must we pray,
    For lo! the very stars are gone.
Brave Admiral, speak, what shall I say? "
    " Why, say, ' Sail on! sail on! and on! ' "

" My men grow mutinous day by day;
    My men grow ghastly wan and weak."
The stout mate thought of home; a spray
    Of salt wave washed his swarthy cheek.

JOAQUIN MILLER

"What shall I say, brave Admiral, say,
  If we sight naught but seas at dawn?"
"Why, you shall say at break of day,
  'Sail on! sail on! sail on! and on!'"

They sailed and sailed, as winds might blow,
  Until at last the blanched mate said:
"Why, now not even God would know
  Should I and all my men fall dead.
These very winds forget their way,
  For God from these dread seas is gone.
Now speak, brave Admiral, speak and say" —
  He said: "Sail on! sail on! and on!"

They sailed. They sailed. Then spake the mate:
  "This mad sea shows his teeth to-night.
He curls his lip, he lies in wait,
  With lifted teeth, as if to bite!
Brave Admiral, say but one good word:
  What shall we do when hope is gone?"
The words leapt like a leaping sword:
  "Sail on! sail on! sail on! and on!"

Then, pale and worn, he kept his deck,
  And peered through darkness. Ah, that night
Of all dark nights! And then a speck —
  A light! A light! A light! A light!
It grew, a starlit flag unfurled!
  It grew to be Time's burst of dawn.
He gained a world; he gave that world
  Its grandest lesson: "On! sail on!"

JOAQUIN MILLER

208. *At the Grave of Walker*

HE lies low in the levelled sand,
  Unsheltered from the tropic sun,
And now of all he knew not one
Will speak him fair in that far land.
Perhaps 'twas this that made me seek,
Disguised, his grave one winter-tide;
A weakness for the weaker side,
A siding with the helpless weak.

A palm not far held out a hand,
Hard by a long green bamboo swung,
And bent like some great bow unstrung,
And quivered like a willow wand;
Perched on its fruits that crooked hand,
Beneath a broad banana's leaf,
A bird in rainbow splendor sang
A low, sad song, of tempered grief.

No sod, no sign, no cross nor stone,
But at his side a cactus green
Upheld its lances long and keen;
It stood in sacred sands alone,
Flat-palmed and fierce with lifted spears;
One bloom of crimson crowned its head,
A drop of blood, so bright, so red,
Yet redolent as roses' tears.

In my left hand I held a shell,
All rosy lipped and pearly red;
I laid it by his lowly bed,
For he did love so passing well

The grand songs of the solemn sea.
O shell! sing well, wild, with a will,
When storms blow loud and birds be still,
The wildest sea-song known to thee!

I said some things with folded hands,
Soft whispered in the dim sea-sound,
And eyes held humbly to the ground,
And frail knees sunken in the sands.
He had done more than this for me,
And yet I could not well do more:
I turned me down the olive shore,
And set a sad face to the sea.

209.   *Westward Ho!*

WHAT strength! what strife! what rude unrest!
      What shocks! what half-shaped armies met!
A mighty nation moving west,
With all its steely sinews set
Against the living forests. Hear
The shouts, the shots of pioneer,
The rended forests, rolling wheels,
As if some half-checked army reels,
Recoils, redoubles, comes again,
Loud-sounding like a hurricane.

O bearded, stalwart, westmost men,
So tower-like, so Gothic built!
A kingdom won without the guilt
Of studied battle, that hath been
Your blood's inheritance. . . . Your heirs
Know not your tombs: the great ploughshares

Cleave softly through the mellow loam
Where you have made eternal home,
And set no sign. Your epitaphs
Are writ in furrows. Beauty laughs
While through the green ways wandering
Beside her love, slow gathering
White, starry-hearted May-time blooms
Above your lowly levelled tombs;
And then below the spotted sky
She stops, she leans, she wonders why
The ground is heaved and broken so,
And why the grasses darker grow
And droop and trail like wounded wing.

Yea, Time, the grand old harvester,
Has gathered you from wood and plain.
We call to you again, again;
The rush and rumble of the car
Comes back in answer. Deep and wide
The wheels of progress have passed on;
The silent pioneer is gone.
His ghost is moving down the trees,
And now we push the memories
Of bluff, bold men who dared and died
In foremost battle, quite aside.

210.   *A California Christmas*

BEHOLD where Beauty walks with Peace!
    Behold where Plenty pours her horn
Of fruits, of flowers, fat increase,
As generous as light of morn.

JOAQUIN MILLER

Green Shasta, San Diego, seas
Of bloom and green between them rolled.
Great herds in grasses to their knees,
And green earth garmented in gold.

White peaks that prop the sapphire blue
Look down on Edens, such as when
That fair first spot perfection knew,
And God walked perfect earth with men.

I say God's kingdom is at hand
Right here, if we but lift our eyes;
I say there lies no line or land
Between this land and Paradise.

EDWARD ROWLAND SILL

1841–1887

211.   *The Fool's Prayer*

THE royal feast was done; the King
    Sought some new sport to banish care,
And to his jester cried: "Sir Fool,
    Kneel now, and make for us a prayer!"

The jester doffed his cap and bells,
    And stood the mocking court before;
They could not see the bitter smile
    Behind the painted grin he wore.

He bowed his head, and bent his knee
    Upon the monarch's silken stool;
His pleading voice arose: "O Lord,
    Be merciful to me, a fool!

" No pity, Lord, could change the heart
    From red with wrong to white as wool:
The rod must heal the sin; but, Lord,
    Be merciful to me, a fool!

" 'Tis not by guilt the onward sweep
    Of truth and right, O Lord, we stay;
'Tis by our follies that so long
    We hold the earth from heaven away.

" These clumsy feet, still in the mire,
    Go crushing blossoms without end;
These hard, well-meaning hands we thrust
    Among the heart-strings of a friend.

" The ill-timed truth we might have kept —
    Who knows how sharp it pierced and stung!
The word we had not sense to say —
    Who knows how grandly it had rung!

" Our faults no tenderness should ask,
    The chastening strips must cleanse them all;
But for our blunders — oh, in shame
    Before the eyes of heaven we fall.

" Earth bears no balsam for mistakes;
    Men crown the knave, and scourge the tool
That did his will; but Thou, O Lord,
    Be merciful to me, a fool! "

The room was hushed; in silence rose
    The King, and sought his gardens cool,
And walked apart, and murmured low,
    " Be merciful to me, a fool! "

212.   *Her Explanation*

SO you have wondered at me, — guessed in vain
     What the real woman is you know so well?
I am a lost illusion. Some strange spell
Once made your friend there, with his fine disdain
Of fact, conceive me perfect. He would fain
(But could not) see me always, as befell
His dream to see me, plucking, asphodel
In saffron robes, on some celestial plain.
All that I was he marred and flung away
In quest of what I was not, could not be, —
Lilith, or Helen, or Antigone.
Still he may search; but I have had my day,
And now the Past is all the part for me
That this world's empty stage has left to play.

213.   *Opportunity*

THIS I beheld, or dreamed it in a dream:
     There spread a cloud of dust along a plain;
And underneath the cloud, or in it, raged
A furious battle, and men yelled, and swords
Shocked upon swords and shields. A prince's banner
Wavered, then staggered backward, hemmed by foes.
A craven hung along the battle's edge,
And thought, " Had I a sword of keener steel —
That blue blade that the king's son bears, — but this
Blunt thing —! " he snapt and flung it from his hand,
And cowering crept away and left the field.

EDWARD ROWLAND SILL

Then came the king's son, wounded, sore bestead,
And weaponless, and saw the broken sword,
Hilt-buried in the dry and trodden sand,
And ran and snatched it, and with battle shout
Lifted afresh he hewed his enemy down,
And saved a great cause that heroic day.

CHARLES GOODRICH WHITING

1842–

214. *Blue Hills Beneath the Haze*

BLUE hills beneath the haze
   That broods o'er distant ways,
Whether ye may not hold
Secrets more dear than gold, —
This is the ever new
Puzzle within your blue.

Is't not a softer sun
Whose smiles yon hills have won?
Is't not a sweeter air
That folds the fields so fair?
Is't not a finer rest
That I so fain would test?

The far thing beckons most,
The near becomes the lost.
Not what we have is worth,
But that which has no birth
Or breath within the ken
Of transitory men.

374

SIDNEY LANIER

1842–1881

215.   *Song of the Chattahoochee*

OUT of the hills of Habersham,
    Down the valleys of Hall,
I hurry amain to reach the plain,
Run the rapid and leap the fall,
Split at the rock and together again,
Accept my bed, or narrow or wide,
And flee from folly on every side
With a lover's pain to attain the plain
        Far from the hills of Habersham,
        Far from the valleys of Hall.

        All down the hills of Habersham,
        All through the valleys of Hall,
The rushes cried *Abide, abide,*
The willful waterweeds held me thrall,
The laving laurel turned my tide,
The ferns and the fondling grass said *Stay,*
The dewberry dipped for to work delay,
And the little reeds sighed *Abide, abide,*
        Here in the hills of Habersham,
        Here in the valleys of Hall.

        High o'er the hills of Habersham,
        Veiling the valleys of Hall,
The hickory told me manifold
Fair tales of shade, the poplar tall
Wrought me her shadowy self to hold,

375

SIDNEY LANIER

The chestnut, the oak, the walnut, the pine,
Overleaning, with flickering meaning and sign,
Said, *Pass not, so cold, these manifold*
Deep shades of the hills of Habersham,
These glades in the valleys of Hall.

And oft in the hills of Habersham,
And oft in the valleys of Hall,
The white quartz shone, and the smooth brook-stone
Did bar me of passage with friendly brawl,
And many a luminous jewel lone
— Crystals clear or a-cloud with mist,
Ruby, garnet and amethyst —
Made lures with the lights of streaming stone
In the clefts of the hills of Habersham,
In the beds of the valleys of Hall.

But oh, not the hills of Habersham,
And oh, not the valleys of Hall
Avail: I am fain for to water the plain.
Downward the voices of Duty call —
Downward, to toil and be mixed with the main,
The dry fields burn, and the mills are to turn,
And a myriad flowers mortally yearn,
And the lordly main from beyond the plain
Calls o'er the hills of Habersham,
Calls through the valleys of Hall.

SIDNEY LANIER

216.   *Opposition*

OF fret, of dark, of thorn, of chill,
    Complain no more; for these, O heart,
Direct the random of the will
    As rhymes direct the rage of art.

The lute's fixt fret, that runs athwart
    The strain and purpose of the string,
For governance and nice consort
    Doth bar his wilful wavering.

The dark hath many dear avails;
    The dark distils divinest dews;
The dark is rich with nightingales,
    With dreams, and with the heavenly Muse.

Bleeding with thorns of petty strife,
    I'll ease (as lovers do) my smart
With sonnets to my lady Life
    Writ red in issues from the heart.

What grace may lie within the chill
    Of favor frozen fast in scorn!
When Good's a-freeze, we call it Ill!
    This rosy Time is glacier-born.

Of fret, of dark, of thorn, of chill,
    Complain thou not, O heart; for these
Bank-in the current of the will
    To uses, arts, and charities.

217. *A Ballad of Trees and the Master*

INTO the woods my Master went,
   Clean forspent, forspent.
Into the woods my Master came,
Forspent with love and shame.
But the olives they were not blind to Him,
The little gray leaves were kind to Him:
The thorn-tree had a mind to Him
When into the woods He came.

Out of the woods my Master went,
And He was well content.
Out of the woods my Master came,
Content with death and shame.
When Death and Shame would woo Him last,
From under the trees they drew Him last:
'Twas on a tree they slew Him — last
When out of the woods He came.

218. *Evening Song*

LOOK off, dear Love, across the sallow sands,
   And mark yon meeting of the sun and sea,
How long they kiss in sight of all the lands.
   Ah, longer, longer, we.

Now in the sea's red vintage melts the sun,
   As Egypt's pearl dissolved in rosy wine,
And Cleopatra night drinks all. 'Tis done,
   Love, lay thine hand in mine.

378

Come forth, sweet stars, and comfort heaven's heart;
  Glimmer, ye waves, round else unlighted sands.
O night! divorce our sun and sky apart
      Never our lips, our hands.

219.   *The Stirrup-Cup*

DEATH, thou'rt a cordial old and rare:
  Look how compounded, with what care!
Time got his wrinkles reaping thee
Sweet herbs from all antiquity.

David to thy distillage went,
Keats, and Gotama excellent,
Omar Khayyam, and Chaucer bright,
And Shakspere for a king-delight.

Then, Time, let not a drop be spilt:
Hand me the cup whene'er thou wilt;
'Tis thy rich stirrup-cup to me;
I'll drink it down right smilingly.

CHARLES WARREN STODDARD
1843–1909
220. *The Royal Mummy to Bohemia*

WHEREFORE these revels that my dull eyes greet?
  These dancers, dancing at my fleshless feet;
The harpers, harping vainly at my ears
Deaf to the world, lo, thrice a thousand years!

CHARLES WARREN STODDARD

Time was when even I was blithe: I knew
The murmur of the flowing wave, where grew
The lean, lithe rushes; I have heard the moan
Of Nilus in prophetic undertone.

My sire was monarch of a mighty race:
Daughter of Pharaoh, I! before my face
Myriads of groveling creatures crawled, to thrust
Their fearful foreheads in the desert dust.

Above me gleamed and glowed my palace walls:
There bloomed my bowers; and there, my waterfalls
Lulled me in languors; slaves with feather flails
Fretted the tranquil air to gentle gales.

O, my proud palms! my royal palms that stood
In stately groups, a queenly sisterhood!
And O, my sphinxes, gazing eye in eye,
Down the dim vistas of eternity!

Where be ye now? And where am I at last?
With gay Bohemia is my portion cast:
Born of the oldest East, I seek my rest
In the fair city of the youngest West.

Farewell, O Egypt! Naught can thee avail:
What tarries now to tell thy sorry tale?
A sunken temple that the sands have hid
The tapering shadow of a pyramid!

And now, my children, harbor me not ill:
I was a princess, am a woman still.
Gibe me no gibes, but greet me at your best,
As I was wont to greet the stranger guest.

CHARLES WARREN STODDARD

Feast well, drink well, make merry while ye may,
For e'en the best of you must pass my way.
The elder as the youngster, fair to see,
Must gird his marble loins and follow me.

221. *The Cocoa-Tree*

CAST on the water by a careless hand,
   Day after day the winds persuaded me:
  Onward I drifted till a coral tree
Stayed me among its branches, where the sand
   Gathered about me, and I slowly grew,
  Fed by the constant sun and the inconstant dew.

The sea-birds build their nests against my root,
   And eye my slender body's horny case.
  Widowed within this solitary place
Into the thankless sea I cast my fruit;
   Joyless I thrive, for no man may partake
  Of all the store I bear and harvest for his sake.

No more I heed the kisses of the morn;
   The harsh winds rob me of the life they gave;
  I watch my tattered shadow in the wave,
And hourly droop and nod my crest forlorn,
   While all my fibres stiffen and grow numb
  Beckoning the tardy ships, the ships that never come!

JOHN BOYLE O'REILLY

1844-1890

222.   ## A White Rose

THE red rose whispers of passion,
    And the white rose breathes of love;
Oh, the red rose is a falcon,
    And the white rose is a dove.

But I send you a cream-white rosebud
    With a flush on its petal tips;
For the love that is purest and sweetest
    Has a kiss of desire on the lips.

223.   ## A Savage

DIXON, a Choctaw, twenty years of age,
    Had killed a miner in a Leadville brawl;
Tried and condemned, the rough-beards curb their rage,
    And watch him stride in freedom from the hall.

"Return on Friday, to be shot to death!"
    So ran the sentence, — it was Monday night.
The dead man's comrades drew a well-pleased breath;
    Then all night long the gambling-dens were bright.

The days sped slowly; but the Friday came,
    And flocked the miners to the shooting-ground;
They chose six riflemen of deadly aim,
    And with low voices sat and lounged around.

382

JOHN BOYLE O'REILLY

"He will not come." "He's not a fool." "The men
  Who set the savage free must face the blame."
A Choctaw brave smiled bitterly, and then
  Smiled proudly, with raised head, as Dixon came.

Silent and stern, a woman at his heels,
  He motions to the brave, who stays her tread.
Next minute flame the guns, — the woman reels
  And drops without a moan: Dixon is dead.

MAURICE THOMPSON

1844–1901

224. On A Fly-Leaf of Theocritus

THOSE were good times, in olden days,
    Of which the poet has his dreams,
When gods beset the woodland ways,
    And lay in wait by all the streams.

One could be sure of something then
    Severely simple, simply grand,
Or keenly, subtly sweet, as when
    Venus and Love went hand in hand.

Now I would give (such is my need)
    All the world's store of rhythm and rhyme
To see Pan fluting on a reed
    And with his goat-hoof keeping time!

MAURICE THOMPSON

Where the green walnut's outer rind
Gives precious bitterness to the wind;

There lurks the sweet creative power,
As lurks the honey in the flower.

In winter's bud that bursts in spring,
In nut of autumn's ripening,

In acrid bulb beneath the mold,
Sleeps the elixir, strong and old,

That Rosicrucians sought in vain, —
Life that renews itself again!

What bottled perfume is so good
As fragrance of split tulip-wood?

What fabled drink of God or muse
Was rich as purple mulberry juice?

And what school-polished gem of thought
Is like the rune from Nature caught?

He is a poet strong and true
Who loves wild thyme and honey-dew;

And like a brown bee works and sings
With morning freshness on his wings,

And a gold burden on his thighs, —
The pollen-dust of centuries!

MAURICE THOMPSON

227.   *Atalanta*

W̶HEN spring grows old, and sleepy winds
    Set from the south with odors sweet,
I see my love in green cool groves
Speed down dusk aisles with shining feet.

She throws a kiss, and bids me run
In accents sweet as roses' breath.
I know I cannot win the race,
And at the end, I know, is death.

Yet joyfully I bare my limbs,
Anoint me with the tropic breeze,
And feel through every sinew thrill
The vigor of Hippomenes.

O race of love, we all have run
Thy happy cause through groves of spring,
And cared not, when at last we lost,
For life or death or any thing.

RICHARD   WATSON   GILDER
1844–1909
228.   *Ode*

I

I AM the spirit of the morning sea;
  I am the awakening and the glad surprise;
I fill the skies
With laughter and with light.
Not tears, but jollity
At birth of day brim the strong man-child's eyes.

RICHARD WATSON GILDER

Behold the white
Wide three-fold beams that from the hidden sun
Rise swift and far, —
One where Orion keeps
His arméd watch, and one
That to the midmost starry heaven upleaps;
The third blots out the firm-fixed Northern Star.
    I am the wind that shakes the glittering wave,
Hurries the snowy spume along the shore
And dies at last in some far-murmuring cave.
My voice thou hearest in the breaker's roar —
That sound which never failed since time began,
And first around the world the shining tumult ran.

II

    I light the sea and wake the sleeping land.
My footsteps on the hills make music, and my hand
Plays like a harper's on the wind-swept pines.

    With the wind and the day
I follow round the world — away! away!
Wide over lake and plain my sunlight shines
And every wave and every blade of grass
Doth know me as I pass;
And me the western sloping mountains know, and me
The far-off, golden sea.

    O sea, whereon the passing sun doth lie!
O man, who watchest by that golden sea!
Grieve not, — O grieve not thou, but lift thine eye
And see me glorious in the sunset sky!

RICHARD WATSON GILDER

III

I love not the night
Save when the stars are bright,
Or when the moon
Fills the white air with silence like a tune.
Yea, even the night is mine
When the Northern Lights outshine,
And all the wild heavens throb in ecstasy divine; —
Yea, mine deep midnight, though the black sky lowers,
When the sea burns white and breaks on the shore in
    starry showers.

IV

I am the laughter of the new-born child
On whose soft-breathing sleep an angel smiled.
And I all sweet first things that are:
First songs of birds, not perfect as at last, —
Broken and incomplete, —
But sweet, oh, sweet!
And I the first faint glimmer of a star
To the wrecked ship that tells the storm is past;
The first keen smells and stirrings of the Spring;
First snow-flakes, and first May-flowers after snow;
The silver glow
Of the new moon's ethereal ring;
The song the morning stars together made,
And the first kiss of lovers under the first June shade.

V

My sword is quick, my arm is strong to smite
In the dread joy and fury of the fight.

I am with those who win, not those who fly;
With those who live I am, not those who die.
Who die? Nay, nay, that word
Where I am is unheard;
For I am the spirit of youth that cannot change,
Nor cease, nor suffer woe;
And I am the spirit of beauty that doth range
Through natural forms and motions, and each show
Of outward loveliness. With me have birth
All gentleness and joy in all the earth.
Raphael knew me, and showed the world my face;
Me Homer knew, and all the singing race, —
For I am the spirit of light, and life, and mirth.

229.   *The Celestial Passion*

O WHITE and midnight sky! O starry bath!
      Wash me in thy pure, heavenly, crystal flood;
Cleanse me, ye stars, from earthly soil and scath;
Let not one taint remain in spirit or blood!
Receive my soul, ye burning, awful deeps;
Touch and baptize me with the mighty power
That in ye thrills, while the dark planet sleeps;
Make me all yours for one blest, secret hour!
O glittering host! O high angelic choir!
Silence each tone that with thy music jars;
Fill me even as an urn with thy white fire
Till all I am is kindred to the stars!
Make me thy child, thou infinite, holy night —
So shall my days be full of heavenly light!

230.   *I Count My Time by Times That I Meet Thee*

I COUNT my time by times that I meet thee;
  These are my yesterdays, my morrows, noons,
And nights; these my old moons and my new moons.
Slow fly the hours, or fast the hours do flee,
If thou art far from or art near to me:
If thou art far, the bird tunes are no tunes;
If thou art near, the wintry days are Junes, —
Darkness is light, and sorrow cannot be.
Thou art my dream come true, and thou my dream;
The air I breathe, the world wherein I dwell;
My journey's end thou art, and thou the way;
Thou art what I would be, yet only seem;
Thou art my heaven and thou art my hell;
Thou art my ever-living judgment-day.

231.   *On the Life-Mask of Lincoln*

THIS bronze doth keep the very form and mould
  Of our great martyr's face. Yes, this is he:
That brow all wisdom, all benignity;
That human, humorous mouth; those cheeks that hold
Like some harsh landscape all the summer's gold;
That spirit fit for sorrow, as the sea
For storms to beat on; the lone agony
Those silent, patient lips too well foretold.
Yes, this is he who ruled a world of men
As might some prophet of the elder day —
Brooding above the tempest and the fray
With deep-eyed thought and more than mortal ken.
A power was his beyond the touch of art
Or armëd strength — his pure and mighty heart.

232   *Sherman*

GLORY and honor and fame and everlasting lauda-
tion
For our captains who loved not war, but fought for the
life of the nation;
Who knew that, in all the land, one slave meant strife,
not peace;
Who fought for freedom, not glory; made war that war
might cease.

Glory and honor and fame; the beating of muffled
drums;
The wailing funeral dirge, as the flag-wrapped coffin
comes;
Fame and honor and glory; and joy for a noble soul,
For a full and splendid life, and laurelled rest at the
goal.

Glory and honor and fame; the pomp that a soldier
prizes;
The league-long waving line as the marching falls and
rises;
Rumbling of caissons and guns; the clatter of horses' feet,
And a million awe-struck faces far down the waiting street.

But better than martial woe, and the pageant of civic
sorrow;
Better than praise of to-day, or the statue we build
to-morrow;
Better than honor and glory, and history's iron pen,
Was the thought of duty done and the love of his
fellow-men.

392

JOHN BANISTER TABB

233. *Evolution*

OUT of the dusk a shadow,
  Then, a spark;
Out of the cloud a silence,
  Then, a lark;
Out of the heart a rapture,
  Then, a pain;
Out of the dead, cold ashes,
  Life again.

234. *Anonymous*

ANONYMOUS — nor needs a name
  To tell the secret whence the flame,
With light, and warmth, and incense, came
A new creation to proclaim.

So was it when, His labor done,
God saw His work, and smiled thereon:
His glory in the picture shone,
But name upon the canvas, none.

235. *Clover*

LITTLE masters, hat in hand
  Let me in your presence stand,
Till your silence solve for me
This your threefold mystery.

Tell me — for I long to know —
How, in darkness there below,
Was your fairy fabric spun,
Spread and fashioned, three in one.

Did your gossips gold and blue,
Sky and Sunshine, choose for you,
Ere your triple forms were seen,
Suited liveries of green?

Can ye, — if ye dwelt indeed
Captives of a prison seed, —
Like the Genie, once again
Get you back into the grain?

Little masters, may I stand
In your presence, hat in hand,
Waiting till you solve for me
This your threefold mystery?

236.   *A Child's Prayer*

MAKE me, dear Lord, polite and kind
    To every one, I pray.
And may I ask you how you find
    Yourself, dear Lord, to-day?

394

JOHN HENRY BONER

1845–1903

237. *Poe's Cottage at Fordham*

HERE lived the soul enchanted
   By melody of song;
Here dwelt the spirit haunted
   By a demoniac throng;
Here sang the lips elated;
Here grief and death were sated;
Here loved and here unmated
   Was he, so frail, so strong.

Here wintry winds and cheerless
   The dying firelight blew,
While he whose song was peerless
   Dreamed the drear midnight through,
And from dull embers chilling
Crept shadows darkly filling
The silent place, and thrilling
   His fancy as they grew.

Here, with brow bared to heaven,
   In starry night he stood,
With the lost star of seven
   Feeling sad brotherhood.
Here in the sobbing showers
Of dark autumnal hours
He heard suspected powers
   Shriek through the stormy wood.

JOHN HENRY BONER

From visions of Apollo
   And of Astarte's bliss,
He gazed into the hollow
   And hopeless vale of Dis;
And though earth were surrounded
By heaven, it still was mounded
With graves. His soul had sounded
   The dolorous abyss.

Proud, mad, but not defiant,
   He touched at heaven and hell.
Fate found a rare soul pliant
   And rung her changes well.
Alternately his lyre,
Stranded with strings of fire,
Led earth's most happy choir,
   Or flashed with Israfel.

No singer of old story
   Luting accustomed lays,
No harper for new glory,
   No mendicant for praise,
He struck high chords and splendid,
Wherein were fiercely blended
Tones that unfinished ended
   With his unfinished days.

Here through this lowly portal,
   Made sacred by his name,
Unheralded immortal
   The mortal went and came.

And fate that then denied him,
And envy that decried him,
And malice that belied him,
    Have cenotaphed his fame.

JOSEPH I. C. CLARKE

1846–1925

238.   *The Fighting Race*

"READ out the names!" and Burke sat back,
    And Kelly drooped his head.
While Shea — they call him Scholar Jack —
    Went down the list of the dead.
Officers, seamen, gunners, marines,
    The crews of the gig and yawl,
The bearded man and the lad in his teens,
    Carpenters, coal passers — all.
Then, knocking the ashes from out his pipe,
    Said Burke in an offhand way:
"We're all in that dead man's list, by Cripe!
    Kelly and Burke and Shea."
"Well, here's to the Maine, and I'm sorry for Spain,"
    Said Kelly and Burke and Shea.

"Wherever there's Kellys there's trouble," said Burke.
    "Wherever fighting's the game,
Or a spice of danger in grown man's work,"
    Said Kelly, "you'll find my name."
"And do we fall short," said Burke, getting mad,
    "When it's touch and go for life?"
Said Shea, "It's thirty-odd years, bedad,
    Since I charged to drum and fife

JOSEPH I. C. CLARKE

Up Marye's Heights, and my old canteen
   Stopped a rebel ball on its way.
There were blossoms of blood on our sprigs of green —
   Kelly and Burke and Shea —
And the dead didn't brag." "Well, here's to the flag!"
   Said Kelly and Burke and Shea.

" I wish't was in Ireland, for there's the place,"
   Said Burke, " that we'd die by right,
In the cradle of our soldier race,
   After one good stand-up fight.
My grandfather fell on Vinegar Hill,
   And fighting was not his trade;
But his rusty pike's in the cabin still,
   With Hessian blood on the blade."
" Aye, aye," said Kelly, " the pikes were great
   When the word was ' clear the way!'
We were thick on the roll in ninety-eight —
   Kelly and Burke and Shea."
" Well, here's to the pike and the sword and the like!"
   Said Kelly and Burke and Shea.

And Shea, the scholar, with rising joy,
   Said, " We were at Ramillies;
We left our bones at Fontenoy
   And up in the Pyrenees;
Before Dunkirk, on Landen's plain,
   Cremona, Lille, and Ghent,
We're all over Austria, France, and Spain,
   Wherever they pitched a tent.
We've died for England from Waterloo
   To Egypt and Dargai;

And still there's enough for a corps or crew,
   Kelly and Burke and Shea."
" Well, here is to good honest fighting blood! "
   Said Kelly and Burke and Shea.

" Oh, the fighting races don't die out,
   If they seldom die in bed,
For love is first in their hearts, no doubt,"
   Said Burke; then Kelly said:
" When Michael, the Irish Archangel, stands,
   The angel with the sword,
And the battle-dead from a hundred lands
   Are ranged in one big horde,
Our line, that for Gabriel's trumpet waits,
   Will stretch three deep that day,
From Jehoshaphat to the Golden Gates —
   Kelly and Burke and Shea."
" Well, here's thank God for the race and the sod! "
   Said Kelly and Burke and Shea.

JAMES JEFFREY ROCHE
1847–1908

239.   *The Kearsarge*

IN the gloomy ocean bed
   Dwelt a formless thing, and said,
In the dim and countless eons long ago,
   " I will build a stronghold high,
   Ocean's power to defy,
And the pride of haughty man to lay low."

Crept the minutes for the sad,
Sped the cycles for the glad,
But the march of time was neither less nor more;
While the formless atom died,
Myriad millions by its side,
And above them slowly lifted Roncador.

Roncador of Carribee,
Coral dragon of the sea,
Ever sleeping with his teeth below the wave;
Woe to him who breaks the sleep!
Woe to them who sail the deep!
Woe to ship and man that fear a shipman's grave!

Hither many a galleon old,
Heavy-keeled with guilty gold,
Fled before the hardy rover smiting sore;
But the sleeper silent lay
Till the preyer and his prey
Brought their plunder and their bones to Roncador.

Be content, O conqueror!
Now our bravest ship of war,
War and tempest who had often braved before,
All her storied prowess past,
Strikes her glorious flag at last
To the formless thing that builded Roncador.

HENRY AUGUSTIN BEERS

1847–1926

240.   *Ecce in Deserto*

THE wilderness a secret keeps
    Upon whose guess I go:
Eye hath not seen, ear hath not heard;
    And yet I know, I know,

Some day the viewless latch will lift,
    The door of air swing wide
To one lost chamber of the wood
    Where those shy mysteries hide, —

One yet unfound, receding depth,
    From which the wood-thrush sings,
Still luring in to darker shades,
    In — in to colder springs.

There is no wind abroad to-day.
    But hark! — the pine-tops' roar,
That sleep and in their dreams repeat
    The music of the shore.

What wisdom in their needles stirs?
    What song is that they sing?
Those airs that search the forest's heart,
    What rumor do they bring?

A hushed excitement fills the gloom,
    And, in the stillness, clear
The vireo's tell-tale warning rings:
    " 'Tis near — 'tis near — 'tis near! "

HENRY AUGUSTIN BEERS

As, in the fairy-tale, more loud
    The ghostly music plays
When, toward the enchanted bower, the prince
    Draws closer through the maze.

Nay — nay. I track a fleeter game,
    A wilder than ye know,
To lairs beyond the inmost haunt
    Of thrush or vireo.

This way it passed: the scent lies fresh;
    The ferns still lightly shake.
Ever I follow hard upon,
    But never overtake.

To other woods the trail leads on,
    To other worlds and new,
Where they who keep the secret here
    Will keep the promise too.

THOMAS NELSON PAGE

1853–1922

241. *Uncle Gabe's White Folks*

SARVENT, Marster! Yes, sah, dat's me —
    Ole Unc' Gabe's my name;
I thankee, Marster, I'm 'bout, yo' see.
    "An' de ole 'ooman? " She's much de same,
Po'ly an' 'plainin', thank de Lord!
But de Marster's gwine ter come back from 'broad.

"Fine ole place? " Yes, sah, 'tis so;
　　An' mighty fine people my white folks war —
But you ought ter 'a' seen it years ago,
　　When de Marster an' de Mistis lived up dyah;
When de niggers'd stan' all roun' de do',
Like grains o' corn on de cornhouse flo.'

"Live mons'ous high? " Yes, Marster, yes;
　　Cut 'n' onroyal 'n' gordly dash;
Eat an' drink till you couldn' res'.
　　My folks war 'n' none o' yo' po'-white-trash;
No, sah, dey was ob high degree —
Dis heah nigger am quality!

"Tell you 'bout 'em? " You mus' 'a' hearn
　　'Bout my ole white folks, sho'!
I tell you, suh, dey was gre't an' stern;
D' didn' have nuttin' at all to learn;
　　D' knowed all dar was to know;
Gol' ober de' head an' onder dey feet;
An' silber! dey sowed 't like folks sows wheat.

"Use ter be rich? " Dat warn' de wud!
　　Jes' wallowed an' roll' in wealf.
Why, none o' my white folks ever stir'd
　　Ter lif' a han' for d'self;
De niggers use ter be stan'in' roun'
Jes' d' same ez leaves when dey fus' fall down;
De stable-stalls up heah at home
Looked like teef in a fine-toof comb;
De cattle was p'digious — mus' tell de fac'!
An' de hogs mecked de hillsides look like black;

403

An' de flocks ob sheep was so gre't an' white
Dey 'peared like clouds on a moonshine night.
An' when my ole Mistis use' ter walk —
    Jes' ter her kerridge (dat was fur
      Ez ever she walked) — I tell you, sir,
You could almos' heah her silk dress talk;
Hit use' ter soun' like de mornin' breeze,
When it wakes an' rustles de Gre't House trees.
An' de Marster's face! — de Marster's face,
    Whenever de Marster got right pleased —
Well, I 'clar' ter Gord, 't would shine wid grace
    De same ez his countenance had been greased.
De cellar, too, had de bes' ob wine,
An' brandy, an' sperrits dat yo' could fine;
An' ev'ything in dyah was stored,
'Skusin' de glory of de Lord!

"Warn' dyah a son?" Yes, sah, you knows
    He's de young Marster now;
But we heah dat dey tooken he very clo'es
    Ter pay what ole Marster owe;
He's done been gone ten year, I s'pose.
But he's comin' back some day, of co'se;
An' my ole 'ooman is aluz pyard,
    An' meckin' de Blue-Room baid,
An' ev'y day dem sheets is ayard,
    An' will be till *she's* daid;
An' de styars she'll scour,
    An' dat room she'll ten',
      Ev'y blessed day dat de Lord do sen'!

What say, Marster? Yo' say, you knows? —
  He's young an' slender-like an' fyah;
Better-lookin' 'n you, of co'se!
Hi! you's he? 'Fo Gord, 'tis him!
  'Tis de very voice an' eyes an' hyah,
An' mouf an' smile, on'y yo' ain' so slim —
I wonder whah — whah's de ole 'ooman?
Now let my soul
  Depart in peace,
For I behol'
Dy glory, Lord! — I knowed you, chile —
  I knowed you soon's I see'd your face!
Whar has you been dis blessed while?
  Done come back an' buy de place?
  Oh, bless de Lord for all his grace!
De ravins shell hunger, an' shell not lack,
De Marster, de young Marster's done come back!

242.   *Ashcake*

WELL, yes, sir, dat am a comical name —
    It are so, for a fac' —
But I knowed one, down in Ferginyer,
  Could 'a' toted dat on its back.

" What was it? " I'm gwine to tell you —
  'Twas mons'us long ago:
'Twas " Ashcake," sah; an' all on us
  Use' ter call 'im jes' " Ashcake," so.

You see, sir, my ole Marster, he
   Was a pow'ful wealfy man,
Wid mo' plantations dan hyahs on you haid —
   Gre't acres o' low-groun' lan'.

Jeems River bottoms, dat used ter stall
   A fo'-hoss plough, no time;
An' he'd knock you down ef you jes' had dyared
   Ter study 'bout guano 'n' lime.

De corn used ter stan' in de row dat thick
   You jes' could follow de balk;
An' rank! well, I 'clar 'ter de king, I'se seed
   Five 'coons up a single stalk!

He owned mo' niggers 'n arr' a man
   About dyar, black an' bright;
He owned so many, b'fo' de Lord,
   He didn' know all by sight!

Well, sir, one evelin', long to'ds dusk,
   I seen de Marster stan'
An' watch a yaller boy pass de gate
   Wid a ashcake in his han'.

He never had no mammy at all —
   Leastways, she was daid by dat —
An' de cook an' de hands about on de place
   Used ter see dat de boy kep' fat.

Well, he trotted along down de parf dat night,
   An' de Marster he seen him go,
An' hollered, " Say, boy — say, what's yer name? "
   " A — ashcake, sir," says Joe.

It 'peared ter tickle de Marster much,
  An' he called him up to de do'.
"Well, dat is a curisome name," says he;
  "But I guess it suits you, sho'."

"Whose son are you?" de Marster axed.
  "Young Jane's," says Joe; "she's daid."
A sperrit cudden 'a' growed mo' pale,
  An' "By Gord!" I heerd him said.

He tuk de child 'long in de house,
  Jes' 'count o' dat ar whim;
An', dat-time-out, you never see
  Sich sto' as he sot by him.

An' Ashcake swung his cradle, too,
  As clean as ever you see;
An' stuck as close ter ole Marster's heel
  As de shadder sticks to de tree.

'Twel one dark night, when de river was out,
  De Marster an' Ashcake Joe
Was comin' home an' de skiff upsot,
  An' Marster 'd 'a' drownded, sho',

Excusin' dat Ashcake cotch'd him hard
  An' gin him holt o' de boat,
An' saved him so; but 't was mo'n a week
  B'fo' *his* body comed afloat.

An' de Marster he grieved so 'bouten dat thing,
  It warn' long, sah, befo' he died;
An' he's sleep, way down in Ferginyer,
  Not fur from young Ashcake's side.

JOHN VANCE CHENEY

1848–1922

243.   *The Happiest Heart*

WHO drives the horses of the sun
　　Shall lord it but a day;
Better the lowly deed were done,
　　And kept the humble way.

The rust will find the sword of fame,
　　The dust will hide the crown;
Ay, none shall nail so high his name
　　Time will not tear it down.

The happiest heart that ever beat
　　Was in some quiet breast
That found the common daylight sweet,
　　And left to Heaven the rest.

244.   *The Strong*

DOST deem him weak that owns his strength is tried?
　　Nay, we may safely lean on him that grieves:
The pine has immemorially sighed,
　　The enduring poplar's are the trembling leaves.

To feel, and bow the head, is not to fear;
　　To cheat with jest — that is the coward's art:
Beware the laugh that battles back the tear;
　　He's false to all that's traitor to his heart.

408

JOHN VANCE CHENEY

He of great deeds does grope amid the throng
 Like him whose steps toward Dagon's temple bore;
There's ever something sad about the strong ——
 A look, a moan, like that on ocean's shore.

EMMA LAZARUS

1849–1887

245. *The Banner of the Jew*

WAKE, Israel, wake! Recall to-day
  The glorious Maccabean rage,
The sire heroic, hoary-gray,
 His five-fold lion-lineage;
The Wise, the Elect, the Help-of-God,
The Burst-of-spring, the Avenging Rod.

From Mizpeh's mountain-ridge they saw
 Jerusalem's empty streets, her shrine
Laid waste where Greeks profaned the Law
 With idol and with pagan sign.
Mourners in tattered black were there,
With ashes sprinkled on their hair.

Then from the stony peak there rang
 A blast to ope the graves: down poured
The Maccabean clan, who sang
 Their battle-anthem to the Lord.
Five heroes lead, and, following, see
Ten thousand rush to victory!

Oh for Jerusalem's trumpet now,
    To blow a blast of shattering power,
To wake the sleepers high and low,
    And rouse them to the urgent hour!
No hand for vengeance — but to save,
A million naked swords should wave.

Oh deem not dead that martial fire,
    Say not the mystic flame is spent!
With Moses' law and David's lyre,
    Your ancient strength remains unbent.
Let but an Ezra rise anew,
To lift the *Banner of the Jew!*

A rag, a mock at first — erelong,
    When men have bled and women wept,
To guard its precious folds from wrong,
    Even they who shrunk, even they who slept,
Shall leap to bless it, and to save.
Strike! for the brave revere the brave!

246. *The Crowing of the Red Cock*

ACROSS the Eastern sky has glowed
    The flicker of a blood-red dawn;
Once more the clarion cock has crowed,
    Once more the sword of Christ is drawn.
A million burning roof-trees light
The world-wide path of Israel's flight.

EMMA LAZARUS

Where is the Hebrew's fatherland?
   The folk of Christ is sore bestead;
The Son of Man is bruised and banned,
   Nor finds whereon to lay his head.
His cup is gall, his meat is tears,
His passion lasts a thousand years.

Each crime that wakes in man the beast,
   Is visited upon his kind.
The lust of mobs, the greed of priest,
   The tyranny of kings, combined
To root his seed from earth again,
His record is one cry of pain.

When the long roll of Christian guilt
   Against his sires and kin is known,
The flood of tears, the life-blood spilt,
   The agony of ages shown,
What oceans can the stain remove
From Christian law and Christian love?

Nay, close the book; not now, not here,
   The hideous tale of sin narrate;
Reëchoing in the martyr's ear,
   Even he might nurse revengeful hate,
Even he might turn in wrath sublime,
With blood for blood and crime for crime.

Coward? Not he, who faces death,
   Who singly against worlds has fought,
For what? A name he may not breathe,
   For liberty of prayer and thought.
The angry sword he will not whet,
His nobler task is — to forget.

FRANCIS SALTUS SALTUS

247. *Pastel*

AMONG the priceless gems and treasures rare
   Old Versailles shelters in its halls sublime,
I can recall one faded image fair,
A girl's sad face, praised once in every clime.
Poets have sung, in rich and happy rhyme,
Her violet eyes, the wonder of her hair.
An art-bijou it was, but dimmed by time,
A dreamy pastel of La Valliere!
I, too, remember in my heart a face
Whose charm I deemed would ever with me dwell;
But as the days went by, its peerless grace
Fled like those dreams that blooming dawn dispel,
Till of its beauty there was left no trace,
Time having blurred it like that pale pastel!

248. *The Sphinx Speaks*

CARVED by a mighty race whose vanished hands
   Formed empires more destructible than I,
In sultry silence I forever lie,
Wrapped in the shifting garment of the sands.
Below me, Pharaoh's scintillating bands
With clashings of loud cymbals have passed by,
And the eternal reverence of the sky
Falls royally on me and all my lands.

The record of the future broods in me;
I have with worlds of blazing stars been crowned,
But none my subtle mystery hath known
Save one, who made his way through blood and sea,
The Corsican, prophetic and renowned,
To whom I spake, one awful night alone!

249.   *The Bayadere*

NEAR strange, weird temples, where the Ganges' tide
   Bathes domed Lahore, I watched, by spice-trees
   fanned,
Her agile form in some quaint saraband,
A marvel of passionate chastity and pride.
Nude to the loins, superb and leopard-eyed,
With fragrant roses in her jewelled hand,
Before some Kaât-drunk Rajah, mute and grand,
Her flexile body bends, her white feet glide.
The dull Kinoors throb one monotonous tune,
And wail with zeal as in a hasheesh trance;
Her scintillant eyes in vague, ecstatic charm
Burn like black stars below the Orient moon,
While the suave, dreamy languor of the dance
Lulls the grim, drowsy cobra on her arm.

EUGENE FIELD

1850–1895

250.   *Little Boy Blue*

THE little toy dog is covered with dust,
    But sturdy and staunch he stands;
And the little toy soldier is red with rust,
    And his musket moulds in his hands.
Time was when the little toy dog was new,
    And the soldier was passing fair;
And that was the time when our Little Boy Blue
    Kissed them and put them there.

" Now, don't you go till I come," he said,
    " And don't you make any noise! "
So, toddling off to his trundle-bed,
    He dreamt of the pretty toys;
And, as he was dreaming, an angel song
    Awakened our Little Boy Blue —
Oh! the years are many, the years are long,
    But the little toy friends are true!

Ay, faithful to Little Boy Blue they stand,
    Each in the same old place,
Awaiting the touch of a little hand,
    The smile of a little face;
And they wonder, as waiting the long years through
    In the dust of that little chair,
What has become of our Little Boy Blue,
    Since he kissed them and put them there.

251.   *Nightfall in Dordrecht*

THE mill goes toiling slowly around
     With steady and solemn creak,
And my little one hears in the kindly sound
     The voice of the old mill speak.
While round and round those big white wings
     Grimly and ghostlike creep,
My little one hears that the old mill sings
     " Sleep, little tulip, sleep! "

The sails are reefed and the nets are drawn,
     And, over his pot of beer,
The fisher, against the morrow's dawn,
     Lustily maketh cheer.
He mocks at the winds that caper along
     From the far-off clamorous deep, —
But we — we love their lullaby song
     Of " Sleep, little tulip, sleep! "

Old dog Fritz in slumber sound
     Groans of the stony mart:
To-morrow how proudly he'll trot you round,
     Hitched to our new milk-cart!
And you shall help me blanket the kine
     And fold the gentle sheep,
And set the herring a-soak in brine, —
     But now, little tulip, sleep!

A Dream-One comes to button the eyes
     That wearily droop and blink,
While the old mill buffets the frowning skies
     And scolds at the stars that wink;

415

Over your face the misty wings
　　Of that beautiful Dream-One sweep,
And rocking your cradle she softly sings
　　" Sleep, little tulip, sleep! "

252.　　　　*Dibdin's Ghost*

D EAR wife, last midnight, whilst I read
　　　The tomes you so despise,
A spectre rose beside the bed,
　　And spake in this true wise:
" From Canaan's beatific coast
　　I've come to visit thee,
For I am Frognall Dibdin's ghost,"
　　Says Dibdin's ghost to me.

I bade him welcome, and we twain
　　Discussed with buoyant hearts
The various things that appertain
　　To bibliomaniac arts.
" Since you are fresh from t'other side,
　　Pray tell me of that host
That treasured books before they died,"
　　Says I to Dibdin's ghost.

" They've entered into perfect rest;
　　For in the life they've won
There are no auctions to molest,
　　No creditors to dun.
Their heavenly rapture has no bounds
　　Beside that jasper sea;
It is a joy unknown to Lowndes,"
　　Says Dibdin's ghost to me.

Much I rejoiced to hear him speak
   Of biblio-bliss above,
For I am one of those who seek
   What bibliomaniacs love.
" But tell me, for I long to hear
   What doth concern me most,
Are wives admitted to that sphere? "
   Says I to Dibdin's ghost.

" The women folk are few up there;
   For 'twere not fair, you know,
That they our heavenly joy should share
   Who vex us here below.
The few are those who have been kind
   To husbands such as we;
They knew our fads, and didn't mind,"
   Says Dibdin's ghost to me.

" But what of those who scold at us
   When we would read in bed?
Or, wanting victuals, make a fuss
   If we buy books instead?
And what of those who've dusted not
   Our motley pride and boast, —
Shall they profane that sacred spot? "
   Says I to Dibdin's ghost.

" Oh, no! they tread that other path,
   Which leads where torments roll,
And worms, yes, bookworms, vent their wrath
   Upon the guilty soul.

Untouched of bibliomaniac grace,
    That saveth such as we,
They wallow in that dreadful place,"
    Says Dibdin's ghost to me.

" To my dear wife will I recite
    What things I've heard you say;
She'll let me read the books by night
    She's let me buy by day.
For we together by and by
    Would join that heavenly host;
She's earned a rest as well as I,"
    Says I to Dibdin's ghost.

GEORGE PARSONS LATHROP

1851–1898

253.   *Keenan's Charge*

I

THE sun had set;
    The leaves with dew were wet:
Down fell a bloody dusk
On the woods, that second of May,
Where Stonewall's corps, like a beast of prey,
Tore through, with angry tusk.

" They've trapped us, boys! "
Rose from our flank a voice.
With a rush of steel and smoke
On came the rebels straight,
Eager as love and wild as hate;
And our line reeled and broke:

418

GEORGE PARSONS LATHROP

Broke and fled.
No one stayed — but the dead!
With curses, shrieks, and cries,
Horses and wagons and men
Tumbled back through the shuddering glen,
And above us the fading skies.

There's one hope still, —
Those batteries parked on the hill!
" Battery, wheel! " (mid the roar)
" Pass pieces; fix prolonge to fire
Retiring. Trot! " In the panic dire
A bugle rings " Trot! " — and no more.

The horses plunged,
The cannon lurched and lunged,
To join the hopeless rout.
But suddenly rode a form
Calmly in front of the human storm,
With a stern, commanding shout:

" Align those guns! "
(We knew it was Pleasonton's.)
The cannoneers bent to obey,
And worked with a will at his word:
And the black guns moved as if *they* had heard.
But ah the dread delay!

" To wait is crime;
O God, for ten minutes' time! "
The General looked around.

EDWIN MARKHAM

1852–

254. *The Man with the Hoe*

God made man in His own image, in the image of God
made He him. — GENESIS.

Written after seeing the Painting by Millet

BOWED by the weight of centuries he leans
 Upon his hoe and gazes on the ground,
The emptiness of ages in his face,
And on his back the burden of the world.
Who made him dead to rapture and despair,
A thing that grieves not and that never hopes,
Stolid and stunned, a brother to the ox?
Who loosened and let down this brutal jaw?
Whose was the hand that slanted back this brow?
Whose breath blew out the light within this brain?

Is this the Thing the Lord God made and gave
To have dominion over sea and land;
To trace the stars and search the heavens for power;
To feel the passion of Eternity?
Is this the Dream He dreamed who shaped the suns
And pillared the blue firmament with light?
Down all the stretch of Hell to its last gulf
There is no shape more terrible than this —
More tongued with censure of the world's blind greed —
More filled with signs and portents for the soul —
More fraught with menace to the universe.

What gulfs between him and the seraphim!
Slave of the wheel of labor, what to him
Are Plato and the swing of Pleiades?

EDWIN MARKHAM

What the long reaches of the peaks of song,
The rift of dawn, the reddening of the rose?
Through this dread shape the suffering ages look;
Time's tragedy is in that aching stoop;
Through this dread shape humanity betrayed,
Plundered, profaned, and disinherited,
Cries protest to the Judges of the World,
A protest that is also prophecy.

O masters, lords, and rulers in all lands,
Is this the handiwork you give to God,
This monstrous thing distorted and soul-quenched?
How will you ever straighten up this shape;
Touch it again with immortality;
Give back the upward looking and the light;
Rebuild in it the music and the dream;
Make right the immemorial infamies,
Perfidious wrongs, immedicable woes?

O masters, lords, and rulers in all lands,
How will the Future reckon with this Man?
How answer his brute question in that hour
When whirlwinds of rebellion shake the world?
How will it be with kingdoms and with kings —
With those who shaped him to the thing he is —
When this dumb Terror shall reply to God,
After the silence of the centuries?

255. *The Invisible Bride*

THE low-voiced girls that go
    In gardens of the Lord,
Like flowers of the field they grow
    In sisterly accord.

Their whispering feet are white
    Along the leafy ways;
They go in whirls of light
    Too beautiful for praise.

And in their band forsooth
    Is one to set me free —
The one that touched my youth —
    The one God gave to me.

She kindles the desire
    Whereby the gods survive —
The white ideal fire
    That keeps my soul alive.

Now at the wondrous hour,
    She leaves her star supreme,
And comes in the night's still power,
    To touch me with a dream.

Sibyl of mystery
    On roads unknown to men,
Softly she comes to me,
    And goes to God again.

HENRY VAN DYKE

1852–

256.   *An Angler's Wish*

I

WHEN tulips bloom in Union Square,
  And timid breaths of vernal air
  Go wandering down the dusty town,
Like children lost in Vanity Fair;

When every long, unlovely row
Of westward houses stands aglow,
  And leads the eyes towards sunset skies
Beyond the hills where green trees grow, —

Then weary seems the street parade,
And weary books, and weary trade:
  I'm only wishing to go a-fishing;
For this the month of May was made.

II

I guess the pussy-willows now
Are creeping out on every bough
  Along the brook; and robins look
For early worms behind the plough.

The thistle-birds have changed their dun
For yellow coats, to match the sun;
  And in the same array of flame
The dandelion show's begun.

425

The flocks of young anemones
Are dancing round the budding trees:
 Who can help wishing to go a-fishing
In days as full of joy as these?

III

I think the meadow-lark's clear sound
Leaps upward slowly from the ground,
 While on the wing the blue-birds ring
Their wedding-bells to woods around.

The flirting chewink calls his dear
Behind the bush; and very near,
 Where water flows, where green grass grows,
Song-sparrows gently sing, " Good cheer."

And, best of all, through twilight's calm
The hermit-thrush repeats his psalm.
 How much I'm wishing to go a-fishing
In days so sweet with music's balm!

IV

'Tis not a proud desire of mine;
I ask for nothing superfine;
 No heavy weight, no salmon great,
To break the record — or my line:

Only an idle little stream,
Whose amber waters softly gleam,
 Where I may wade, through woodland shade,
And cast the fly, and loaf, and dream:

Only a trout or two, to dart
From foaming pools, and try my art:
　　No more I'm wishing — old-fashioned fishing,
And just a day on Nature's heart.

257.　　　　*The Veery*

THE moonbeams over Arno's vale in silver flood were
　　pouring,
When first I heard the nightingale a long-lost love de-
　　ploring.
So passionate, so full of pain, it sounded strange and eerie;
I longed to hear a simpler strain, — the wood-notes of
　　the veery.

The laverock sings a bonny lay above the Scottish heather;
It sprinkles down from far away like light and love to-
　　gether;
He drops the golden notes to greet his brooding mate, his
　　dearie;
I only know one song more sweet, — the vespers of the
　　veery.

In English gardens, green and bright and full of fruity
　　treasure,
I heard the blackbird with delight repeat his merry meas-
　　ure:
The ballad was a pleasant one, the tune was loud and
　　cheery,
And yet, with every setting sun, I listened for the veery.

There! little girl, don't cry!
They have broken your heart, I know;
   And the rainbow gleams
   Of your youthful dreams
Are things of the long ago;
   But Heaven holds all for which you sigh. —
   There! little girl, don't cry!

262.   *On the Death of Little*
          Mahala Ashcraft

" LITTLE Haly! Little Haly! " cheeps the robin in
    the tree;
" Little Haly! " sighs the clover, " Little Haly! " moans
    the bee;
" Little Haly! Little Haly! " calls the kill-deer at twi-
    light;
And the katydids and crickets hollers " Haly! " all the
    night.

The sunflowers and the hollyhawks droops over the garden
    fence;
The old path down the garden-walks still holds her foot-
    prints' dents;
And the well-sweep's swingin' bucket seems to wait fer
    her to come
And start it on its wortery errant down the old bee-gum.

The bee-hives all is quiet; and the little Jersey steer,
When any one comes nigh it, acts so lonesome-like and
    queer;

434

And the little Banty chickens kindo' cutters faint and low,
Like the hand that now was feedin' 'em was one they didn't
know.
They's sorrow in the wavin' leaves of all the apple-trees;
And sorrow in the harvest-sheaves, and sorrow in the
breeze;
And sorrow in the twitter of the swallers 'round the shed;
And all the song her red-bird sings is " Little Haly's
dead! "

The medder 'pears to miss her, and the pathway through
the grass,
Whare the dewdrops ust to kiss her little bare feet as she
passed;
And the old pin in the gate-post seems to kindo'-sorto'
doubt
That Haly's little sunburnt hands 'll ever pull it out.

Did her father er her mother ever love her more'n me,
Er her sisters er her brother prize her love more tendurly?
I question — and what answer? — only tears, and tears
alone,
And ev'ry neghbor's eyes is full o' teardrops as my own.

" Little Haly! Little Haly! " cheeps the robin in the
tree;
" Little Haly! " sighs the clover; " Little Haly! " moans
the bee;
" Little Haly! Little Haly! " calls the kill-deer at twilight,
And the katydids and crickets hollers " Haly! " all the
night.

An' little Orphant Annie says, when the blaze is blue,
An' the lampwick sputters, an' the wind goes woo-oo!
An' you hear the crickets quit, an' the moon is gray,
An' the lightnin' bugs in dew is all squenched away, —
You better mind yer parents, and yer teachers fond and
    dear,
An' churish them 'at loves you, an' dry the orphant's tear,
An' he'p the pore an' needy ones 'at clusters all about,
Er the Gobble-uns 'll git you

        Ef you
          Don't
            Watch
              Out!

265. *Old John Henry*

OLD John's jes' made o' the commonest stuff —
    Old John Henry —
He's tough, I reckon, — but none too tough —
Too tough though's better than not enough!
    Says old John Henry.
He does his best, and when his best's bad,
He don't fret none, ner he don't git sad —
He simply 'lows it's the best he had:
    Old John Henry —

His doctern's jes' o' the plainest brand —
    Old John Henry —
A smilin' face and a hearty hand
'S religen 'at all folks understand,
    Says old John Henry.

He's stove up some with the rhumatiz,
And they hain't no shine on them shoes o' his,
And his hair hain't cut — but his eye-teeth is:
Old John Henry!

He feeds hisse'f when the stock's all fed —
Old John Henry —
And sleeps like a babe when he goes to bed —
And dreams o' heaven and home-made bread,
Says old John Henry.

He hain't refined as he'd ort to be
To fit the statutes o' poetry,
Ner his clothes don't fit him — but *he* fits *me:*
Old John Henry.

266. A Man by the Name of Bolus

A MAN by the name of Bolus — (all 'at we'll ever
know
Of the stranger's name, I reckon — and I'm kindo' glad
it's so!) —
Got off here, Christmas morning, looked 'round the town,
and then
Kindo' sized up the folks, I guess, and — went away again!

The fac's is, this man Bolus got " run in," Christmas-day;
The town turned out to see it, and cheered, and blocked
the way;
And they dragged him 'fore the Mayor — fer he couldn't
er wouldn't walk —
And socked him down fer trial — though he couldn't er
wouldn't talk!

Drunk? They was no doubt of it! — W'y, the marshal
of the town
Laughed and testified 'at he fell *up*-stairs 'stid o' *down!*
This man by the name of Bolus? — W'y, he even drapped
his jaw
And snored on through his " hearin' " — drunk as you
ever saw!

One feller spit in his boot-leg, and another 'n' drapped a
small
Little chunk o' ice down his collar, — but he didn't wake
at all!
And they all nearly split when his Honor said, in one of
his witty ways,
To " chalk it down fer him, ' Called away — be back in
thirty days! ' "

That's where this man named Bolus slid, kindo' like in a
fit,
Flat on the floor; and — drat my ears! — I hear 'em
a-laughin' yit!
Somebody fetched Doc Sifers from jest across the hall, —
And all Doc said was, " Morphine! We're too late! " and
that's all!

That's how they found his name out — piece of a letter
'at read:
" Your wife has lost her reason, and little Nathan's
dead —
Come ef you kin, — fergive *her* — but Bolus, as fer *me*,
This hour I send a bullet through where my heart *ort* to
be! "

440

Man by the name of Bolus! — As his revilers broke
Fer the open air, 'peared like, to me, I heard a voice 'at
    spoke —
Man by the name of Bolus! git up from where you lay —
Git up and smile white at 'em with your hands crossed
    thataway!

267.   *An Old Sweetheart*

A S one who cons at evening o'er an album all alone,
    And muses on the faces of the friends that he has
    known,
So I turn the leaves of fancy till, in shadowy design,
I find the smiling features of an old sweetheart of mine.

The lamplight seems to glimmer with a flicker of surprise,
As I turn it low to rest me of the dazzle in my eyes,
And light my pipe in silence, save a sigh that seems to
    yoke
Its fate with my tobacco and to vanish with the smoke.

'Tis a fragrant retrospection — for the loving thoughts
    that start
Into being are like perfume from the blossom of the
    heart;
And to dream the old dreams over is a luxury divine —
When my truant fancy wanders with that old sweetheart
    of mine.

Though I hear, beneath my study, like a fluttering **of**
      wings,
The voices of my children, and the mother as she sings,
I feel no twinge of conscience to deny me any theme
When Care has cast her anchor in the harbor of a dream.

In fact, to speak in earnest, I believe it adds a charm
To spice the good a trifle with a little dust of harm —
For I find an extra flavor in memory's mellow wine
That makes me drink the deeper to that old sweetheart
      of mine.

A face of lily beauty, with a form of airy grace,
Floats out of my tobacco as the genii from the vase;
And I thrill beneath the glances of a pair of azure eyes
As glowing as the summer and as tender as the skies.

I can see the pink sunbonnet and the little checkered dress
She wore when first I kissed her and she answered the
      caress
With the written declaration that, " as surely as the vine
Grew round the stump," she loved me — that old sweet-
      heart of mine.

And again I feel the pressure of her slender little hand,
As we used to talk together of the future we had
      planned —
When I should be a poet, and with nothing else to do
But write the tender verses that she set the music to:

When we should live together in a cozy little cot
Hid in a nest of roses, with a fairy garden-spot
Where the vines were ever fruited, and the weather ever
fine,
And the birds were ever singing for that old sweetheart
of mine:

When I should be her lover forever and a day,
And she my faithful sweetheart till the golden hair was
gray;
And we should be so happy that when either's lips were
dumb
They would not smile in Heaven till the other's kiss had
come.

But, ah! my dream is broken by a step upon the stair,
And the door is softly opened, and — my wife is standing
there;
Yet with eagerness and rapture all my visions I resign
To greet the living presence of that old sweetheart of
mine.

GEORGE EDWARD WOODBERRY

1855–

268.   *At Gibraltar*

I

ENGLAND, I stand on thy imperial ground,
  Not all a stranger; as thy bugles blow,
I feel within my blood old battles flow, —
The blood whose ancient founts in thee are found.

GEORGE EDWARD WOODBERRY

Still surging dark against the Christian bound
Wide Islam presses; well its peoples know
Thy heights that watch them wandering below;
I think how Lucknow heard their gathering sound.
I turn, and meet the cruel, turbaned face.
England, 'tis sweet to be so much thy son!
I feel the conqueror in my blood and race;
Last night Trafalgar awed me, and to-day
Gibraltar wakened; hark, thy evening gun
Startles the desert over Africa!

II

Thou art the rock of empire, set mid-seas
Between the East and West, that God has built;
Advance thy Roman borders where thou wilt,
While run thy armies true with his decrees;
Law, justice, liberty, — great gifts are these:
Watch that they spread where English blood is spilt,
Lest, mixed and sullied with his country's guilt,
The soldier's life-stream flow, and Heaven displease!
Two swords there are: one naked, apt to smite,
Thy blade of war; and, battle-storied, one
Rejoices in the sheath, and hides from light.
American I am; would wars were done!
Now westward, look, my country bids good-night, —
Peace to the world from ports without a gun!

HENRY CUYLER BUNNER
1855–1896

269.   *The Way to Arcady*

OH, *what's the way to Arcady,*
  To Arcady, to Arcady;
Oh, what's the way to Arcady,
  Where all the leaves are merry?

Oh, what's the way to Arcady?
The spring is rustling in the tree, —
The tree the wind is blowing through, —
  It sets the blossoms flickering white.
I knew not skies could burn so blue
  Nor any breezes blow so light.
They blow an old-time way for me,
Across the world to Arcady.

Oh, what's the way to Arcady?
Sir Poet, with the rusty coat,
Quit mocking of the song-bird's note.
How have you heart for any tune,
You with the wayworn russet shoon?
Your scrip, a-swinging by your side,
Gapes with a gaunt mouth hungry-wide.
I'll brim it well with pieces red,
If you will tell the way to tread.

Oh, I am bound for Arcady,
And if you but keep pace with me
You tread the way to Arcady.

And where away lies Arcady,
And how long yet may the journey be?

445

Ah, that (quoth he) *I do not know:*
Across the clover and the snow —
Across the frost, across the flowers —
Through summer seconds and winter hours,
I've trod the way my whole life long,
  And know not now where it may be;
My guide is but the stir to song,
That tells me I cannot go wrong,
    Or clear or dark the pathway be
    Upon the road to Arcady.

But how shall I do who cannot sing?
  I was wont to sing, once on a time, —
There is never an echo now to ring
  Remembrance back to the trick of rhyme.

'Tis strange you cannot sing (quoth he), —
The folk all sing in Arcady.

But how may he find Arcady
Who hath nor youth nor melody?

What, know you not, old man (quoth he), —
  Your hair is white, your face is wise, —
  That Love must kiss that Mortal's eyes
Who hopes to see fair Arcady?
No gold can buy you entrance there;
But beggared Love may go all bare —
No wisdom won with weariness;
But Love goes in with Folly's dress —
No fame that wit could ever win;
But only Love may lead Love in
    To Arcady, to Arcady.

HENRY CUYLER BUNNER

Ah, woe is me, through all my days
   Wisdom and wealth I both have got,
And fame and name, and great men's praise;
   But Love, ah Love! I have it not.
There was a time, when life was new —
   But far away and half forgot —
I only know her eyes were blue;
   But Love — I fear I knew it not.
We did not wed, for lack of gold,
And she is dead, and I am old.
All things have come since then to me,
Save Love, ah Love! and Arcady.

Ah, then I fear we part (quoth he), —
My way's for Love and Arcady.

But you, you fare alone, like me;
   The gray is likewise in your hair.
   What love have you to lead you there,
To Arcady, to Arcady?

Ah, no, not lonely do I fare;
   My true companion's Memory.
With Love he fills the Spring-time air;
   With Love he clothes the Winter tree.
Oh, past this poor horizon's bound
   My song goes straight to one who stands, —
Her face all gladdening at the sound, —
   To lead me to the Spring-green lands,
To wander with enlacing hands.

447

The songs within my breast that stir
Are all of her, are all of her.
My maid is dead long years (quoth he), —
She waits for me in Arcady.

Oh, yon's the way to Arcady,
*   To Arcady, to Arcady;*
Oh, yon's the way to Arcady,
*   Where all the leaves are merry.*

270.　　　*To a Dead Woman*

NOT a kiss in life; but one kiss, at life's end,
　　I have set on the face of Death in trust for thee.
Through long years keep it fresh on thy lips, O friend!
　　At the gate of Silence give it back to me.

271.　　　*Strong as Death*

O DEATH, when thou shalt come to me
　　From out thy dark, where she is now,
Come not with graveyard smell on thee,
　　Or withered roses on thy brow.

Come not, O Death, with hollow tone,
　　And soundless step, and clammy hand —
Lo, I am now no less alone
　　Than in thy desolate, doubtful land;

But with that sweet and subtle scent
　　That ever clung about her (such
As with all things she brushed was blent);
　　And with her quick and tender touch.

With the dim gold that lit her hair,
　　Crown thyself, Death; let fall thy tread
So light that I may dream her there,
　　And turn upon my dying bed.

And through my chilling veins shall flame
　　My love, as though beneath her breath;
And in her voice but call my name,
　　And I will follow thee, O Death.

272.　　　　*Triumph*

THE dawn came in through the bars of the blind, —
　　And the winter's dawn is gray, —
And said, " However you cheat your mind,
　　The hours are flying away."

A ghost of a dawn, and pale, and weak, —
　　" Has the sun a heart," I said,
" To throw a morning flush on the cheek
　　Whence a fairer flush has fled? "

As a gray rose-leaf that is fading white
　　Was the cheek where I set my kiss;
And on that side of the bed all night
　　Death had watched, and I on this.

I kissed her lips, they were half apart,
  Yet they made no answering sign;
Death's hand was on her failing heart,
  And his eyes said, " She is mine."

I set my lips on the blue-veined lid,
  Half-veiled by her death-damp hair;
And oh, for the violet depths it hid
  And the light I longed for there!

Faint day and the fainter life awoke,
  And the night was overpast;
And I said, " Though never in life you spoke,
  Oh, speak with a look at last! "

For the space of a heart-beat fluttered her breath,
  As a bird's wing spread to flee;
She turned her weary arms to Death,
  And the light I longed for there!

HARRISON SMITH MORRIS

1856–

273. *Always*

IS love, then only liking
  That lasts while beauty is;
Or while the clock is striking
  Forgetful hours of bliss?

Is love the cheek that wrinkles,
  The eye that saddens, oh —
Is love the star that twinkles
  But with the dawn must go?

HARRISON SMITH MORRIS

Ah, happy, who have found it
    In other measure made,
With tender ties around it
    And tranquil with the shade;

With hope and home and laughter
    And — whether beauty stay
Or blacken with the rafter —
    A true love all the way.

EDWARD SANFORD MARTIN

1856–

274.   *A Girl of Pompeii*

A PUBLIC haunt they found her in:
    She lay asleep, a lovely child;
The only thing left undefiled
Where all things else bore taint of sin.

Her charming contours fixed in clay
    The universal law suspend,
    And turn Time's chariot back, and blend
A thousand years with yesterday.

A sinless touch, austere yet warm,
    Around her girlish figure pressed,
    Caught the sweet imprint of her breast,
And held her, surely clasped, from harm.

Truer than work of sculptor's art
    Comes this dear maid of long ago,
    Sheltered from woeful chance, to show
A spirit's lovely counterpart,

451

CHARLES HENRY LUDERS

Wind of the East,
Wind of the sunrise seas,
Wind of the clinging mists and gray, harsh rains, —
Blow moist and chill across the wastes of brine,
And shut the sun out, and the moon and stars,
And lash the boughs against the dripping eaves,
Yet keep thou from my love.

But thou, sweet wind!
Wind of the fragrant South,
Wind from the bowers of jasmine and of rose, —
Over magnolia blooms and lilied lakes
And flowering forests come with dewy wings,
And stir the petals at her feet, and kiss
The low mound where she lies.

RICHARD BURTON

1861–

278.   *Black Sheep*

FROM their folded mates they wander far,
    Their ways seem harsh and wild:
They follow the beck of a baleful star,
    Their paths are dream-beguiled.

Yet haply they sought but a wider range,
    Some loftier mountain slope,
And little recked of the country strange
    Beyond the gates of hope.

454

And haply a bell with a luring call
   Summoned their feet to tread
Midst the cruel rocks, where the deep pitfall
   And the lurking snare are spread.

Maybe, in spite of their tameless days
   Of outcast liberty,
They're sick at heart for the homely ways
   Where their gathered brothers be.

And oft at night, when the plains fall dark
   And the hills loom large and dim,
For the shepherd's voice they mutely hark,
   And their souls go out to him.

Meanwhile, " Black sheep! black sheep! " we cry,
   Safe in the inner fold;
And maybe they hear, and wonder why,
   And marvel, out in the cold.

279.   *The Forefather*

HERE at the country inn,
   I lie in my quiet bed,
And the ardent onrush of armies
   Throbs and throbs in my head.

Why, in this calm, sweet place,
   Where only silence is heard,
Am I 'ware of the crash of conflict, —
   Is my blood to battle stirred?

RICHARD BURTON

Without, the night is blessed
    With the smell of pines, with stars;
Within, is the mood of slumber,
    The healing of daytime scars.

'Tis strange, — yet I am thrall
    To epic agonies;
The tumult of myriads dying
    Is borne to me on the breeze.

Mayhap in the long ago
    My forefather grim and stark
Stood in some hell of carnage,
    Faced forward, fell in the dark;

And I, who have always known
    Peace with her dove-like ways,
Am gripped by his martial spirit
    Here in the after days.

I cannot rightly tell:
    I lie, from all stress apart,
And the ardent onrush of armies
    Surges hot through my heart.

WALLACE RICE

1859-

280.   *Under the Stars*

*TELL me what sail the seas
        Under the stars?*
Ships, and ships' companies,
    Off to the wars.

WALLACE RICE

Steel are the ship's great sides,
    Steel are her guns,
Backward she thrusts the tides,
    Swiftly she runs;

Steel is the sailor's heart,
    Stalwart his arm,
His the Republic's part
    Through cloud and storm.

Tell me what standard rare
    Streams from the spars?
Red stripes and white they bear,
    Blue, with bright stars:

Red for brave hearts that burn
    With liberty,
White for the peace they earn
    Making men free,

Stars for the Heaven above, —
    Blue for the deep,
Where, in their country's love,
    Heroes shall sleep.

Tell me why on the breeze
    These banners blow?
Ships, and ships' companies,
    Eagerly go

Warring, like all our line,
    Freedom to friend
Under this starry sign,
    True to the end.

WALLACE RICE

Fair is the Flag's renown,
  Sacred her scars,
Sweet the death she shall crown
  Under the stars.

ROBERT MOWRY BELL

1860–

281.   *The Second Volume*

IN the groined alcoves of an ancient tower
  Amid a wealth of treasured tomes I found
A little book, in choicest vellum bound:
Therein a romance of such magic power
It held me rapt through many a trancëd hour;
And then, the threads of interest all unwound,
Abruptly closed. I searched that palace round,
And for its mate still earth's preserves I scour.
Perchance that was the whole? Then purposeless
The pain of conflict, and the bitter doubt
But half resolved; love in a dire distress,
Deserted, baffled, with its joy left out.
Could life so end, half told; its school so fail?
Soul, soul, there is a sequel to thy tale!

HAMLIN GARLAND

1860–

282.   *The Ute Lover*

BENEATH the burning brazen sky,
  The yellowed tepees stand.
Not far away a singing river
Sets through the sand.

458

HAMLIN GARLAND

Within the shadow of a lonely elm tree
The tired ponies keep.
The wild land, throbbing with the sun's hot magic,
Is rapt as sleep.

From out a clump of scanty willows
A low wail floats, —
The endless repetition of a lover's
Melancholy notes,
So sad, so sweet, so elemental,
All lovers' pain
Seems borne upon its sobbing cadence, —
The love-song of the plain.
From frenzied cry forever falling,
To the wind's wild moan,
It seems the voice of anguish calling
Alone! alone!

Caught from the winds forever moaning
On the plain,
Wrought from the agonies of woman
In maternal pain,
It holds within its simple measure
All death of joy,
Breathed though it be by smiling maiden
Or lithe brown boy.

It hath this magic, sad though its cadence
And short refrain —
It helps the exiled people of the mountain
Endure the plain;

THOMAS FLEMING DAY

1861-

292. *The Coasters*

OVERLOADED, *undermanned,*
    Trusting to a lee,
Playing I-spy with the land,
    Jockeying the sea —
That's the way the Coaster goes,
    Through calm and hurricane:
Everywhere the tide flows,
Everywhere the wind blows,
    From Mexico to Maine.

O East and West! O North and South!
    We ply along the shore,
From famous Fundy's foggy mouth,
    From floes of Labrador;
Through pass and strait, on sound and sea,
    From port to port we stand —
The rocks of Race fade on our lee,
    We hail the Rio Grande.
Our sails are never lost to sight;
    On every gulf and bay
They gleam, in winter wind-cloud white,
    In summer rain-cloud gray.

We hold the coast with slippery grip;
    We dare from cape to cape:
Our leaden fingers feel the dip
    And trace the channel's shape.

470

THOMAS FLEMING DAY

We sail or bide as serves the tide;
  Inshore we cheat its flow,
And side by side at anchor ride
  When stormy head-winds blow.
We are the offspring of the shoal,
  The hucksters of the sea;
From customs theft and pilot toll
  Thank God that we are free.

  Legging on and off the beach,
    Drifting up the strait,
  Fluking down the river reach,
    Towing through the gate —
  That's the way the Coaster goes,
    Flirting with the gale:
  Everywhere the tide flows,
  Everywhere the wind blows,
    From York to Beavertail.

  Here and there to get a load,
    Freighting anything;
  Running off with spanker stowed,
    Loafing wing-a-wing —
  That's the way the Coaster goes,
    Chumming with the land:
  Everywhere the tide flows,
  Everywhere the wind blows,
    From Ray to Rio Grande.

We split the swell where rings the bell
  On many a shallow's edge,
We take our flight past many a light
  That guards the deadly ledge;

THOMAS FLEMING DAY

We greet Montauk across the foam,
   We work the Vineyard Sound,
The Diamond sees us running home,
   The Georges outward bound;
Absecom hears our canvas beat
   When tacked off Brigantine;
We raise the Gulls with lifted sheet,
   Pass wing-and-wing between.

Off Monomoy we fight the gale,
   We drift off Sandy Key;
The watch of Fenwick sees our sail
   Scud for Henlopen's lee.
With decks awash and canvas torn
   We wallow up the Stream;
We drag dismasted, cargo borne,
   And fright the ships of steam.
Death grips us with his frosty hands
   In calm and hurricane;
We spill our bones on fifty sands
   From Mexico to Maine.

Cargo reef in main and fore,
   Manned by half a crew,
Romping up the weather shore,
   Edging down the Blue —
   That's the way the Coaster goes,
   Scouting with the lead:
Everywhere the tide flows,
Everywhere the wind blows,
   From Cruz to Quoddy Head.

LOUISE IMOGEN GUINEY

1861–1920

293.   *The Wild Ride*

I HEAR in my heart, I hear in its ominous pulses,
  All day, on the road, the hoofs of invisible horses;
All night, from their stalls, the importunate tramping and
    neighing.

Let cowards and laggards fall back! but alert to the saddle,
Straight, grim, and abreast, go the weather-worn, gallop-
    ing legion,
With a stirrup-cup each to the lily of women that loves
    him.

The trail is through dolor and dread, over crags and
    morasses;
There are shapes by the way, there are things that appal
    or entice us:
What odds? We are knights, and our souls are but bent
    on the riding.

I hear in my heart, I hear in its ominous pulses,
All day, on the road, the hoofs of invisible horses;
All night, from their stalls, the importunate tramping and
    neighing.

We spur to a land of no name, out-racing the storm-wind;
We leap to the infinite dark, like the sparks from the
    anvil.
Thou leadest, O God! All's well with Thy troopers that
    follow.

LOUISE IMOGEN GUINEY

294.   *Irish Peasant Song*

I TRY to knead and spin, but my life is low the while.
  Oh, I long to be alone, and walk abroad a mile;
Yet if I walk alone, and think of naught at all,
Why from me that's young should the wild tears fall?

The shower-stricken earth, the earth-colored streams,
They breathe on me awake, and moan to me in dreams;
And yonder ivy fondling the broke castle-wall,
It pulls upon my heart till the wild tears fall.

The cabin-door looks down a furze-lighted hill,
And far as Leighlin Cross the fields are green and still;
But once I hear the blackbird in Leighlin hedges call,
The foolishness is on me, and the wild tears fall!

295.   *Athassel Abbey*

FOLLY and Time have fashioned
    Of thee a songless reed;
O not-of-earth-impassioned!
Thy music's mute indeed.

Red from the chantry crannies
The orchids burn and swing,
And where the arch began is
Rest for a raven's wing;

And up the bossy column
Quick tails of squirrels wave,
And black, prodigious, solemn,
A forest fills the nave.

Still faithfuller, still faster,
To ruin give thy heart:
Perfect before the Master
Aye as thou wert, thou art.

But I am wind that passes
In ignorant wild tears,
Uplifted from the grasses,
Blown to the void of years,

Blown to the void, yet sighing
In thee to merge and cease,
Last breath of beauty's dying,
Of sanctity, of peace!

Tho' use nor place forever
Unto my soul befall,
By no beloved river
Set in a saintly wall,

Do thou by builders given
Speech of the dumb to be,
Beneath thine open heaven,
Athassel, pray for me!

296.   *Open, Time*

OPEN, Time, and let him pass
    Shortly where his feet would be!
Like a leaf of Michaelmas
Swooning from the tree,

LOUISE IMOGEN GUINEY

Ere its hour the manly mind
Trembles in a sure decrease,
Nor the body now can find
Any hold on peace.

Take him, weak and overworn;
Fold about his dying dream
Boyhood, and the April morn,
And the rolling stream:

Weather on a sunny ridge,
Showery weather, far from here;
Under some deep-ivied bridge,
Water rushing clear:

Water quick to cross and part,
(Golden light on silver sound),
Weather that was next his heart
All the world around!

Soon upon his vision break
These, in their remembered blue;
He shall toil no more, but wake
Young, in air he knew.

He has done with roofs and men.
Open, Time, and let him pass,
Vague and innocent again,
Into country grass.

297. *When on the Marge of Evening*

WHEN on the marge of evening the last blue light
    is broken,
And winds of dreamy odor are loosened from afar,
Or when my lattice opens, before the lark has spoken,
On dim laburnum-blossoms, and morning's dying star,

I think of thee, (O mine the more if other eyes be
    sleeping!)
Whose great and noonday splendor the many share and
    see,
While sacred and forever, some perfect law is keeping
The late and early twilight alone and sweet for me.

298. *To a Dog's Memory*

THE gusty morns are here,
    When all the reeds ride low with level spear;
And on such nights as lured us far of yore,
Down rocky alleys yet, and through the pine,
The Hound-star and the pagan Hunter shine;
But I and thou, ah, field-fellow of mine,
Together roam no more.

Soft showers go laden now
With odors of the sappy orchard-bough,
And brooks begin to brawl along the march;
The late frost steams from hollow sedges high;
The finch is come, the flame-blue dragon-fly,
The cowslip's common gold that children spy,
The plume upon the larch.

477

There is a music fills
The oaks of Belmont and the Wayland hills
Southward to Dewing's little bubbly stream,
The heavenly weather's call! O, who alive
Hastes not to start, delays not to arrive,
Having free feet that never felt a gyve
Weigh, even in a dream?

But thou, instead, hast found
The sunless April uplands underground,
And still, wherever thou art, I must be.
My beautiful! arise in might and mirth,
For we were tameless travellers from our birth;
Arise against thy narrow door of earth,
And keep the watch for me.

299.   *Two Epitaphs*

I

TWO white heads the grasses cover;
  Dorcas, and her lifelong lover.
While they graced their country closes
Simply as the brooks and roses,
Where was lot so poor, so trodden,
But they cheered it of a sudden?
Fifty years at home together,
Hand in hand, they went elsewhither,
Then first leaving hearts behind
Comfortless. Be thou as kind.

II

Praise thou the Mighty Mother for what is wrought,
    not me,
A nameless nothing-caring head asleep against her knee.

300.   *The Kings*

A MAN said unto his angel;
    "My spirits are fallen through,
And I cannot carry this battle;
O brother, what shall I do?

"The terrible Kings are on me,
With spears that are deadly bright,
Against me so from the cradle
Do fate and my fathers fight."

Then said to the man his angel:
"Thou wavering, foolish soul,
Back to the ranks! What matter
To win or to lose the whole,

"As judged by the little judges
Who hearken not well, nor see?
Not thus by the other issue,
The Wise shall interpret thee.

"Thy will is the very, the only,
The solemn event of things;
The weakest of hearts defying
Is stronger than all these Kings.

EDITH MATILDA THOMAS

1854–1925

Isaiah xxxviii. 15

303.   *The Quiet Pilgrim*

WHEN on my soul in nakedness
    His swift, avertless hand did press,
Then I stood still, nor cried aloud,
Nor murmured low in ashes bowed;
And, since my woe is utterless,
To supreme quiet I am vowed;
Afar from me be moan and tears, —
I shall go softly all my years.

Whenso my quick, light-sandaled feet
Bring me where Joys and Pleasures meet,
I mingle with their throng at will;
They know me not an alien still,
Since neither words nor ways unsweet
Of storëd bitterness I spill;
Youth shuns me not, nor gladness fears, —
For I go softly all my years.

Whenso I come where Griefs convene,
And in my ear their voice is keen,
They know me not, as on I glide,
That with Arch Sorrow I abide.
They haggard are, and drooped of mien,
And round their brows have cypress tied:
Such shows I leave to light Grief's peers, —
I shall go softly all my years.

482

Yea, softly! heart of hearts unknown.
Silence hath speech that passeth moan,
More piercing-keen than breathëd cries
To such as heed, made sorrow-wise.
But save this voice without a tone,
That runs before me to the skies,
And rings above thy ringing spheres,
Lord, I go softly all my years!

304.   *Lyric*

TELL me, is there sovereign cure
      For heart-ache, heart-ache, —
Cordial quick and potion sure,
      For heart-ache, heart-ache?

Fret thou not. If all else fail
      For heart-ache, heart-ache,
One thing surely will avail, —
      That's heart-break, heart-break!

305.   *If Still They Live*

IF still they live, whom touch nor sight
      Nor any subtlest sense can prove,
Though dwelling past our day and night,
      At farthest star's remove, —

Oh, not because these skies they change
      For upper deeps of sky unknown,
Shall that which made them ours grow strange,
      For spirit holds its own;

483

Whether it pace this earth around,
  Or cross, with printless, buoyant feet,
The unreverberant Profound
  That hath no name nor mete!

306. *Rank and File*

YOU might have painted that picture,
  I might have written that song:
Not ours, but another's, the triumph,
  'Tis done and well done — so 'long!

You might have fought in the vanguard,
  I might have struck at foul Wrong:
What matters whose hand was the foremost?
  'Tis done and well done — so 'long!

So 'long, and into the darkness,
  With the immemorial throng —
Foil to the few and the splendid:
  All's done and well done — so 'long!

Yet, as we pass, we will pledge them —
  The bold, and the bright, and the strong,
(Ours was never black envy:)
  All's done and well done — so 'long!

GERTRUDE HALL

1863-

307.　　*How Shall We Tell an Angel*

HOW shall we tell an angel
　　From another guest?
How, from the common worldly herd,
　One of the blest?

Hint of suppressëd halo,
　Rustle of hidden wings,
Wafture of heavenly frankincense, —
　Which of these things?

The old Sphinx smiles so subtly:
　"I give no golden rule, —
Yet would I warn thee, World: treat well
　Whom thou call'st fool."

308.　　　　*The Dust*

IT settles softly on your things,
　Impalpable, fine, light, dull, gray:
Her dingy dust-clout Betty brings,
　And singing brushes it away:

And it's a queen's robe, once so proud,
　And it's the moths fed in its fold,
It's leaves, and roses, and the shroud
　Wherein an ancient saint was rolled.

485

And it is Beauty's golden hair,
    And it is Genius' crown of bay,
And it is lips once warm and fair
    That kissed in some forgotten May. . . .

309.   *My Old Counselor*

THE Sun looked from his everlasting skies,
   He laughed into my daily-dying eyes;
He said to me, the brutal shining Sun:
" Poor, fretful, hot, rebellious, little one!

" Thou shalt not find it, yet there shall be truth;
Thou shalt grow old, but yet there shall be youth;
Thou shalt not do, yet great deeds shall be done, —
Believe me, child, I am an old, old Sun!

" Thou mayst go blind, yet fair will bloom the spring;
Thou mayst not hear them, but the birds will sing;
Thou mayst despair, no less will hope be rife;
Thou must lie dead, but many will have life.

" Thou mayst declare of love: it is a dream!
Yet long with love, my love, the Earth will teem:
Let not thy foolish heart be borne so low, —
Lift up thy heart! Exult that it is so! "

310. *How Dreary Looks the Ivied Cot*

HOW dreary looks the ivied cot,
  (Yet all is flush with May!)
How sad the little garden plot,
  Since Mary went away.

At morning to her window side
  A flock of sparrows comes:
They wait and wonder, " Where can bide
  That Mary of the crumbs? "

Below, the poor neglected flowers
  In languid whispers sigh,
" Where's Mary of the grateful showers,
  Will she come by and by? "

And every night down in the lane,
  Just past the gate, there stands
A youth whose face, wet with his pain,
  Is hidden in his hands.

311. *In the Art Museum*

HE stands where the white light showers,
  In his wonted high recess;
The dust has woven a soft veil
  Over his comeliness.

Beneath the pensive eyebrows
  And lids that never beat,
The same glance floats forever —
  So sad and solemn-sweet;

487

The same peace seals forever
　　The full lips finely curled, —
I'm come to this his dwelling
　　To bring him news of the world:

"Once more the spring hath mantled
　　With green the lasting hills —
Hast thou no faint remembrance
　　Of daisies and daffodils?

"Their stems still lengthen sunward
　　As when thou wast of us, —
My heart swells with its sorrow
　　For thee — Antinous."

312.　　　　　*To a Weed*

YOU bold thing! thrusting 'neath the very nose
　　Of her fastidious majesty the rose,
Ev'n in the best ordainëd garden-bed,
　　Unauthorized, your smiling little head!

The gardener, — mind, — will come in his big boots
And drag you up by your rebellious roots,
And cast you forth to shrivel in the sun,
Your daring quelled, your little weed's life done.

And when the noon cools and the sun drops low,
He'll come again with his big wheelbarrow
And trundle you, — I don't know clearly where, —
But *off* — outside the dew, the light, the air.

Meantime — ah, yes! the air is very blue,
And gold the light and diamond the dew, —
You laugh and curtsey in your worthless way,
And you are gay — ah, so exceeding gay!

You argue in your manner of a weed,
You did not make yourself grow from a seed,
You fancy you've a claim to standing-room,
You dream yourself a right to breathe and bloom.

The Sun loves you, you think, just as the rose,
He never scorned you for a weed, — *he knows*,
The green-gold flies rest on you, and are glad,
It's only cross old gardeners find you bad.

You know, you weed, *I quite agree with you,*
I am a weed myself, and I laugh too, —
Both, just as long as we can shun his eye,
Let's sniff at the old gardener trudging by!

313.   *A King's Daughter*

A FAIR King's daughter once possessed
   A bird in whom she took delight;
And everything a bird loves best
She gave that favored one, but flight!

It was her joy to smooth his wings,
To watch those eyes that waxed and waned,
To tender him choice offerings
And have him feed from her white hand.

489

And every day she loved him more. . . .
But when at last she loved him most,
She opened wide his prison door,
Content that he to her were lost.

LIZETTE WOODWORTH REESE

1856–

314.   *Lydia*

BREAK forth, break forth, O Sudbury town,
     And bid your yards be gay
Up all your gusty streets and down,
     For Lydia comes to-day!

I hear it on the wharves below;
     And if I buy or sell,
The good folk as they churchward go
     Have only this to tell.

My mother, just for love of her,
     Unlocks her carvëd drawers;
And sprigs of withered lavender
     Drop down upon the floors.

For Lydia's bed must have the sheet
     Spun out of linen sheer,
And Lydia's room be passing sweet
     With odors of last year.

The violet flags are out once more
     In lanes salt with the sea;
The thorn-bush at Saint Martin's door
     Grows white for such as she.

So, Sudbury, bid your gardens blow,
    For Lydia comes to-day;
Of all the words that I do know,
    I have but this to say.

315.   *Daffodils*

FATHERED by March, the daffodils are here.
    First, all the air grew keen with yesterday,
And once a thrush from out some hollow gray
On a field's edge, where whitening stalks made cheer,
Fluted the last unto the budding year;
Now that the wind lets loose from orchard spray
Plum bloom and peach bloom down the dripping way,
Their punctual gold through the wet blades they rear.
Oh, fleet and sweet! A light to all that pass
Below, in the cramped yard, close to the street,
Long-stemmed ones flame behind the palings bare,
The whole of April in a tuft of grass.
Scarce here, soon will it be — oh, sweet and fleet! —
Gone like a snatch of song upon the stair.

316.   *Tears*

WHEN I consider Life and its few years —
    A wisp of fog betwixt us and the sun;
A call to battle, and the battle done
Ere the last echo dies within our ears;
A rose choked in the grass; an hour of fears;
The gusts that past a darkening shore do beat;
The burst of music down an unlistening street —
I wonder at the idleness of tears.

491

Ye old, old dead, and ye of yesternight,
Chieftains, and bards, and keepers of the sheep,
By every cup of sorrow that you had,
Loose me from tears, and make me see aright
How each hath what once he stayed to weep;
Homer his sight, David his little lad!

317. *Trust*

I AM Thy grass, O Lord!
   I grow up sweet and tall
But for a day, beneath Thy sword
   To lie at evenfall.

Yet have I not enough
   In that brief day of mine?
The wind, the bees, the wholesome stuff
   The sun pours out like wine.

Behold, this is my crown, —
   Love will not let me be;
Love holds me here; Love cuts me down;
   And it is well with me.

Lord, Love, keep it but so;
   Thy purpose is full plain:
I die that after I may grow
   As tall, as sweet again.

LIZETTE WOODWORTH REESE

318.   *A Holiday*

ALONG the pastoral ways I go,
    To get the healing of the trees,
The ghostly news the hedges know;
To hive me honey like the bees,
Against the time of snow.

The common hawthorn that I see,
Beside the sunken wall astir,
Or any other blossoming tree,
Is each God's fair white gospeller,
His book upon the knee.

A gust-broken bough; a pilfered nest;
Rumors of orchard or of bin;
The thrifty things of east and west, —
The countryside becomes my Inn,
And I its happy guest.

CHARLOTTE PERKINS STETSON

319.   *A Common Inference*

A NIGHT: mysterious, tender, quiet, deep;
    Heavy with flowers; full of life asleep;
Thrilling with insect voices; thick with stars;
No cloud between the dewdrops and red Mars;
The small earth whirling softly on her way,
The moonbeams and the waterfalls at play;
A million million worlds that move in peace,
A million mighty laws that never cease;

And one small ant-heap, hidden by small weeds,
Rich with eggs, slaves, and store of millet seeds.
   They sleep beneath the sod
     And trust in God.

A day: all glorious, royal, blazing bright;
Heavy with flowers; full of life and light;
Great fields of corn and sunshine; courteous trees;
Snow-sainted mountains; earth-embracing seas;
Wide golden deserts; slender silver streams;
Clear rainbows where the tossing fountain gleams;
And everywhere, in happiness and peace,
A million forms of life that never cease;
And one small ant-heap, crushed by passing tread,
Hath scarce enough alive to mourn the dead!
   They shriek beneath the sod,
     " There is no God! "

320.   *A Conservative*

THE garden beds I wandered by
   One bright and cheerful morn,
When I found a new-fledged butterfly,
   A-sitting on a thorn,
A black and crimson butterfly,
   All doleful and forlorn.

I thought that life could have no sting
   To infant butterflies,
So I gazed on this unhappy thing
   With wonder and surprise,
While sadly with his waving wing
   He wiped his weeping eyes.

CHARLOTTE PERKINS STETSON

Said I, " What can the matter be?
  Why weepest thou so sore?
With garden fair and sunlight free
  And flowers in goodly store: " —
But he only turned away from me
  And burst into a roar.

Cried he, " My legs are thin and few
  Where once I had a swarm!
Soft fuzzy fur — a joy to view —
  Once kept my body warm,
Before these flapping wing-things grew,
  To hamper and deform! "

At that outrageous bug I shot
  The fury of mine eye;
Said I, in scorn all burning hot,
  In rage and anger high,
" You ignominious idiot!
  Those wings are made to fly! "

" I do not want to fly," said he,
  " I only want to squirm! "
And he drooped his wings dejectedly,
  But still his voice was firm:
" I do not want to be a fly!
  I want to be a worm! "

O yesterday of unknown lack!
  To-day of unknown bliss!
I left my fool in red and black,
  The last I saw was this, —
The creature madly climbing back
  Into his chrysalis.

321.   *An Obstacle*

I WAS climbing up a mountain path
    With many things to do,
Important business of my own,
    And other people's too,
When I ran against a Prejudice
    That quite cut off the view.

My work was such as could not wait,
    My path quite clearly showed,
My strength and time were limited,
    I carried quite a load;
And there that hulking Prejudice
    Sat all across the road.

I spoke to him politely,
    For he was huge and high,
And begged that he would move a bit
    And let me travel by.
He smiled, but as for moving! —
    He didn't even try.

And then I reasoned quietly
    With that colossal mule:
My time was short — no other path —
    The mountain winds were cool.
I argued like a Solomon;
    He sat there like a fool.

CHARLOTTE PERKINS STETSON

Then I flew into a passion,
    I danced and howled and swore.
I pelted and belabored him
    Till I was stiff and sore;
He got as mad as I did —
    But he sat there as before.

And then I begged him on my knees;
    I might be kneeling still
If so I hoped to move that man
    Of obdurate ill-will —
As well invite the monument
    To vacate Bunker Hill.

So I sat before him helpless,
    In an ecstasy of woe —
The mountain mists were rising fast,
    The Sun was sinking slow —
When a sudden inspiration came,
    As sudden winds do blow.

I took my hat, I took my stick,
    My load I settled fair,
I approached that awful incubus
    With an absent-minded air —
And I walked directly through him,
    As if he wasn't there.

322.   *Similar Cases*

THERE was once a little animal,
    No bigger than a fox,
And on five toes he scampered
    Over Tertiary rocks.
They called him Eohippus,
    And they called him very small,
And they thought him of no value —
    When they thought of him at all;
    For the lumpish old Dinoceras
    And Coryphodon so slow
Were the heavy aristocracy
    In days of long ago.

Said the little Eohippus,
    " I am going to be a horse!
And on my middle finger-nails
    To run my earthly course!
I'm going to have a flowing tail!
    I'm going to have a mane!
I'm going to stand fourteen hands high
    On the psychozoic plain! "

The Coryphodon was horrified,
    The Dinoceras was shocked;
And they chased young Eohippus,
    But **he** skipped away and mocked.
Then they laughed enormous laughter,
    And they groaned enormous groans,
And they bade young Eohippus
    Go view his father's bones.

CHARLOTTE PERKINS STETSON

Said they, " You always were as small
   And mean as now we see,
And that's conclusive evidence
   That you're always going to be.
What! Be a great, tall, handsome beast,
   With hoofs to gallop on?
Why! You'd have to change your nature! "
   Said the Loxolophodon.

They considered him disposed of,
   And retired with gait serene;
That was the way they argued
   In " the early Eocene."

There was once an Anthropoidal Ape,
   Far smarter than the rest,
And everything that they could do
   He always did the best;
So they naturally disliked him,
   And they gave him shoulders cool,
And when they mentioned him at all
   They said he was a fool.

Cried this pretentious Ape one day,
   " I'm going to be a Man!
And stand upright, and hunt, and fight,
   And conquer all I can!
I'm going to cut down forest trees,
   And make my houses higher!
I'm going to kill the Mastodon!
   I'm going to make a fire! "

CHARLOTTE PERKINS STETSON

Loud screamed the Anthropoidal Apes
　　With laughter wild and gay;
They tried to catch the boastful one,
　　But he always got away.
So they yelled at him in chorus,
　　Which he minded not a whit;
And they pelted him with cocoanuts,
　　Which didn't seem to hit.

And when they gave him reasons
　　Which they thought of much avail,
To prove how his preposterous
　　Attempt was sure to fail.
Said the sages, " In the first place,
　　The thing cannot be done!
And, second, if it *could* be,
　　It would not be any fun!

And third and most conclusive,
　　And admitting no reply,
You would have to change your nature!
　　We should like to see you try! "
They chuckled then triumphantly,
　　These lean and hairy shapes,
For these things passed as arguments
　　With the Anthropoidal Apes.

There was once a Neolithic Man,
　　An enterprising wight,
Who made his chopping implements
　　Unusually bright.

CHARLOTTE PERKINS STETSON

Unusually clever he,
  Unusually brave,
And he drew delightful Mammoths
  On the borders of his cave.

To his Neolithie neighbors,
  Who were startled and surprised,
Said he, " My friends, in course of time,
  We shall be civilized!
" We are going to live in cities!
  We are going to fight in wars!
We are going to eat three times a day
  Without the natural cause!

We are going to turn life upside down
  About a thing called gold!
We are going to want the earth, and take
  As much as we can hold!
" We are going to wear great piles of stuff
  Outside our proper skins!
We are going to have Diseases!
  And Accomplishments!! And Sins!!! "

Then they all rose up in fury
  Against their boastful friend,
For prehistoric patience
  Cometh quickly to an end.
Said one, " This is chimerical!
  Utopian! Absurd! "
Said another, " What a stupid life!
  Too dull, upon my word! "

Cried all, " Before such things can come,
   You idiotic child,
You must alter Human Nature! "
   And they all sat back and smiled.
Thought they, "An answer to that last
   It will be hard to find! "
It was a clinching argument
   To the Neolithic Mind.

LILLA CABOT PERRY

323. *Meeting After Long Absence*

I

As she feared it would be

HERE in this room where first we met,
   And where we said farewell with tears,
Here, where you swore " Though you forget,
   My love shall deeper grow with years,"

Here, where the pictures on the wall,
   The very rugs upon the floor,
The smallest objects you recall, —
   I am awaiting you once more.

The books that we together read, —
   From off their shelves they beckon me.
All here seems living! What is dead?
   What is the ghost I fear to see?

LILLA CABOT PERRY

Unchanged am I. Did you despise
   My love as " small " ? — it fills my heart!
You come — a stranger from your eyes
   Looks out — and, meeting, first we part.

II

As it was

I told myself in singing words
   That you were changed and I was true;
I would not trust winds, waves, and birds
   That change was not in you.

I sang Love's dirge before we met, —
   " As murdered corpse in river bed
In eyes my heart cannot forget
   I see Love lying dead! "

You came — one look — no word was spoken,
   Our hands, once clasped, forgot to part,
And, though our silence is unbroken,
   Heart has found rest on heart.

CAROLINE DUER

324.   *A Portrait*

A MAN more kindly, in his careless way,
   Than many who profess a higher creed;
Whose fickle love might change from day to day,
   And yet be faithful to a friend in need;
Whose manners covered, through life's outs and ins,
Like charity, a multitude of sins.

MARY McNEIL FENOLLOSA

Is it of birds from the blue above,
Or fish from the depths that be?
Or is it the ghosts
In silver hosts
Of birds that were drowned at sea?

LANGDON ELWYN MITCHELL

1862–

327.   *To One Being Old*

HER aged hands are worn with works of love;
Dear aged hands that oft on me are laid;
Her heart's below, but, oh, her love's above,
As flowers do sunward turn though in the shade.

The set of sun is dear that lasts not long,
And she is sweeter far than light that dies:
But if her aged body's weak, she's strong;
Her folly, wisdom in a softer guise.

The very smile of love is hers, and she
Hath him long known where others knew a shade;
Forget thine eyes, and learn herewith to see
Within this time-worn sheath the snowy blade.

Upon her lovely cheek there still doth play
A maiden's blush, for her heart grows not old;
Her silver locks go sweetly all astray;
Though silver are her locks, her heart is gold!

LANGDON ELWYN MITCHELL

328.   *The Wayside Virgin*

France

I AM the Virgin; from this granite ledge
   A hundred weary winters have I watched
The lonely road that wanders at my feet;
And many days I've sat here, in my lap
A little heap of snow, and overheard
The dry, dead voices of sere, rustling leaves;
While scarce a beggar creaked across the way.
How very old I am! I have forgot
The day they fixed me here; and whence I came,
With crown of gold, and all my tarnished blue.

How green the grass is now, and all around
Blossoms the May; but it is cold in here,
Sunless and cold. — Now comes a little maid
To kneel among the asters at my feet;
What a sweet noise she makes, like murmurings
Of bees in June! I wonder what they say,
These rosy mortals, when they look at me?
I wonder why
They call me Mary and bow down to me?
Oh, I am weary of my painted box, —
Come, child,
And lay thy warm face on my wooden cheek,
That I may feel it glow as once of yore
It glowed when I, a cedar's happy heart,
Felt the first sunshine of the early spring!

329. *Written At the End of a Book*

THIS is the end of the book
  Written by God.
I am the earth he took,
  I am the sod,
The wood and iron which he struck
  With his sounding rod.

I am the reed that he blew:
  Once quietly
By the riverside I grew,
  Till one day he
Rooted me up and breathed a new
  Delirium in me.

Would he had left me there,
  Where all is still;
To lean on the heavy air,
  Silent, at will
To be, and joy, yet not to share,
  The avenging thrill.

I am the reed that he blew,
  Which yet he blows,
(For this is his breath too,
  And these, like those,
Are his own words blown unto you,
  — Hearken if you choose!)

LANGDON ELWYN MITCHELL

This is the end of the book;
  And, if you read
Ought that is evil, why, look,
  I but obeyed,
— When deep his voice in my ear shook,
  I blew as he said!

GEORGE SANTAYANA

1863–

330. *On the Death of a Metaphysician*

UNHAPPY dreamer, who outwinged in flight
  The pleasant region of the things I love,
And soared beyond the sunshine, and above
The golden cornfields and the dear and bright
Warmth of the hearth, — blasphemer of delight,
Was your proud bosom not at peace with Jove,
That you sought, thankless for his guarded grove,
The empty horror of abysmal night?
Ah, the thin air is cold above the moon!
I stood and saw you fall, befooled in death,
As, in your numbëd spirit's fatal swoon,
You cried you were a god, or were to be;
I heard with feeble moan your boastful breath
Bubble from depths of the Icarian sea.

331. *On a Piece of Tapestry*

HOLD high the woof, dear friends, that we may see
  The cunning mixture of its colors rare.
Nothing in nature purposely is fair, —
Her mingled beauties never quite agree;

But here all vivid dyes that garish be,
To that tint mellowed which the sense will bear,
Glow, and not wound the eye that, resting there,
Lingers to feed its gentle ecstasy.
Crimson and purple and all hues of wine,
Saffron and russet, brown and sober green
Are rich the shadowy depths of blue between;
While silver threads with golden intertwine,
To catch the glimmer of a fickle sheen, —
All the long labor of some captive queen.

332.   *Faith*

O WORLD, thou choosest not the better part!
    It is not wisdom to be only wise,
And on the inward vision close the eyes,
But it is wisdom to believe the heart.
Columbus found a world, and had no chart,
Save one that faith deciphered in the skies;
To trust the soul's invincible surmise
Was all his science and his only art.
Our knowledge is a torch of smoky pine
That lights the pathway but one step ahead
Across a void of mystery and dread.
Bid, then, the tender light of faith to shine
By which alone the mortal heart is led
Unto the thinking of the thought divine.

333. *These Strewn Thoughts by the Mountain Pathway Sprung*

THESE strewn thoughts, by the mountain pathway
    sprung,
I conned for comfort, till I ceased to grieve,
And with these flowering thorns I dare to weave
The crown, great Mother, on thine altar hung.
Teach thou a larger speech to my loosed tongue,
And to mine opened eyes thy secrets give,
That in thy perfect love I learn to live,
And in thine immortality be young.
The soul is not on earth an alien thing
That hath her life's rich sources otherwhere;
She is a parcel of the sacred air.
She takes her being from the breath of spring,
The glance of Phoebus is her fount of light,
And her long sleep a draught of primal night.

334. *We Needs Must be Divided in the Tomb*

WE needs must be divided in the tomb,
    For I would die among the hills of Spain,
And o'er the treeless melancholy plain
Await the coming of the final gloom.
But thou — O pitiful! — wilt find scant room
Among thy kindred by the northern main,
And fade into the drifting mist again,
The hemlocks' shadow, or the pines' perfume.

Let gallants lie beside their ladies' dust
In one cold grave, with mortal love inurned;
Let the sea part our ashes, if it must,
The souls fled thence which love immortal burned,
For they were wedded without bond of lust,
And nothing of our heart to earth returned.

335.   *To W. P.*

I

CALM was the sea to which your course you kept,
    Oh, how much calmer than all southern seas!
Many your nameless mates, whom the keen breeze
Wafted from mothers that of old have wept.
All souls of children taken as they slept.
Are your companies, partners of your ease,
And the green souls of all these autumn trees
Are with you through the silent spaces swept.
Your virgin body gave its gentle breath
Untainted to the gods. Why should we grieve,
But that we merit not your holy death?
We shall not loiter long, your friends and I;
Living you made it goodlier to live,
Dead you will make it easier to die.

II

With you a part of me hath passed away;
For in the peopled forest of my mind
A tree made leafless by this wintry wind
Shall never don again its green array.

Chapel and fireside, country road and bay,
Have something of their friendliness resigned;
Another, if I would, I could not find,
And I am grown much older in a day.
But yet I treasure in my memory
Your gift of charity, your mellow ease,
And the dear honor of your amity;
To these once mine, my life is rich with these.
And I scarce know which part may greater be, —
What I keep of you, or you rob from me.

III

Your bark lies anchored in the peaceful bight
Until a kinder wind unfurl her sail;
Your docile spirit, wingèd by this gale,
Hath at the dawning fled into the light.
And I half know why heaven deemed it right
Your youth, and this my joy in youth, should fail;
God hath them still, for ever they avail,
Eternity hath borrowed that delight.
For long ago I taught my thoughts to run
Where all the great things live that lived of yore,
And in eternal quiet float and soar;
There all my loves are gathered into one,
Where change is not, nor parting any more,
Nor evolution of the moon and sun.

IV

In my deep heart these chimes would still have rung
To toll your passing, had you not been dead;
For time a sadder mask than death may spread
Over the face that ever should be young.

GEORGE SANTAYANA

The bough that falls with all its trophies hung
Falls not too soon, but lays its flower-crowned head
Most royal in the dust, with no leaf shed
Unhallowed or unchiselled or unsung —
And though the after world may never hear
The happy name of one so gently true,
Nor chronicles write large this fatal year,
Yet we who loved you, though we be but few,
Keep you in whatsoe'er is good, and dear
In our weak virtues monuments of you.

RICHARD HOVEY

1864-1900

336. *Song*

(*From "The Marriage of Guenevere"*)

THE flower-born Blodueda,
     Great joy of love was hers;
Now lonely is the life she leads
Among the moonlit firs.

The white enchantress, Arianrod,
The daughter of King Don,
Hath hidden in a secret place
And borne a goodly son.

But he shall have nor name nor arms
Wherewith to get him fame,
Unless his mother's heart relent
And give him arms and name.

RICHARD HOVEY

Twice hath she cursed him from her heart —
Twice and yet once again,
That he shall never take a wife
Of all the seed of men.

Yet all unwitting she gave him arms,
When the foe was in the land;
And all unwitting a goodly name,
Llew of the Steady Hand.

And Gwydion, the son of Don,
Hath wrought with mighty charms
A mystery of maidenhood
To lie within his arms.

He took the blossoms of the oak
And the blossoms of the broom
And the blossoms of the meadow-sweet
And fashioned her therefrom.

Of all the maidens on the earth
She was by far most fair,
And the memory of the meadow-sweet
Was odors in her hair.

But she hath given her heart away
To the stout lord of Penllyn,
And he is slain by Cynvall's banks,
Betrayed by all his kin.

And oh, and she were light of heart
Had they but slain her so!
In likeness of a mournful owl,
She grieves her nightly woe.

The motherless Blodueda
Shall never find release;
From eve till morn she makes her moan
Among the moonlit trees.

337.   *The Wander-Lovers*

DOWN the world with Marna!
   That's the life for me!
Wandering with the wandering wind,
Vagabond and unconfined!
Roving with the roving rain
Its unboundaried domain!
Kith and kin of wander-kind,
Children of the sea!

Petrels of the sea-drift!
Swallows of the lea!
Arabs of the whole wide girth
Of the wind-encircled earth!
In all climes we pitch our tents,
Cronies of the elements,
With the secret lords of birth
Intimate and free.

All the seaboard knows us
From Fundy to the Keys;
Every bend and every creek
Of abundant Chesapeake;

RICHARD HOVEY

Ardise hills and Newport coves
And the far-off orange groves,
Where Floridian oceans break,
Tropic tiger seas.

Down the world with Marna,
Tarrying there and here!
Just as much at home in Spain
As in Tangier or Touraine!
Shakespeare's Avon knows us well,
And the crags of Neufchâtel;
And the ancient Nile is fain
Of our coming near.

Down the world with Marna,
Daughter of the air!
Marna of the subtle grace,
And the vision in her face!
Moving in the measures trod
By the angels before God!
With her sky-blue eyes amaze
And her sea-blue hair!

Marna with the trees' life
In her veins a-stir!
Marna of the aspen heart
Where the sudden quivers start!
Quick-responsive, subtle, wild!
Artless as an artless child,
Spite of all her reach of art!
Oh, to roam with her!

Marna with the wind's will,
Daughter of the sea!
Marna of the quick disdain,
Starting at the dream of stain!
At a smile with love aglow,
At a frown a statued woe,
Standing pinnacled in pain
Till a kiss sets free!

Down the world with Marna,
Daughter of the fire!
Marna of the deathless hope,
Still alert to win new scope
Where the wings of life may spread
For a flight unhazarded!
Dreaming of the speech to cope
With the heart's desire!

Marna of the far quest
After the divine!
Striving ever for some goal
Past the blunder-god's control!
Dreaming of potential years
When no day shall dawn in fears!
That's the Marna of my soul,
Wander-bride of mine!

RICHARD HOVEY

338.   *The Sea Gypsy*

I AM fevered with the sunset,
  I am fretful with the bay,
For the wander-thirst is on me
And my soul is in Cathay.

There's a schooner in the offing,
With her topsails shot with fire,
And my heart has gone aboard her
For the Islands of Desire.

I must forth again to-morrow!
With the sunset I must be
Hull down on the trail of rapture
In the wonder of the sea.

339.   *Unmanifest Destiny*

TO what new fates, my country, far
  And unforeseen of foe or friend,
Beneath what unexpected star,
  Compelled to what unchosen end,

Across the sea that knows no beach
  The Admiral of Nations guides
Thy blind obedient keels to reach
  The harbor where thy future rides!

The guns that spoke at Lexington
  Knew not that God was planning then
The trumpet word of Jefferson
  To bugle forth the rights of men.

To them that wept and cursed Bull Run,
  What was it but despair and shame?
Who saw behind the cloud the sun?
  Who knew that God was in the flame?

Had not defeat upon defeat,
  Disaster on disaster come,
The slave's emancipated feet
  Had never marched behind the drum.

There is a Hand that bends our deeds
  To mightier issues that we planned,
Each son that triumphs, each that bleeds,
  My country, serves Its dark command.

I do not know beneath what sky
  Nor on what seas shall be thy fate;
I only know it shall be high,
  I only know it shall be great.

340.   *From "Taliesin"*

Voices of Unseen Spirits

HERE falls no light of sun nor stars;
  No stir nor striving here intrudes;
No moan nor merry-making mars
  The quiet of these solitudes.

Submerged in sleep, the passive soul
  Is one with all the things that seem
Night blurs in one confusëd whole
  Alike the dreamer and the dream.

RICHARD HOVEY

O dwellers in the busy town!
  For dreams you smile, for dreams you weep.
Come out, and lay your burdens down!
  Come out; there is no God but Sleep.

Sleep, and renounce the vital day;
  For evil is the child of life.
Let be the will to live, and pray
  To find forgetfulness of strife.

Beneath the thicket of these leaves
  No light discriminates each from each.
No Self that wrongs, no Self that grieves,
  Hath longer deed nor creed nor speech.

Sleep on the mighty Mother's breast!
  Sleep, and no more be separate!
Then, one with Nature's ageless rest,
  There shall be no more sin to hate.

Taliesin

Spirits of Sleep,
    That swell and sink
        In the sea of Being
Like waves on the deep,
Forming, crumbling,
Fumbling, and tumbling
        Forever, unseeing,
    From brink to brink!

Perishing voices,
    That call and call
        From the coves of dream
With hollow noises!

Teach me these things, through whose high knowledge,
    I, —
    When Death hath poured oblivion through my veins,
And brought me home, as all are brought, to lie
    In that vast house, common to serfs and Thanes, —
I shall not die, I shall not utterly die,
    For beauty born of beauty — *that* remains.

343.   *Comradery*

WITH eyes hand-arched he looks into
        The morning's face, then turns away
With schoolboy feet, all wet with dew,
    Out for a holiday.

The hill brook sings, incessant stars,
    Foam-fashioned, on its restless breast;
And where he wades its water-bars
    Its song is happiest.

A comrade of the chinquapin,
    He looks into its knotted eyes
And sees its heart; and, deep within,
    Its soul that makes him wise.

The wood-thrush knows and follows him,
    Who whistles up the birds and bees;
And round him all the perfumes swim
    Of woodland loam and trees.

Where'er he pass, the supple springs'
Foam-people sing the flowers awake;
And sappy lips of bark-clad things
Laugh ripe each fruited brake.

His touch is a companionship;
His word, an old authority:
He comes, a lyric at his lip,
Unstudied Poesy.

344.   *Dirge*

WHAT shall her silence keep
    Under the sun?
Here, where the willows weep
    And waters run;
Here, where she lies asleep,
    And all is done.

Lights, when the tree-top swings;
    Scents that are sown;
Sounds of the wood-bird's wings;
    And the bee's drone:
These be her comfortings
    Under the stone.

What shall watch o'er her here
    When day is fled?
Here, when the night is near
    And skies are red;
Here, where she lieth dear
    And young and dead.

Shadows, and winds that spill
Dew, and the tune
Of the wild whippoorwill,
And the white moon, —
These be the watchers still
Over her stone.

PHILIP HENRY SAVAGE

1858–1899

345.   *Silkweed*

LIGHTER than dandelion down,
        Or feathers from the white moth's wing,
Out of the gates of bramble-town
        The silkweed goes a-gypsying.

Too fair to fly in autumn's rout,
        All winter in the sheath it lay;
But now, when spring is pushing out,
        The zephyr calls, "Away! away!"

Through mullein, bramble, brake, and fern,
        Up from their cradle-spring they fly,
Beyond the boundary wall to turn
        And voyage through the friendly sky.

Softly, as if instinct with thought,
        They float and drift, delay and turn;
And one avoids and one is caught
        Between an oak-leaf and a fern.

528

And one holds by an airy line
    The spider drew from tree to tree;
And if the web is light and fine,
    'Tis not so light and fine as he!

And one goes questing up the wall
    As if to find a door; and then,
As if he did not care at all,
    Goes over, and adown the glen.

And all in airiest fashion fare
    Adventuring, as if, indeed,
'Twere not so grave a thing to bear
    The burden of a seed!

346.   *New England*

WHOE'ER thou art, who walkest there
    Where God first taught my feet to roam,
Breathe but my name into the air,
    I am content, for that is home.

A sense, a color comes to me,
    Of baybushes that heavy lie
With juniper along the sea,
    And the blue sea along the sky.

New England is my home; 'tis there
    I love the pagan Sun and Moon.
'Tis there I love the growing year,
    December and young-summer June.

EUGENE RICHARD WHITE

When the Sea has swallowed up the Sun
   And the white gulls glint — was it they who spoke?
Wes'-Sou' West from the Devil's Quay:

"Fell through a crack in the Floor of the Sea"?

Of the old-time Band there's not a man
   Who has ever told how the ship went down.
Were they marked by God with the fearsome ban?
   Butchered they priests in a sun-white town?
Do they harry Hell where they may be:

"Fell through a crack in the Floor of the Sea"?

Though ye searched the West to the guttering sun,
   Or the East till the baffled lights burn black,
Or North to the bergs till the South be won,
   The changeling shadows answer back,
And their trembling lips pale piteously:

"Fell through a crack in the Floor of the Sea"?

And when the great grim Finger becks
   The whining Seas from their ancient bed,
Shall some tongue speak from the world-old wrecks
   To read the log of the Thwarted Dead?
Is there never an end on the mystery:

"Fell through a crack in the Floor of the Sea"?

538

ELAINE GOODALE EASTMAN

1863–

353. A Countrywoman of Mine

HANDSOME? I hardly know. Her profile's fine —
  Delightful, intellectual, aquiline.

Her keen eyes light it; keen, yet often kind;
Her fair hair crowns it to an artist's mind.

Fine figure and fine manners, without doubt,
Determine half her charm, and bear me out.

Learned? Well, rather. See them for yourself —
Mill, Spencer, Darwin, on her favorite shelf.

Well educated, certainly well read;
Well born, of course, and (not of course) well bred.

Provincial? Never! Cockney? Not at all.
Her world is small enough, yet not too small.

To prove she knows it, only watch a while
That humorous, tender, half-sarcastic smile.

Accomplished? She says not; but who can tell?
She does some simple things, and does them well.

She walks well, stands well, sits well — things so rare,
To praise as they deserve I hardly dare!

She rows, rides, dances — admirably done!
Delights in each, and yet depends on none.

539

Verily, he doth lift up
Matter, like a sacred cup.
Into deep substance he reached, and lo
Where ye were not, ye were; and so
Out of useless nothing, ye
Groaned and laughed and came to be.
And I use you, as I can,
Wonderful uses, made for man,
Iron pot and brazen pan.

V

What are ye?
I know not;
Nor what I really do
When I move and govern you.
There is no small work unto God.
He requires of us greatness;
Of his least creature
A high angelic nature,
Stature superb and bright completeness.
He sets to us no humble duty.
Each act that he would have us do
Is haloed round with strangest beauty.
Terrific deeds and cosmic tasks
Of his plainest child he asks.
When I polish the brazen pan
I hear a creature laugh afar
In the gardens of a star,
And from his burning presence run
Flaming wheels of many a sun.
Whoever makes a thing more bright,
He is an angel of all light.

ANNA HEMPSTEAD BRANCH

When I cleanse this earthen floor
My spirit leaps to see
Bright garments trailing over it.
Wonderful lustres cover it,
A cleanness made by me.
Purger of all men's thoughts and ways,
With labor do I sound Thy praise,
My work is done for Thee.
Whoever makes a thing more bright,
He is an angel of all light.
Therefore let me spread abroad
The beautiful cleanness of my God.

VI

One time in the cool of dawn
Angels came and worked with me.
The air was soft with many a wing.
They laughed amid my solitude
And cast bright looks on everything.
Sweetly of me did they ask
That they might do my common task.
And all were beautiful — but one
With garments whiter than the sun
Had such a face
Of deep, remembered grace,
That when I saw I cried — "Thou art
The great Blood-Brother of my heart.
Where have I seen thee?" — And he said,
"When we are dancing 'round God's throne,
How often thou art there.

Beauties from thy hands have flown
Like white doves wheeling in mid-air.
Nay — thy soul remembers not?
Work on, and cleanse thy iron pot."

VII

What are we? I know not.

361. *Songs for My Mother*

I

MY mother's hands are cool and fair,
   They can do anything.
Delicate mercies hide them there
   Like flowers in the spring.

When I was small and could not sleep,
   She used to come to me,
And with my cheek upon her hand
   How sure my rest would be.

For everything she ever touched
   Of beautiful or fine,
Their memories living in her hands
   Would warm that sleep of mine.

Her hands remember how they played
   One time in meadow streams, —
And all the flickering song and shade
   Of water took my dreams.

ANNA HEMPSTEAD BRANCH

Swift through her haunted fingers pass
   Memories of garden things; —
I dipped my face in flowers and grass
   And sounds of hidden wings.

One time she touched the cloud that kissed
   Brown pastures bleak and far; —
I leaned my cheek into a mist
   And thought I was a star.

All this was very long ago
   And I am grown; but yet
The hand that lured my slumber so
   I never can forget.

For still when drowsiness comes on
   It seems so soft and cool,
Shaped happily beneath my cheek,
   Hollow and beautiful.

II

My mother has the prettiest tricks
   Of words and words and words.
Her talk comes out as smooth and sleek
   As breasts of singing birds.

She shapes her speech all silver fine
   Because she loves it so.
And her own eyes begin to shine
   To hear her stories grow.

And if she goes to make a call
    Or out to take a walk
We leave our work when she returns
    And run to hear her talk.

We had not dreamed these things were so
    Of sorrow and of mirth.
Her speech is as a thousand eyes
    Through which we see the earth.

God wove a web of loveliness,
    Of clouds and stars and birds,
But made not any thing at all
    So beautiful as words.

They shine around our simple earth
    With golden shadowings,
And every common thing they touch
    Is exquisite with wings.

There's nothing poor and nothing small
    But is made fair with them.
They are the hands of living faith
    That touch the garment's hem.

They are as fair as bloom or air,
    They shine like any star,
And I am rich who learned from her
    How beautiful they are.

WILLA SIBERT CATHER

362.   *In Rose Time*

OH this is the joy of the rose;
  That it blows
   And goes.

Winter lasts a five-month,
 Spring-time stays but one;
Yellow blow the rye-fields
 When the rose is done.

Pines are clad at Yuletide
 When the birch is bare,
And the holly's greenest
 In the frosty air.

Sorrow keeps a stone house
 Builded grim and gray;
Pleasure hath a straw thatch
 Hung with lanterns gay.

On her petty savings
 Niggard Prudence thrives,
Passion, ere the moonset,
 Bleeds a thousand lives.

Virtue hath a warm heart —
 Folly's dead and drowned;
Friendship hath her own when
 Love is underground.

Ah, for me the madness
   Of the spendthrift flower,
Burning myriad sunsets
   In a single hour.

For this is the joy of the rose;
   That it blows,
     And goes.

363.   *In Media Vita*

STREAMS of the spring a-singing,
   Winds of the May that blow,
Birds from the Southland winging,
   Buds in the grasses below.
Clouds that speed hurrying over,
   And the climbing rose by the wall
Singing of bees in the clover,
   And the dead, under all!

Lads and their sweethearts lying
   In the cleft of the windy hill;
Hearts that hushed of their sighing,
   Lips that are tender and still.
Stars in the purple gloaming,
   Flowers that suffice and fall,
Twitter of bird-mates homing,
   And the dead, under all!

Herdsman abroad with his collie,
　Girls on their way to the fair,
Hot lads a-chasing their folly,
　Parsons a-praying their prayer.
Children their kites a-flying,
　Grandsires that nod by the wall,
Mothers soft lullabies sighing,
　And the dead, under all!

364.　*Poppies in Ludlow Castle*

THROUGH halls of vanished pleasure,
　And hold of vanished power,
And crypt of faith forgotten,
　I came to Ludlow tower.

A-top of arch and stairway,
　Of crypt and donjon cell,
Of council hall and chamber,
　Of wall and ditch and well,

High over grated arches
　Where clinging ivies run,
A thousand scarlet poppies
　Enticed the rising sun.

Upon the topmost turret,
　With death and damp below, —
Three hundred years of spoilage, —
　The crimson poppies grow.

559

The man Flammonde saw none of that,
And what he saw we wondered at —
That none of us, in her distress,
Could hide or find our littleness.

There was a boy that all agreed
Had shut within him the rare seed
Of learning. We could understand,
But none of us could lift a hand.
The man Flammonde appraised the youth,
And told a few of us the truth;
And thereby, for a little gold,
A flowered future was unrolled.

There were two citizens who fought
For years and years, and over nought;
They made life awkward for their friends,
And shortened their own dividends.
The man Flammonde said what was wrong
Should be made right; nor was it long
Before they were again in line,
And had each other in to dine.

And these I mention are but four
Of many out of many more.
So much for them. But what of him —
So firm in every look and limb?
What small satanic sort of kink
Was in his brain? What broken link
Withheld him from the destinies
That came so near to being his?

EDWIN ARLINGTON ROBINSON

What was he, when we came to sift
His meaning, and to note the drift
Of incommunicable ways
That make us ponder while we praise?
Why was it that his charm revealed
Somehow the surface of a shield?
What was it that we never caught?
What was he, and what was he not?

How much it was of him we met
We cannot ever know; nor yet
Shall all he gave us quite atone
For what was his, and his alone;
Nor need we now, since he knew best,
Nourish an ethical unrest;
Rarely at once will nature give
The power to be Flammonde and live.

We cannot know how much we learn
From those who never will return,
Until a flash of unforeseen
Remembrance falls on what has been.
We've each a darkening hill to climb;
And this is why, from time to time
In Tilbury Town, we look beyond
Horizons for the man Flammonde.

T. A. DALY
1871–

378. *A Child's Christmas Song*

L ORD, I'm just a little boy
   Born one day like You,
And I've got a mother dear
   And a birthday, too.
But my birthday comes in spring,
   When the days are long,
And the robin in the tree
   Wakens me with song.
Since the birds are all away,
   Lord, when You are born,
Let Your angels waken me
   On Your birthday morn.

Lord, I'm just a little boy,
   Hidden in the night;
Let Your angels spy me out
   Long before it's light.
I would be the first to wake
   And the first to raise
In this quiet house of ours
   Songs of love and praise.
You shall hear me first, dear Lord,
   Blow my Christmas horn;
Let Your angels waken me
   On Your birthday morn.

T. A. DALY

379. *For Old Lovers*

THE sap is bubbling in the tree,
    The pink buds herald spring.
Yet winter holds for you and me
    One charm to which we cling.
The April sun grows warm by noon,
    Its daylight skies are bright;
But the cool evenings bring the boon
    Of a wood fire at night.

The greening sod of April days
    Is lovely to the eye,
But firmer, lovelier turf is May's
    And kindlier glows the sky.
Let striplings to the greenwood go
    For April's chill delight,
But we two still shall bless the glow
    Of a wood fire at night.

AMY LOWELL

1874-1925

380. *Venus Transiens*

TELL me,
    Was Venus more beautiful
Than you are,
When she topped
The crinkled waves,
Drifting shoreward
On her plaited shell?

577

Was Botticelli's vision
Fairer than mine;
And were the painted rosebuds
He tossed his lady,
Of better worth
Than the words I blow about you
To cover your too great loveliness
As with a gauze
Of misted silver?

For me,
You stand poised
In the blue and buoyant air,
Cinctured by bright winds,
Treading the sunlight.
And the waves which precede you
Ripple and stir
The sands at your feet.

381. *Madonna of the Evening Flowers*

ALL day long I have been working,
    Now I am tired.
I call: "Where are you?"
But there is only the oak tree rustling in the wind.
The house is very quiet,
The sun shines in on your books,
On your scissors and thimble just put down,
But you are not there.
Suddenly I am lonely:
Where are you?
I go about searching.

Then I see you,
Standing under a spire of pale blue larkspur,
With a basket of roses on your arm.
You are cool, like silver,
And you smile.
I think the Canterbury bells are playing little tunes,
You tell me that the peonies need spraying,
That the columbines have overrun all bounds,
That the pyrus japonica should be cut back and
    rounded.
You tell me these things.
But I look at you, heart of silver,
White heart-flame of polished silver,
Burning beneath the blue steeples of the larkspur,
And I long to kneel instantly at your feet,
While all about us peal the loud, sweet, Te Deums of the
    Canterbury bells.

382.   *Patterns*

I WALK down the garden-paths,
    And all the daffodils
Are blowing, and the bright blue squills.
I walk down the patterned garden-paths
In my stiff, brocaded gown.
With my powdered hair and jewelled fan,
I too am a rare
Pattern. As I wander down
The garden-paths.

Before my feet the dusty, rough-paved way
Flushes beneath its gray.
My steps fall ringed with light,
   So bright
It seems a myriad suns are strown
About the town.

You blazen me with jewelled insignia.
A flaming nebula
Rims in my life. And yet
You set
The word upon me, unconfessed,
To go unguessed.

384.   *The Precinct — Rochester*

THE tall yellow hollyhocks stand,
   Still and straight,
With their round blossoms spread open,
In the quiet sunshine.
And still is the old Roman wall,
Rough with jagged bits of flint,
And jutting stones,
Old and cragged,
Quite still in its antiquity.
The pear-trees press their branches against it,
And feeling it warm and kindly,
The little pears ripen to yellow and red.
They hang heavy, bursting with juice,
Against the wall.

So old, so still!
The sky is still.
The clouds make no sound
As they slide away
Beyond the Cathedral Tower
To the river,
And the sea,
It is very quiet
Very sunny.
The myrtle flowers stretch themselves in the sunshine,
But make no sound.
The roses push their little tendrils up,
And climb higher and higher.
In spots they have climbed over the wall.
But they are very still,
They do not seem to move.
And the old wall carries them
Without effort, and quietly
Ripens and shields the vines and blossoms.

A bird in a plane-tree
Sings a few notes,
Cadenced and perfect
They weave into the silence.
The Cathedral bell knocks,
One, Two, Three, and again,
And then again.
It is a quiet sound,
Calling to prayer,
Hardly scattering the stillness,
Only making it close in more densely.
The gardener picks ripe gooseberries

For the Dean's supper tonight.
It is very quiet
Very regulated and mellow.
But the wall is old.
It has known many days.
It is a Roman wall,
Left-over and forgotten.
Beyond the Cathedral close
Yelp and mutter the discontents of people not mellow,
Not well-regulated.
People who care more for bread than for beauty,
Who would break the tombs of saints,
And give the painted windows of churches
To their children for toys.
People who say:
"They are dead, we live!
The world is for the living."

Fools! It is always the dead who breed,
Crush the ripe fruit, and cast it aside
Yet its seeds shall fructify,
And trees rise where your huts were standing.
But the little people are ignorant,
They chaffer, and swarm.
They gnaw like rats,
And the foundations of the Cathedral are honey-combed.

The Dean is in the Chapter House;
He is reading the architect's bill
For the completed restoration of the Cathedral,
He will have ripe gooseberries for supper,

And then he will walk up and down the path
By the wall,
And admire the snapdragons and dahlias,
Thinking how quiet and peaceful
The garden is.
The old wall will watch him,
Very quietly and patiently it will watch.
For the wall is old,
It is a Roman wall.

JOSEPHINE PRESTON PEABODY

1874–1922

385.   *The Cloud*

THE islands called me far away,
    The valleys called me home.
The rivers with a silver voice
    Drew on my heart to come.

The paths reached tendrils to my hair
    From every vine and tree.
There was no refuge anywhere
    Until I came to thee.

There is a northern cloud I know,
    Along a mountain crest;
And as she folds her wings of mist,
    So I could make my rest.

587

There is no chain to bind her so
    Unto that purple height;
And she will shine and wander, slow,
    Slow, with a cloud's delight.

Would she begone? She melts away,
    A heavenly joyous thing.
Yet day will find the mountain white,
    White-folded with her wing.

As you may see, but half aware
    If it be late or soon,
Soft breathing on the day-time air,
    The fair forgotten Moon.

And though love cannot bind me, Love,
    — Ah no! — yet I could stay
Maybe, with wings forever spread,
    — Forever, and a day.

386. *A Song of Solomon*

KING SOLOMON was the wisest man
    Of all that have been kings.
He built an House unto the Lord;
    And he sang of creeping things.

Of creeping things, of things that fly,
    Or swim within the seas;
Of the little weed along the wall,
    And of the cedar-trees.

And happier he, without mistake,
　　Than all men since alive.
God's House he built; and he did make
　　A thousand songs and five.

THEODOSIA GARRISON

1874-

387.　　　*A Love Song*

MY love it should be silent, being deep —
　　And being very peaceful should be still —
Still as the utmost depths of ocean keep —
Serenely silent as some mighty hill.

Yet is my love so great it needs must fill
With very joy the inmost heart of me,
The joy of dancing branches on the hill
The joy of leaping waves upon the sea.

388.　　　*The Dreamers*

THE gypsies passed her little gate —
　　She stopped her wheel to see —
A brown-faced pair who walked the road,
Free as the wind is free;
And suddenly her tidy room
A prison seemed to be.

Her shining plates against the walls,
Her sunlit sanded floor,
The brass-bound wedding chest that held
Her linen's snowy store,
The very wheel whose humming died, —
Seemed only chains she bore.

She watched the foot-free gypsies pass;
She never knew or guessed
The wistful dream that drew them close —
The longing in each breast
Some day to know a home like hers,
Wherein their hearts might rest.

ROBERT FROST

1875–

389.   *Storm Fear*

WHEN the wind works against us in the dark,
    And pelts with snow
The lower chamber window on the east,
And whispers with a sort of stifled bark,
    The beast,
" Come out! Come out! " —
It costs no inward struggle not to go,
    Ah, no!
I count our strength,
    Two and a child,
Those of us not asleep subdued to mark
How the cold creeps as the fire dies at length, —
    How drifts are piled,

Dooryard and road ungraded,
Till even the comforting barn grows far away
And my heart owns a doubt
Whether 'tis in us to arise with day
And save ourselves unaided.

390.   *The Telephone*

WHEN I was just as far as I could **walk**
    From here today,
There was an hour
All still
When leaning with my head against a flower
I heard you talk.
Don't say I didn't, for I heard you say —
You spoke from that flower on the window sill —
Do you remember what it was you said? "

" First tell me what it was you thought you heard."

" Having found the flower and driven a bee away,
I leaned my head,
And holding by the stalk,
I listened and I thought I caught the word —
What was it?   Did you call me by my name?
Or did you say —
Someone said 'Come' — I heard it as I bowed."

" I may have thought as much, but not aloud."

  " Well, so I came."

591

391.   *The Road Not Taken*

TWO roads diverged in a yellow wood,
     And sorry I could not travel both
And be one traveler, long I stood
And looked down one as far as I could
To where it bent in the undergrowth;

Then took the other, as just as fair,
And having perhaps the better claim,
Because it was grassy and wanted wear;
Though as for that the passing there
Had worn them really about the same,

And both that morning equally lay
In leaves no step had trodden black.
Oh, I kept the first for another day!
Yet knowing how way leads on to way,
I doubted if I should ever come back.

I shall be telling this with a sigh
Somewhere ages and ages hence:
Two roads diverged in a wood, and I —
I took the one less traveled by,
And that has made all the difference.

392.   *Good-bye and Keep Cold*

THIS saying good-bye on the verge of the dark
    And cold to an orchard so young in the bank,
Reminds me of all that can happen to harm
An orchard away at the end of the farm
All winter cut off by a hill from the house.
I don't want it girdled by rabbit and mouse,
I don't want it dreamily nibbled for browse
By deer, and I don't want it budded by grouse,
(If certain it wouldn't be idle to call,
I'd summon grouse, rabbit and deer to the wall
And warn them away with a stick for a gun.)
I don't want it spitted by the heat of the sun.
(We made it secure against being, I hope,
By setting it out on a northerly slope.)
No orchard's the worse for the wintriest storm,
But one thing about it, it mustn't get warm.
"How often already you've had to be told
Keep cold, young orchard. Good-bye and keep cold.
Dread fifty above more than fifty below."
I have to be gone for a season or so;
My business awhile is with different trees,
Less carefully nurtured, less fruitful than these
And such as is done to their wood with an ax —
Maples and birches and tamaracks.
I wish I could promise to lie in the night
And share in an orchard's arboreal plight,
When slowing (and nobody comes with a light!)
Its heart sinks lower under the sod;
But something has to be left to God.

393.   *The Onset*

ALWAYS the same when on a fated night
    At last the gathered snow lets down as white
As may be in dark woods and with a song
It shall not make again all winter long —
Of hissing on the yet uncovered ground, —
I almost stumble looking up and round,
As one who, overtaken by the end,
Give's up his errand and lets death descend
Upon him where he is, with nothing done
To evil, no important triumph won
More than if life had never been begun.
Yet all the precedent is on my side:
I know that winter death has never tried
The earth but it has failed; the snow may heap
In long storms an undrifted four feet deep
As measured against maple, birch and oak;
It cannot check the Peeper's silver croak;
And I shall see the snow all go down the hill
In water of a slender April rill
That flashes tail through last year's withered brake
And dead weeds like a disappearing snake.
Nothing will be left white but here a birch
And there a clump of houses with a church.

394. *My November Guest*

MY sorrow, when she's here with me,
  Thinks these dark days of autumn rain
Are beautiful as days can be;
She loves the bare, the withered tree;
  She walks the sodden pasture lane.

Her pleasure will not let me stay.
  She talks and I am fain to list:
She's glad the birds are gone away,
She's glad her simple worsted grey
  Is silver now with clinging mist.

The desolate, deserted trees,
  The faded earth, the heavy sky,
The beauties she so truly sees,
She thinks I have no eye for these,
  And vexes me for reason why.

Not yesterday I learned to know
  The love of bare November days
Before the coming of the snow;
But it were vain to tell her so,
  And they are better for her praise.

1874–

399.   *The Trail Makers*

NORTH and west along the coast among the misty
      islands,
   Sullen in the grip of night and smiling in the day:
Nunivak and Akutan, with Nome against the highlands,
      On we drove with plated prow agleam with frozen
      spray.

Loud we sang adventuring and lustily we jested;
   Quarreled, fought, and then forgot the taunt, the blow,
      the jeers;
Named a friend and clasped a hand — a compact sealed,
      attested;
   Shared tobacco, yarns, and drink, and planned surpassing
      years.

Then — the snow that locked the trail where famine's
      shadow followed
   Out across the blinding white and through the stabbing
      cold,
Past tents along the tundra over faces blotched and hol-
      lowed;
   Toothless mouths that babbled foolish songs of hidden
      gold.

Wisdom, lacking sinews for the toil, gave over trying;
   Fools, with thews of iron, blundered on and won the
      fight;

H. H. KNIBBS

Weaklings drifted homeward; else they tarried — worse
  than dying —
  With the painted lips and wastrels on the edges of the
  night.

Berries of the saskatoon were ripening and falling;
  Flowers decked the barren with its timber scant and
  low;
All along the river-trail were many voices calling,
  And e'en the whimpering Malemutes they heard — and
  whined to go.

Eyelids seared with fire and ice and frosted parka-edges;
  Firelight like a spray of blood on the faces lean and
  brown;
Shifting shadows of the pines across our loaded sledges;
  And far behind the fading trail, the lights and lures of
  town.

So we played the bitter game nor asked for praise or pity:
  Wind and wolf they found the bones that blazed out
  lonely trails. . . .
Where a dozen shacks were set, today there blooms a city;
  Now where once was empty blue, there pass a thousand
  sails.

Scarce a peak that does not mark the grave of those who
  perished
  Nameless, lost to lips of men who followed, gleaning
  fame
From the soundless triumph of adventurers who cherished
  Naught above the glory of a chance to play the game.

Half the toil — and we have won to wealth in other sta-
   tion;
   Rusted out as useless ere our worth was tried and known.
But the Hand that made us caught us up and hewed a
   nation
   From the frozen fastness that so long was His alone.

.   .   .   .

Loud we sang adventuring and lustily, we jested;
   Quarreled, fought, and then forgot the taunt, the blow,
      the jeers;
Sinned and slaved and vanished — we, the giant-men who
      wrested
   Truth from out a dream wherein we planned surpassing
      years.

ADELAIDE CRAPSEY

1878-1914

400.   *Dirge*

NEVER the nightingale,
      Oh, my dear,
   Never again the lark
      Thou wilt hear;
   Though dusk and the morning still
   Tap at thy window-sill,
   Though ever love call and call
   Thou wilt not hear at all,
      My dear, my dear.

ADELAIDE CRAPSEY

401.   *Vendor's Song*

MY songs to sell, good sir!
    I pray you buy.
Here's one will win a lady's tears,
    Here's one will make her gay,
Here's one will charm your true love true
    Forever and a day;
Good sir, I pray you buy!

Oh, no, he will not buy.

My songs to sell, sweet maid!
    I pray you buy.
This one will teach you Lilith's lore,
    And this what Helen knew,
And this will keep your gold hair gold,
    And this your blue eyes blue;
Sweet maid, I pray you buy!

Oh, no, she will not buy.

If I'd as much money as I could tell,
I never would cry my songs to sell,
I never would cry my songs to sell.

VACHEL LINDSAY

1879–

402.   *The Flower of Mending*

WHEN Dragon-fly would fix his wings,
    When Snail would patch his house,
When moths have marred the overcoat
Of tender Mister Mouse,

The pretty creatures go with haste
To the sunlit blue-grass hills
Where the Flower of Mending yields the wax
And webs to help their ills.

The hour the coats are waxed and webbed
They fall into a dream,
And when they wake the ragged robes
Are joined without a seam.

My heart is but a dragon-fly,
My heart is but a mouse,
My heart is but a haughty snail
In a little stony house.

Your hand was honey-comb to heal,
Your voice a web to bind.
You were a Mending Flower to me
To cure my heart and mind.

403. *Abraham Lincoln Walks at Midnight*

IT is portentous, and a thing of state
      That here at midnight, in our little town
A mourning figure walks, and will not rest,
Near the old court-house pacing up and down.

Or by his homestead, or in shadowed yards
He lingers where his children used to play,
Or through the market, on the well-worn stones
He stalks until the dawn-stars burn away.

VACHEL LINDSAY

A bronzed, lank man! His suit of ancient black,
A famous high-top hat and plain worn shawl
Make him the quaint great figure that men love,
The prairie lawyer, master of us all.

He cannot sleep upon his hillside now.
He is among us: — as in times before!
And we who toss and lie awake for long
Breathe deep, and start, to see him pass the door.

His head is bowed. He thinks on men and kins.
Yea, when the sick world cries, how can he sleep?
Too many peasants fight, they know not why,
Too many homesteads in black terror weep.

The sins of all the war-lords burn his heart.
He sees the dreadnaughts scouring every main.
He carries on his shawl-wrapped shoulders now
The bitterness, the folly and the pain.

He cannot rest until a spirit-dawn
Shall come: — the shining hope of Europe free:
The league of sober folk, the Workers' Earth,
Bringing long peace to Cornland, Alp and Sea.

It breaks his heart that kings must murder still,
That all his hours of travail here for men
Seem yet in vain. And who will bring white peace
That he may sleep upon his hill again?

404. *General William Booth Enters into Heaven*

To be sung to the tune of "The Blood of the Lamb"
with indicated instruments.

BOOTH led boldly with his big bass drum.
   Are you washed in the blood of the Lamb?
The saints smiled gravely, and they said, "He's come."
   Are you washed in the blood of the Lamb?   **Bass drums**
Walking lepers followed, rank on rank,
Lurching bravos from the ditches dank,
Drabs from alleyways and drug-fiends pale —
Minds still passion-ridden, soul powers frail!
Vermin-eaten saints with mouldy breath
Unwashed legions with the ways of death —
   Are you washed in the blood of the Lamb?

Every slum has sent its half-a-score
The round world over — Booth had groaned for more.
Every banner that the wide world flies
Bloomed with glory and transcendent dyes.
Big-voiced lasses made their banjos bang!   **Banjos**
Tranced, fanatical, they shrieked and sang,
   Are you washed in the blood of the Lamb?
Hallelujah! It was queer to see
Bull-necked convicts with that land make free!
Loons with bazoos blowing blare, blare, blare —
On, on, upward through the golden air.
   Are you washed in the blood of the Lamb?

Booth died blind, and still by faith he trod,
Eyes still dazzled by the ways of God.   **Bass drums**
Booth led boldly and he looked the chief: **slower and**
                                                    softer

VACHEL LINDSAY

Eagle countenance in sharp relief,
Beard a-flying, air of high command
Unabated in that holy land.
Jesus came from out the Court-House door,
Stretched his hands above the passing poor.
Booth saw not, but led his queer ones there   Flutes
Round and round the mighty Court-House square.
Yet in an instant all that blear review
Marched on spotless, clad in raiment new.
The lame were straightened, withered limbs uncurled
And blind eyes opened on a new sweet world.

Drabs and vixens in a flash made whole!
Gone was the weasel-head, the snout, the jowl;   Bass drums
Sages and sibyls now, and athletes clean,   louder and
Rulers of empires, and of forests green!   faster
The hosts were sandalled and their wings were fire —
    Are you washed in the blood of the Lamb?
But their noise played havoc with the angel-choir
    Are you washed in the blood of the Lamb?
Oh, shout Salvation! it was good to see   Grand
Kings and princes by the Lamb set free.   chorus tam-
The banjos rattled and the tambourines   bourines all
Jin-jing-jingled in the hands of queens!   instruments
                                                 in full blast

And when Booth halted by the curb for prayer   Reverently
He saw his Master through the flag-filled air.   sung—no
Christ came gently with a robe and crown   instruments
For Booth the soldier while the throng knelt down;
He saw King Jesus — they were face to face,
And he knelt a-weeping in that holy place.
    Are you washed in the blood of the lamb?

605

ROBERT HAVEN SCHAUFFLER

405.   *"Scum o' The Earth"*

I

A T the gate of the West I stand,
   On the isle where the nations throng.
We call them " scum o' the earth "!

Stay, are we doing you wrong,
Young fellow from Socrates' land? —
You, like a Hermes so lissome and strong
Fresh from the Master Praxiteles' hand?
So you're Spartan birth?
Descended, perhaps, from one of the band —
Deathless in story and song —
Who combed their long hair at Thermopylae's pass?
Ah, I forget the straits, alas!
More tragic than theirs, more compassion-worth,
That have doomed you to march in our " immigrant class "
Where you're nothing but " scum o' the earth."

II

You Pole with the child on your knee,
What dower bring you to the land of the free?
Hark! does she croon
That sad little tune
That Chopin once found on his Polish lea
And mounted in gold for you and for me?
Now a ragged young fiddler answers
In wild Czech melody
That Dvořák took whole from the dancers.

606

And the heavy faces bloom
In the wonderful Slavic way;
The little, dull eyes, the brows a-gloom,
Suddenly dawn like the day.
While, watching these folk and their mystery,
I forget that they're nothing worth;
That Bohemians, Slovaks, Croatians,
And men of all Slavic nations
Are " polacks " — and " scum o' the earth."

III

Genoese boy of the level brow,
Lad of the lustrous, dreamy eyes
A-stare at Manhattan's pinnacles now
In the first sweet shock of a hushed surprise;
Within your far-rapt seer's eyes
I catch the glow of the wild surmise
That played on the Santa Maria's prow
In that still gray dawn,
Four centuries gone,
When a world from the wave began to rise.
Oh, it's hard to foretell what high emprise
Is the goal that gleams
When Italy's dreams
Spread wing and sweep into the skies.
Caesar dreamed him a world ruled well;
Dante dreamed Heaven out of Hell;
Angelo brought us there to dwell;
And you, are you of a different birth? —
You're only a " dago " — " scum o' the earth "!

IV

Stay, are we doing you wrong
Calling you " scum o' the earth,"
Man of the sorrow-bowed head,
Of the features tender yet strong, —
Man of the eyes full of wisdom and mystery
Mingled with patience and dread?
Have not I known you in history,
Sorrow-bowed head?
Were you the poet-king, worth
Treasures of Ophir unpriced?
Were you the prophet, perchance, whose art
Foretold how the rabble would mock
That shepherd of spirits, erelong,
Who should carry the lambs on his heart
And tenderly feed his flock?
Man — lift that sorrow-bowed head.
Lo! 'tis the face of the Christ!

Countrymen, bend and invoke
Mercy for us blasphemers,
For that we spat on these marvelous folk,
Nations of darers and dreamers,
Scions of singers and seers,
Our peers, and more than our peers.
" Rabble and refuse," we name them.
And " scum o' the earth " to shame them.
Mercy for us of the few young years,
Of the culture so callow and crude,
Of the hands so grasping and rude,

ROBERT HAVEN SCHAUFFLER

The lips so ready for sneers
At the sons of our ancient more-than-peers.
Mercy for us who dare despise
Men in whose loins our Homer lies;
Mothers of men who shall bring to us
The glory of Titian, the grandeur of Huss;
Children in whose frail arms shall rest
Prophets and singers and saints of the West.
Newcomers all from the eastern seas,
Help us incarnate dreams like these.
Forget, and forgive, that we did you wrong.
Help us to father a nation, strong
In the comradeship of an equal birth,
In the wealth of the richest bloods of earth.

DON MARQUIS

1878–

406.   *The Name*

IT shifts and shifts from form to form,
    It drifts and darkles, glooms and glows,
It is the passion of the storm,
    The poignance of the rose;
Through changing shapes, through devious ways,
    By noon or night, through cloud or flame,
My heart hath followed all my days
    Something I cannot name.

In sunlight on some woman's hair,
    Or starlight in some woman's eyne —
Or in low laughter smothered where
    Her red lips wedded mine —

My heart has known, and thrill d to know,
    This unnamed presence that it sought;
And when thy heart hath found it so,
    "Love is the name," I thought.

Sometimes when sudden afterglows
    In futile glory storm the skies
Within their transient gold and rose
    The secret stirs and dies;
Or when the tamping Morn walks o'er
    The troubled seas with feet of flame
My awed heart whispers, " Ask no more,
    For Beauty is the name! "

Or dreaming in old chapels where
    The dim aisles pulse with murmurings
That part are music, part are prayer —
    (Or rush of hidden wings) —
I often lift a startled head
    To some saint's carven countenance,
Half fancying that the lips have said,
    " All names mean God perchance."

407.   *The Nobler Lesson*

CHRIST was of virgin birth, and, being slain,
    The creedists say, He rose from death again.
Oh, futile age-long talk of death and birth! —
His life, that is the one thing wonder-worth;
Not how He came, but how He lived on earth.

For if gods stoop, and with quaint jugglery
Mock nature's laws, how shall that profit thee? —
The nobler lesson is that mortals can
Grow godlike through this baffled front of man!

408.   *The God-Maker, Man*

NEVERMORE
    Shall the shepherds of Arcady follow
Pan's moods as he lolls by the shore
    Of the mere, or lies hid in the hollow;
Nevermore
    Shall they start at the sound of his reed-fashioned flute;

Fallen mute
    Are the strings of Apollo,
His lyre and his lute;
    And the lips of the Memnons are mute
Evermore;
    And the gods of the North, — are they dead or for-
        getful,
Our Odin and Baldur and Thor?
    Are they drunk, or grown weary of worship and fretful,
Our Odin and Baldur and Thor?

And into what night have the Orient deities strayed?
Swart gods of the Nile, in dusk splendors arrayed,
    Brooding Isis and somber Osiris,
    You were gone ere the fragile papyrus,
(That bragged you eternal!) decayed.

Not too hot with a gross belief,
    Nor yet too cold with pride,
I will bow me down where my brothers bow,
    Humble — but open-eyed!

409.   *From the Bridge*

HELD and thrilled by the vision
    I stood, as the twilight died,
Where the great bridge soars like a song
    Over the crawling tide —

Stood on the middle arch —
    And night flooded in from the bay,
And wonderful under the stars
    Before me the city lay;

Girdled with swinging waters —
    Guarded by ship on ship —
A gem that the strong old ocean
    Held in his giant grip;

There was play of shadows above
    And drifting gleams below,
And magic of shifting waves
    That darkle and glance and glow;

Dusky and purple and splendid,
    Banded with loops of light,
The tall towers rose like pillars,
    Lifting the dome of night;

The gliding cars of traffic
   Slid swiftly up and down
Like monsters, fiery mailed,
   Leaping across the town.

Not planned with a thought of beauty;
   Built by a lawless breed;
Builded of lust for power,
   Builded of gold and greed.

Risen out of the trader's
   Brutal and sordid wars —
And yet, behold! a city
   Wonderful under the stars!

AMELIA JOSEPHINE BURR
1878–

410.   *A Song of Living*

BECAUSE I have loved life, I shall have no sorrow to
   die.
I have sent up my gladness on wings, to be lost in the blue
   of the sky.
I have run and leaped with the rain, I have taken the
   wind to my breast.
My cheek like a drowsy child to the face of the earth I
   have pressed.
Because I have loved life, I shall have no sorrow to die.

I have kissed young Love on the lips, I have heard his
   song to the end.
I have struck my hand like a seal in the loyal hand of a
   friend.

I have known the peace of heaven, the comfort of work
   done well.
I have longed for death in the darkness and risen alive
   out of hell.
Because I have loved life, I shall have no sorrow to
   die.

I give a share of my soul to the world where my course is
   run.
I know that another shall finish the task I must leave un-
   done.
I know that no flower, nor flint was in vain on the path
   I trod.
As one looks on a face through a window, through life I
   have looked on God.
Because I have loved life, I shall have no sorrow to die.

WITTER BYNNER

1881–

411.   *Hills of Home*

NAME me no names for my disease,
   With uninforming breath;
I tell you I am none of these,
   But homesick unto death —

Homesick for hills that I had known,
   For brooks that I had crossed,
Before I met this flesh and bone
   And followed and was lost. . . .

And though they break my heart at last,
  Yet name no name of ills.
Say only, " Here is where he passed,
  Seeking again those hills."

412.   *Ghosts of Indians*

INDIAN–FOOTED move the mists
  From the corner of the lake,
Silent, sinuous and bent;
And their trailing feathers shake,
Tremble to forgotten leapings,
While with lingerings or creepings
Down they lean again to slake
The dead thirst of parching mouths,
Lean their pale mouths in the lake.

Indian-footed move the mists
That were hiding in the pine,
But upon the oval lake
In a bent and ghostly line
Lean and drink for better sleeping . . .
Then they turn again and — creeping
Gliding as with fur and fins —
Disappear through woods and water
On a thousand moccasins.

THOMAS S. JONES, Jr.

1882–

413.   *Dusk at Sea*

TO-NIGHT eternity alone is near;
    The sea, the sunset, and the darkening blue;
Within their shelter is no space for fear,
    Only the wonder that such things are true.

The thought of you is like the dusk at sea —
    Space and wide freedom and old shores left far,
The shelter of a lone immensity
    Sealed by the sunset and the evening star.

HERMANN HAGEDORN

1882–

414.   *Doors*

LIKE a young child who to his mother's door
    Runs eager for the welcoming embrace,
    And finds the door shut, and with troubled face
Calls and through sobbing calls, and o'er and o'er
Calling, storms at the panel — so before
    A door that will not open, sick and numb,
    I listen for a word that will not come,
And know, at last, I may not enter more.

Silence! And through the silence and the dark
    By that closed door, the distant sob of tears
        Beats on my spirit, as on fairy shores
The spectral sea; and through the sobbing, hark!
    Down the fair-chambered corridor of years,
        The quiet shutting, one by one, of doors.

618

ARTHUR DAVISON FICKE

415. *To the Harpies*

YOU who with birch or laurel
    Are swift to scourge or bless —
Silence your foolish quarrel
Before her loveliness.

What though she went a-travel
Down paths you do not know?
Your words shall not unravel
Webs that allured her so.

Hush now your foolish babble
Around her golden head.
Shut out the prying rabble.
Be happy. She is dead.

Now give one final kindness
That late you dreamed not of —
Silence, to cloak your blindness —
Peace, since you know not love.

416. *"I am in Love with Far-Seeing Places"*

I AM in love with high far-seeing places
    That look on plains half-sunlight and half-storm —
In love with hours when from the circling faces
Veils pass, and laughing fellowship glows warm.

619

DAVID MORTON

422.   *Old Ships*

THERE is a memory stays upon old ships,
    A weightless cargo in the musty hold, —
Of bright lagoons and prow-caressing lips,
    Of stormy midnights, — and a tale untold.
They have remembered islands in the dawn,
    And windy capes that tried their slender spars,
The torturous channels where their keels have gone,
    And calm, blue nights of stillness and the stars.

Ah, never think that ships forget a shore,
    Or bitter seas, or winds that made them wise;
There is a dream upon them, evermore; —
    And there be some who say that sunk ships rise
To seek familiar harbors in the night,
    Blowing in mists, their spectral sails like light.

ALAN SEEGER
1888-1916

423. *"I Have a Rendezvous with Death"*

I HAVE a rendezvous with Death
    At some disputed barricade,
When Spring comes back with rustling shade
And apple-blossoms fill the air —
I have a rendezvous with Death
When Spring brings back blue days and fair.

ALAN SEEGER

It may be he shall take my hand
And lead me into his dark land
And close my eyes and quench my breath —
It may be I shall pass him still.
I have a rendezvous with Death
On some scarred slope of battered hill,
When Spring comes round again this year
And the first meadow-flowers appear.

God knows 'twere better to be deep
Pillowed in silk and scented down,
Where love throbs out in blissful sleep,
Pulse nigh to pulse, and breath to breath,
Where hushed awakenings are dear. . . .
But I've a rendezvous with Death
At midnight in some flaming town,
When Spring trips north again this year,
And I to my pledged word am true,
I shall not fail that rendezvous.

LOUIS UNTERMEYER

1885–

424.   *Reveille*

WHAT sudden bugle calls us in the night
     And wakes us from a dream that we had shaped;
Flinging us sharply up against a fight
   We thought we had escaped.

It is no easy waking, and we win
   No final peace; our victories are few.
But still imperative forces pull us in
   And sweep us somehow through.

LOUIS UNTERMEYER

Summoned by a supreme and confident power
    That wakes our sleeping courage like a blow,
We rise, half-shaken, to the challenging hour,
    And answer it — and go.

EZRA POUND

1885-

425.   *An Immorality*

SING we for love and idleness,
    Naught else is worth the having.

Though I have been in many a land,
There is naught else in living.

And I would rather have my sweet,
Though rose-leaves die of grieving,

Than do high deeds in Hungary
To pass all men's believing.

JOYCE KILMER

1886-1918

426.   *Rouge Bouquet*

March 7, 1918

IN a wood they call the Rouge Bouquet
    There is a new-made grave today,
Built by never a spade nor pick
Yet covered with earth ten metres thick.

JOYCE KILMER

There lie many fighting men,
　　Dead in their youthful prime,
Never to laugh nor love again
　　Nor taste the Summertime.
For Death came flying through the air
And stopped his flight at the dugout stair,
Touched his prey and left them there,
　　Clay to clay.
He hid their bodies stealthily
In the soil of the land they fought to free
　　And fled away.
Now over the grave abrupt and clear
　　Three volleys ring;
And perhaps their brave young spirits hear
　　The bugle sing:
" Go to sleep!
Go to sleep!)
Slumber well where the shell screamed and fell.
Let your rifles rest on the muddy floor,
You will not need them any more.
Danger's past;
Now at last,
Go to sleep! "

There is on earth no worthier grave
To hold the bodies of the brave
Than this place of pain and pride
Where they nobly fought and nobly died.
Never fear but in the skies
　　Saints and angels stand
Smiling with their holy eyes
　　On this new-come band.

Rich joy and love he got and gave;
His heart was merry as his dress;
Pile laurel wreaths upon his grave
Who did not gain, but was, success!

428.   *Trees*

I THINK that I shall never see
A poem lovely as a tree.

A tree whose hungry mouth is pressed
Against the earth's sweet flowing breast;

A tree that looks at God all day
And lifts her leafy arms to pray;

A tree that may in summer wear
A nest of robins in her hair;

Upon whose bosom snow has lain;
Who intimately lives with the rain.

Poems are made by fools like me,
But only God can make a tree.

CHRISTOPHER MORLEY

1890–

429. *At a Window Sill*

TO write a sonnet needs a quiet mind. . . .
  I paused and pondered, tried again. To write. . . .
Raising the sash, I breathed the winter night:
Papers and small hot room were left behind.
Against the gusty purple, ribbed and spined
With golden slots and vertebrae of light
Men's cages loomed. Down sliding from a height
An elevator winked as it declined.

Coward! There is no quiet in the brain —
If pity burns it not, then beauty will:
Tinder it is for every blowing spark.
Uncertain whether this is bliss or pain
The unresting mind will gaze across the sill
From high apartment windows, in the dark.

430. *In an Auction Room*

*(Letter of John Keats to Fanny Brawne, Anderson
Galleries, March 15, 1920.)*

HOW *about this lot?* said the auctioneer;
  One hundred, may I say, just for a start?
Between the plum-red curtains, drawn apart,
A written sheet was held. . . . And strange to hear

432.   *Wraith*

"THIN Rain, whom are you haunting,
    That you haunt my door? "
— Surely it is not I she's wanting;
    Someone living here before —
" Nobody's in the house but me:
You may come in if you like and see."

Thin as thread, with exquisite fingers —
    Have you seen her, any of you? —
Grey shawl, and leaning on the wind,
    And the garden showing through?

Glimmering eyes, — and silent, mostly,
    Sort of a whisper, sort of a purr,
Asking something, asking it over,
    If you get a sound from her. —

Ever see her, any of you? —
    Strangest thing I've ever known, —
Every night since I moved in,
    And I came to be alone.

" Thin Rain, hush your knocking!
    You may not come in!
This is I that you hear rocking;
    Nobody's with me, nor has been! "

Curious, how she tried the window, —
    Odd, the way she tries the door, —
Wonder just what sort of people
    Could have had this house before. . . .

EDNA ST. VINCENT MILLAY

433.   *Elegy Before Death*

THERE will be rose and rhododendron
    When you are dead and under ground;
Still will be heard from white syringas
    Heavy with bees, a sunny sound;

Still will the tamaracks be raining
    After the rain has ceased, and still
Will there be robins in the stubble,
    Brown sheep upon the warm green hill.

Spring will not ail nor autumn falter;
    Nothing will know that you are gone,
Saving alone some sullen plough-land
    None but yourself sets foot upon;

Saving the may-weed and the pig-weed
    Nothing will know that you are dead, —
These, and perhaps a useless wagon
    Standing beside some tumbled shed.

Oh, there will pass with your great passing
    Little of beauty not your own, —
Only the light from common water,
    Only the grace from simple stone.

LEONORA SPEYER

434. A Note From the Pipes

PAN, blow your pipes and I will be
  Your fern, your pool, your dream, your tree!

I heard you play, caught your swift eye,
"A pretty melody!" called I,
"Hail, Pan!" And sought to pass you by.

Now blow your pipes and I will sing
To your sure lips' accompanying!

Wild God, who lifted me from earth,
Who taught me freedom, wisdom, mirth,
Immortalized my body's worth, —

Blow, blow your pipes! And from afar
I'll come — I'll be your bird, your star,
Your wood, your nymph, your kiss, your rhyme,
And all your godlike summer-time!

435. April on the Battlefields

APRIL now walks the fields again,
  Trailing her tearful leaves
And holding all her frightened buds against her heart:
Wrapt in her clouds and mists,
She walks,
Groping her way among the graves of men.

636

The green of earth is differently green,
A dreadful knowledge trembles in the grass,
And little wide-eyed flowers die too soon;
There is a stillness here —
After a terror of all raving sounds —
And birds sit close for comfort upon the boughs
Of broken trees.

April, thou grief!
What of thy sun and glad high wind,
Thy valiant hills and woods and eager brooks,
Thy thousand-petalled hopes?
The sky forbids thee sorrow, April!
And yet —
I see thee walking listlessly
Across those scars that once were joyous sod,
Those graves,
Those stepping-stones from life to life.

Death is an interruption between two heart-beats,
That I know —
Yet know not how I know —
But April mourns,
Trailing her tender green,
The passion of her green,
Across the passion of those fearful fields.

Yes, all the fields!
No barrier here,
No challenge in the night,
No stranger-land;
She passes with her perfect countersign,
Her green;

She wanders in her mournful garden,
Dropping her buds like tears,
Spreading her lovely grief upon the graves of man.

ALICE CORBIN

436.   *Muy Vieja Mexicana*

I'VE seen her pass with eyes upon the road—
  An old bent woman in a bronze-black shawl,
With skin as dried and wrinkled as a mummy's,
As brown as a cigar-box, and her voice
Like the low vibrant strings of a guitar.
And-I have fancied from the girls about
What she was at their age, what they will be
When they are old as she. But now she sits
And smokes away each night, till dawn comes round,
Thinking, beside the piñons' flame, of days
Long past and gone, when she was young— content
To be no longer young, her epic done:

    For a woman has work and much to do,
    And it's good at the last to know it's through,
    And still have time to sit alone,
    To have some time you can call your own.
    It's good at the last to know your mind
    And travel the paths that you traveled blind,
    To see each turn and even make
    Trips in the byways you did not take—
    But that, por Dios, is over and done,
    It's pleasanter now in the way we've come;
    It's good to smoke and none to say
    What's to be done on the coming day,

No mouths to feed or coat to mend,
And none to call till the last long end.
Though one have sons and friends of one's own,
It's better at last to live alone.
For a man must think of food to buy,
And a woman's thoughts may be wild and high;
But when she is young she must curb her pride,
And her heart is tamed for the child at her side.
But when she is old her thoughts may go
Wherever they will, and none to know.
And night is the time to think and dream,
And not to get up with the dawn's first gleam;
Night is the time to laugh or weep,
And when dawn comes it is time to sleep . . .

When it's all over and there's none to care,
I mean to be like her and take my share
Of comfort when the long day's done,
And smoke away the nights, and see the sun
Far off, a shrivelled orange in a sky gone black,
Through eyes that open inward and look back.

MARGARET WIDDEMER

437. *If You Should Tire of Loving Me*

IF you should tire of loving me
    Some one of our far days,
Oh never start to hide your heart
    Or cover thought with praise.

639

MARGARET WIDDEMER

For every word you would not say
    Be sure my heart has heard,
So go from me all silently
    Without a kiss or word;

For God must give you happiness,
    And oh, it may befall
In listening long to Heaven-song
    I may not care at all!

MARGUERITE WILKINSON

1883–

438.   *The Robber in England*

I AM a robber from over the seas;
  I have come stealing things like these:
The slant of the hills toward Parracombe Town,
The look of the sea from Porlock down,
The patchwork of fields with hedges between
Dividing the new-ploughed red from green
Like a magical quilt-stitch set to bind
Fields upon hills around and behind.
I have come stealing the tilt of the thatches
Where villages doze among the green patches,
Where each little house as the road winds around
Seems to have grown from a root in the ground,
For almost as natural as trees are they
With the dull brown thatch above the stone's old gray,
Of ancient plaster firm and mellow
In quiet tones of cream and yellow.
When I go home I shall carry away
Deep-drawn fragrance of Devon hay,

MARGUERITE WILKINSON

The teasing turn of a path like a dream
And the soothing flavor of Devonshire cream,
The fiery glance of poppies in corn,
The blessed light on a holy book
Through colored windows reverently borne
While overhead the sweet bells shook
For somebody married, somebody dead,
Or another hour of the ages sped.
Into my treasury I shall thrust
Heather-plunder and bracken-rust,
Thorn of holly and ivy-bud
And songs of all the singing brood,
With English voices cheery and sweet
And the patient look of English feet
Clumsily shod and moving slow
Wherever the paths of the good land go,
Or on streets of London that twist and wind
Like the whimsical humor of the English mind.
These and the angels weeping stone tears
In Westminster Abbey forever and ever,
And the knights that sound the hours with spears
In Wells Cathedral prompt and clever,
The combs the Romans used at Bath,
The Cheshire Cheese where Johnson made merry,
The Bloody Tower with its scenes of wrath
And the old Cathedral of Canterbury, —
These I have stolen, stolen away
To make them mine till my dying day;
And neither the King in Buckingham Palace
Nor the gracious Queen with her crown of gold
Will take them from me, for all without malice
What I have taken I mean to hold.

And loitered through the twilight down
The hills that gird some Attic town
Still shining in the early gloam
Beside the murmur of the foam.

What dream is this? I know the croft,
   Deep in this dale, where they were born;
I know their wind-swept hills aloft
   Among the rustling corn;
Yet, while they glimmer slowly by,
A younger earth, a fairer sky
Seem round them, and they move sublime
Among the dews of dawning time.

441. *"Whence Cometh My Help"*

LET me sleep among the shadows of the mountains
    when I die,
  In the murmur of the pines and sliding streams,
Where the long day loiters by
Like a cloud across the sky,
  Where the moon-drenched night is musical with dreams.

Lay me down within a canyon of the mountains, far away,
  In a valley filled with dim and rosy light,
Where the flashing rivers play
Out across the golden day,
  And a noise of many waters brims the night.

All the wisdom, all the beauty I have lived for, unaware,
  Came upon me by the banks of upland rills;
I have seen God walking there
In the solemn soundless air
  When the morning wakened wonder in the hills.

I am what the mountains made me, of their green and
    gold and gray,
  Of the dawnlight and the moonlight and the foam. . . .
Mighty mothers far away,
Ye who washed my soul in spray,
  I am coming, mother mountains, coming home.

When I draw my dreams about me, when I leave the
    darkling plain
  Where my soul forgets to soar and learns to plod,
I shall go back home again
To the kingdoms of the rain,
  To the blue purlieus of heaven, nearer God.

Where the rose of dawn blooms earlier across the miles
    of mist,
  Between the tides of sundown and moonrise,
I shall keep a lover's tryst
With the gold and amethyst,
  With the stars for my companions in the skies.

442.   *Earth-Born*

NO lapidary's heaven, no brazier's hell for me,
    For I am made of dust and dew and stream and plant
    and tree;
I am akin to boulders, I am cousin to the mud,
And all the winds of all the skies made music in my blood.

I want a brook and pine trees; I want a storm to blow
Loud-lunged across the looming hills, with rain and sleet
    and snow.
Put me not off with diadems and thrones of chryso-
    prase . . .
I want the winds of northern nights and wild March days.

My blood runs red with sunset, my body is white with
    rain,
Upon my heart the skies of dawn have set their scarlet
    stain.
My thoughts are green with springtime. Among the
    meadow rue
I think my very soul is growing green and gold and blue.

What will be left, I wonder, when Death has washed me
    clean
Of dust and dew and sundown and April's virgin green?
If there's enough to make a ghost, I'll bring it back again
To the little lovely earth that bore me, body, soul, and
    brain.

CARL SANDBURG

443.   *Under The Harvest Moon*

UNDER the harvest moon,
    When the soft silver
Drips shimmering
Over the garden nights,

CARL SANDBURG

Death, the gray mocker
Comes and whispers to you
As a beautiful friend
Who remembers.
Under the summer roses,
When the flagrant crimson
Lurks in the dusk
Of the wild red leaves,
Love, with little hands,
Comes and touches you
With a thousand memories,
And asks you
Beautiful unanswerable questions.

ROBERT HILLYER

444.   *To a Scarlatti Passepied*

STRANGE little tune, so thin and rare,
    Like scents of roses of long ago,
Quavering lightly upon the strings
Of a violin, and dying there
With a dancing flutter of delicate wings;
Thy courtly joy and thy gentle woe,
Thy gracious gladness and plaintive fears
Are lost in the clamorous age we know,
And pale like a moon in the lurid day;
A phantom of music, strangely fled
From the princely halls of the quiet dead,
Down the long lanes of the vanished years
Echoing frailly and far away.

And thus, O little house that sheltered me,
Dissolve again in wind and rain, to be
Part of the cosmic weird economy.
    And, O, how oft with new life shalt thou lift
    Out of the atom-drift!

447.   *The Poet's Town*

X

BUT still did the Mighty Makers
  Stir in the common sod;
The corn through its awful acres
Trembled and thrilled with God!

More than a man was the sower,
Lured by a man's desire,
For a triune Bride walked close at his side —
Dew and Dust and Fire!

More than a man was the plowman
Shouting his gee and haw;
For a something dim kept pace with him,
And ever the poet saw;

Till the winds of the cosmic struggle
Made of his flesh a flute,
To echo the tune of a whirlwind rune
Unto the million mute.

JOHN G. NEIHARDT

XI

Son of the Mother of mothers,
The womb and the tomb of Life,
With Fire and Air for brothers
And a clinging Dream for a wife;

Ever the soul of the dreamer
Strove with its mortal mesh,
And the lean flame grew till it fretted through
The last thin links of flesh.

Oh, rending the veil asunder,
He fled to mingle again
With the dred Orestean thunder,
The Lear of the driven rain!

XII

Once in a cycle the comet
Doubles its lonesome track.
Enriched with the tears of a thousand years,
Aeschylus wanders back.

Ever inweaving, returning,
The near grows out of the far;
And Homer shall sing once more in a swing
Of the austere Polar Star.

Then what of the lonesome dreamer
With the lean blue flame in his breast?
And who was your clown for a day, O Town,
The strange, unbidden guest?

DANA BURNET

1888–

448. *"Who Dreams Shall Live"*

WHO *dreams* shall live! And if we do not dream
    Then we shall build no Temple into Time.
Yon dust cloud, whirling slow against the sun,
Was yesterday's *cathedral*, stirred to gold
By heedless footsteps of a passing world.
The faiths of *stone* and *steel* are failed of proof,
The King who made religion of a *Sword*
Passes, and is forgotten in a day.
The crown he wore rots at a lily's root,
The rose unfurls her banners o'er his dust.

The dreamer dies, but never dies fair dream,
Though Death shall call the whirlwind to his aid,
Enlist men's passions, trick their hearts with hate,
Still the fair Vision lives! Say nevermore
That *dreams* are fragile things. What else endures
Of all this *broken world save only dreams!*

449. *The Riddle*

WE were laying the road to a Riddle,
    And never a man knew why,
Nor Oleson, nor little Giuseppe,
    Nor Sandy McGregor, nor I;
It lay on the hills before us,
    And the hills were strange with its gleam,
And mayhap the Thing was a City,
    And mayhap 'twas only a dream.

DANA BURNET

We started our picks in the morning,
    We quit when we came to the stars,
We held out our hands to the camp-fire
    And told off the miles by the scars;
Long miles that we laid with our labor.
    And never a man knew why,
Nor Oleson, nor little Giuseppe,
    Nor Sandy McGregor, nor I.

We sat by the fire at twilight
    And guessed at it gleaming there,
With a little red cloud above it
    Like the rose in a woman's hair!
And all of us held by the guesses
    And toiled to the visions they made,
And some of us wondered, and cursed it,
    And some of us wondered — and prayed.

But each of us cherished his vision
    And fought for his guess in the gloam,
And one of us dreamed it was heaven,
    And one of us dreamed it was Home.
Old Sandy McGregor saw heather,
    And moorland and thistle-blown sod —
And little Giuseppe stood forward,
    And guessed it was Naples — or God.

The Oleson, the Swede, broke the silence;
    He surged to his feet like a tide
And said it was Snow on a Mountain,
    And turned to his blanket — and cried.

HERVEY ALLEN

453. *Palmetto Town*

SEA–ISLAND winds sweep through Palmetto Town,
  Bringing with piney tang the old romance
Of Pirates and of smuggling gentlemen;
And tongues as languorous as southern France
Flow down her streets like water-talk at fords;
While through iron gates where pickaninnies sprawl,
The sound floats back, in rippled banjo chords,
From lush magnolia shade where mockers call.
Mornings, the flower-women hawk their wares —
Bronze caryatids of a genial race,
Bearing the bloom-heaped baskets on their heads;
Lithe, with their arms akimbo in wide grace,
Their jasmine nods jestingly at cares —
Turbaned they are, deep-chested, straight and tall,
Bandying old English words now seldom heard,
But sweet as Provençal.
Dreams peer like prisoners through her harp-like gates,
From molten gardens mottled with gray-gloom,
Where lichened sundials shadow ancient dates,
And deep piazzas loom.
Fringing her quays are frayed palmetto posts,
Where clipper ships once moored along the ways,
And fanlight doorways, sunstruck with old ghosts,
Sicken with loves of her lost yesterdays.
Often I halt upon some gabled walk,
Thinking I see the ear-ringed *picaroons*,
Slashed with a sash or Spanish *folderols*,
Gambling for moidores or for gold doubloons.

But they have gone where night goes after day,
And the old streets are gay with whistled tunes,
Bright with the lilt of scarlet parasols,
Carried by honey-voiced young octoroons.

MARGARET LEE ASHLEY

454.   *In April*

IF I am slow forgetting,
    It is because the sun
Has such old tricks of setting
    When April days are done.

The soft spring sunlight traces
    Old patterns — green and gold;
The flowers have no new faces,
    The very buds are old!

If I am slow forgetting —
    Ah, well, come back and see
The same old sunbeams petting
    My garden-plots for me.

Come smell the green things growing,
    The boxwood after rain;
See where old beds are showing
    Their slender spears again.

At dusk, that fosters dreaming —
    Come back at dusk and rest,
And watch our old star gleaming
    Against the primrose west.

INDEX OF AUTHORS

The references are to the numbers of the poems

INDEX OF FIRST LINES

INDEX OF FIRST LINES

INDEX OF FIRST LINES

INDEX OF FIRST LINES

INDEX OF FIRST LINES

INDEX OF FIRST LINES

INDEX OF FIRST LINES

INDEX OF FIRST LINES

676

INDEX OF FIRST LINES

INDEX OF FIRST LINES

INDEX OF FIRST LINES

INDEX OF FIRST LINES